Conforming

Conforming to the Mind of Christ

Jesus the Anointed One

Bishop Gregory Leachman

To my sister with love from the Bishop God Bless You

Conforming

© 2013 by Gregory Leachman.
All rights reserved. No part of this book may be reproduced, stored in a retrieval system or transmitted in any form or by any means without the prior written permission of the publishers, except by a reviewer who may quote brief passages in a review to be printed in a newspaper, magazine or journal.

For more information, please contact Bishop
Gregory Leachman at
(314) 956-8339
Or P.O. Box 93406
St. Louis, MO 63163-3506

Softcover 978-1481164023
PUBLISHED BY REVIVAL WAVES OF GLORY BOOKS & PUBLISHING
www.revivalwavesofglory.com
Litchfield, IL

Printed in the United States of America

Table of Contents

Introduction 8
The Beginning 11
Conforming 13
Thought: You Can't Know Your Enemy Until You Know His god 17
Thought – Betrayal 19
Thought: So Then How Far Are You and Your Anointing Prepared to Go? 21
Thought: God Is Looking for Some Standers 23
Thought: The Missing Link 27
Thought: Praising God on Credit 31
Thought: Naked Not Ashamed 38
Thought: The Lord Has Made for Me to Do 43
Thought: D.N.A. 44
Thought: Never Be Without One 46
Thought: Holy Ghost Pure Fire 48
Thought: The Compelling Kind 50
Thought: My Rock 53
Title: The Inside Man 55
Title: Holy Ghost Have Your Own Way 58
Title: Steer Them In 65
Title: Time Change 68
Title: Your Flesh is Your Number One Enemy 71
Title: Start Here 73
Title: It's Feeding Time 75
Title: Knowing Your Word 77

Title: You Did It Lord, Whatever It Is You Did It Lord 81
Title: Say Something before You Can Get Something, Say What the Bible Says the True Word of God 83
Title: The Blessing Isn't In What You Lost, It's In What You have Left 84
Title: Obey or Receive the Sharp Swords 88
Thought: God Promised To You, If You Do? 90
Title: You Don't Know What You Don't Know 93
Title: Jesus Has a Need 95
Thought: Trust God When You Can't Trace Him 97
Title: Well in the Mean Time, I'll Do This but Not That 99
Title: The Zebra Standard with a Jackass Mentality 102
Title: For Christ Sake 105
Title: Click, Click, Click, Click Turn, Click Turn 108
Title: Boarding Time, You Need the Right Pass 111
Title: Working to God Out of Your Substance That Never Ends 116
Title: The Closer Wants to Bring You Closure, So He Can Bring Closure to His Purpose, He's Place on You 118
Title: The Other Side of Me, It Will Come to Pass 120

Title: Same People Different Books 123
Title: Love That Becomes a Reflex 126
Title: Your Blessing Isn't Here, It's Over There 128
Title: Do I Become Domesticated or Do I Be Myself? 131
Title: In the Beginning, the House Without a Home 137
Thought: Where There is No Revelation, There is No Vision 142
Title: Recognizing Your God Given Love Abilities 146
Title: The Transporter – Jonah Chapters 1, 2, 3 149
Title: The Place of Cutting You Out of the Way 151
Title: Producing the Proof 156
Title: When I Truly Die Then I Can Speak, Never the Less Not I but Christ 160
Title: Go Again Seven Times, Don't Give Up 162
Title: Poison Needs an Antidote the Holy Ghost 166
Title: Filling My Empty Vessels 170
Title: God Said You Are Divinely Designed For His Purpose 175
Title: Discerning the Nature of False Doctrine, Jesus Only Brought His 179
Title: My Plans – Empty Plans 187
Title: A Passing On of the Mantle On Your Head to Mine 191

Title: There is Someone in the Oven and the Lord Has Commanded Them to Come Out. 196
Title: And I Will Dwell in the House of the Lord Forever 205
Title: My God is Jesus 207
Title: Masked Murder 211
Title: The Mirror Man 213
Title: The Dove, the Rock and the Water 216
Title: Delivering Face Value, It's About Your New Nature 222
Title: Learning to Walk in a No Account Kind of Love 225
Title: The Lord Said Let Me Introduce You to My Knife 229
Title: Wonder Working Blood 232
Title: What Kind of Leader Are You from the Inside Out 238
Title: How Many gods do You Preach, Teach or Serve 241
Title: Give Me Water Says the Lord, the Same I Gave You to Drink, Living Water 246
Title: Drawing Power, Using the Jesus Kind 250
Title: Show the Study, Study to Show for it 258
Title: People With a Plan 260
Title: Everybody Knows That There is a God but Few Know the One and Only True, Living God – Jesus Christ 263

True Reflections Come from Within......268
Title Multiplied 1 ½ X 2 ½ = 4 272
Title: Clothed With the Glory of the Lord
....277
Title: Freedom Isn't Right to do as We Please it's the Responsibility to do What We Ought to do 281
Title: The Demonic Side – Affect of an Unholy Spirit 285
Title: You Can Always Add to a Finished Product..290
Title: Working On Something New, Why Don't You Stay out of God's Way 295
Title: If the Devil Can Steal Your Joy, He Can Steal Your Victory..................................298
Title: God in Thee Unexpected.................302
Title: The Sweep, Don't Get Swept Under 306
Title: Watch Out for the One Who Turns 2 Great Wonders – Both Good but ONE Turned Evil..310
Title: I Spoke it and it Was Done, I Commanded it and it Stood Fast 314
Title: Learn How to See it Like Jesus ...339
The Ten Commandments as God See's Them..354
Thought: There is Only ONE Expert 359
Title: Religion...364
Final Thought: Who's in Control 369

Introduction

Dedication to the one and only true and living God, my Jesus!

This book has been written to and for the Glory of my Jesus and always in remembrance of Him.

All that He (Jesus) has done for me knowing that no other can do it. This writing is from the Mind of Christ, through many missions in my life. His first name (Jesus) saves and His other name (Holy Spirit) anoints, they are one and cannot be parted. Whether saved or unsaved Jesus was always there, not always in what I was doing, but always there. He will never leave you nor forsake you that mean me too. Jesus said I will be with you until the end of this world and the beginning of my new one.

Jesus said I was there before your beginning and will be there at your ends choice. The end of your flesh is not always your end. I should be where you begin out of all the many things the Lord allowed me to go through and not die. I understand now that I had to be taken by Jesus for my life's purpose, so we begin in this manner. Life's up and downs and all a rounds will sometimes make you want to give up everything, even life itself. But your purpose wasn't set by you. Jesus said before you knew me, before we were formed in our mother's womb He knows us. Before you came forth out

Conforming

of the door of life, I the Lord your God said what and who you would be. You see it's not all up to you, we must learn how to say yes Lord and do it. Saying yes is easy when you're lying. Doing right in God's sight gets hard, until you get use to it like everything else, over and over until we get God's good at it.

So after years and years of my way I learned through much trial and error. Jesus brought me to a place of humbleness and needing the one and only true guidance of Him and not my fleshly wants. Remember this; the flesh is the want your spirit is the need, to get back with Christ like it was in the beginning amen.

All that's in this man made part of this world is the lust of your flesh, the pride in your life, the lust for things and everything you see. (It's personal) Jesus made it that way.

He said work out your own soul salvation with fear and trembling. Jesus has already set hidden people in place to help you. Saved or unsaved, don't get religious on me. God uses that He sees fit to help you. He will use and has used the unjust to help put and keep in His place. The heathen will tell you that you don't belong doing what they are doing, drugs won't be good any more or sleeping around. When Jesus is calling, you will answer. One way or another he will get your attention.

If you have read my first book (God's Greatest Challenge: Man and His Ungodly Ways) then

Conforming

you will really understand this one. This is the new mind Jesus gave me to help you.

Please read this and do what it says to do. You will find yourself in here some where. That's God's Word and He can't lie.

If the Real Godly truth is what you're looking for you will find it with deliverance too. God's promise: from Him, to me, to you and we all make ONE! Amen

Thanks Bill Vincent for your love and support.

The Beginning

Let's start where God starts at the beginning, His not ours.

In Genesis 1:1 through how far you care to read. God has seen fit to supply and create everything we would need even it's reproduction of itself. Then He even established Himself as the one and only true and living God. So we know that God is a spirit and the words He speaks, they are spirit and life.

When God spoke at His appointed time, let there be and it was, then we were already a spiritual seed in the body of God. That's why He said before you were formed in your mother's womb, I had to prepare you in a body to hold my likeness in you and give you a place to live and food.

Even after the man and the woman messed up because you are one flesh, I the Lord your God fixed it. Then you messed up so much and so long I had to stop you by cleaning my Earth. I baptize my Earth and make it a new. I the Lord your God gave another chance, my mercy and my grace before you understood it. Then you said in your heart, I don't really need God all the time so I had to send you into bondage then you cried and cried for years and years,

Conforming

then I heard you in my heart, I turned my ear on again to listen to your cry.

It got real to me, so I prepared for you a deliverer and I anointed Him. I showed you time after time who I am. I am everything you need and more that you can't see or think of in this life.

Then after a while you still disobeyed me more and more. Then I set up holy men of God whom I chose. I called them priest and they set my standard, then you wouldn't listen right, then came my judges, then more mighty men of valor Godly men, then kings and My prophets who sees with My eyes. I even set up some Godly women to help you. I even used a whore to help you. Then you still didn't get it. Then I knew from the start within Myself, that I had to come down to show you all how to do it right, so you could not blame anyone else but yourself. So let's begin with these writings from God's mind to my heart to you with love. Jesus said to be helpers one to another. Amen.

Conforming

Conforming means to keep changing to become to being into what was designed for you to be like, what was pre-destined for you to be.

To what God chose you to be, before you accepted it. Let change after change keep coming, for your conforming. For without change you can't be like Jesus. Jesus works in cans not cant's.

I can do all things through Christ who strengthens thee and me. Conforming to the mind of Christ, let this same mind that's in Christ Jesus be also in you. Lord I give myself away so You can teach me. More of you Lord less of me, conforming to the mind of Christ on and on and on until Heaven is your home forever in your heart.

In my first book we said (God's Greatest Challenge, Man and His Ungodly Ways) on the front. But on the back said (Out of Darkness and Into His Marvelous Light) and Jesus is the light that cometh into the whole world. He is that spiritual light that lets us see our helplessness without Him to guide us. Jesus said apart from Me you can do nothing. We need Jesus to be in us to do what's right in His sight.

Conforming

Jesus said there is a way that seemeth right to a man or woman, but it' end is death.

One real man in the Bible said, Lord my words are your words and none of them fell to the ground or went no where. The Lord said he sent me out and I would not return to Him void, but I would accomplish that which He sent me to do.

Read – Noah

Genesis 6:5-8 And GOD saw that the wickedness of man *was* great in the earth, and *that* every imagination of the thoughts of his heart *was* only evil continually. And it repented the LORD that he had made man on the earth, and it grieved him at his heart. And the LORD said, I will destroy man whom I have created from the face of the earth; both man, and beast, and the creeping thing, and the fowls of the air; for it repenteth me that I have made them. But Noah found grace in the eyes of the LORD.

Genesis 6:22 Thus did Noah; according to all that God commanded him, so did he.

Genesis 7:1 And the LORD said unto Noah, Come thou and all thy house into the ark; for thee have I seen righteous before me in this generation.

Covenant for Leadership

Joshua 1:1 Now after the death of Moses the servant of the LORD it came to pass, that the

Conforming

LORD spake unto Joshua the son of Nun, Moses' minister, saying,

God's Covenant with Job: I will never change my heart about God no matter what.

I am Jesus' Word for you? I wasn't always His spoken Word before the world was. That's what conforming to the mind of Christ means. You have to truly lose yours to gain all of His. So let me share some of His Words with you. Live in His Spirit.

Covenant

God wants to make one with you. Covenant means – To have a personal agreement and commitment between two, God and you for His Glory.

Covenant for Love – David

Covenant from Discipleship to Apostleship or your God given Office.

Acts 1:8 But ye shall receive power, after that the Holy Ghost is come upon you: and ye shall be witnesses unto me both in Jerusalem, and in all Judaea, and in Samaria, and unto the uttermost part of the earth.

Learn to do My Word and then you can teach others. You don't know until you learn how to do it My right.

Conforming

The Covenant of Protection Daniel in the Lions Den.

God told Noah to prepare an Ark of the Covenant, the covenant for new life.

God made a Faith Covenant with Abraham and changed His name.

The three who had on a fire resistant suit, made from the Holy Ghost.

The Covenant God made with Jacob to let you know it wouldn't be easy.

Isaac's Covenant of Promise - God keeps His promise will you?

Your covenant for Exodus out of Egypt or out of your bondage. Jesus made the sacrifice already, so learn how to come out of yours.

Your Covenant for Priesthood Leviticus, Are you Ready?

The Created Covenant man in God's image – Is He your God, there can only be one.

Conforming

Thought: You Can't Know Your Enemy Until You Know His god

Jeremiah 1:4-9 Then the word of the LORD came unto me, saying, Before I formed thee in the belly I knew thee; and before thou camest forth out of the womb I sanctified thee, *and* I ordained thee a prophet unto the nations. Then said I, Ah, Lord GOD! behold, I cannot speak: for I *am* a child. But the LORD said unto me, Say not, I *am* a child: for thou shalt go to all that I shall send thee, and whatsoever I command thee thou shalt speak. Be not afraid of their faces: for I *am* with thee to deliver thee, saith the LORD. Then the LORD put forth his hand, and touched my mouth. And the LORD said unto me, Behold, I have put my words in thy mouth.

Luke 5:20, 21 And when he saw their faith, he said unto him, Man, thy sins are forgiven thee. And the scribes and the Pharisees began to reason, saying, Who is this which speaketh blasphemies? Who can forgive sins, but God alone?

You must and will choose this every day whom you will serve, Jesus or that false god that makes your flesh feel good – or your gods who tells you wrong is right and right is wrong – or those who preach another Gospel.

Conforming

You must learn how to know no man by the flesh, but by their born – again Spirit or not. Many will say and have said Lord Lord, I did this and that in your name but Jesus said I see the real you, depart from me you workers of sin and your own self-righteousness. Repent or go drive into the Lake of Fire. That which is flesh is flesh and that which is Spirit is Spirit.

The reason why Godly men and women of old were victorious, they learned to listen to the spirit of God and not their own spirit - or someone else how to do everything. In all thy ways Jesus said see Me first, make sure it's Me you are seeking, not your need.

Conforming

Thought – Betrayal

Betrayal Always Leaves a Trail

Betray means to lead a stray or seduce to deliver to an enemy by treachery to fail or desert in time of need, to prove false.

Jesus said it means – putting other things and people before God all the time - letting your trying to serve two masters – have it's way or letting bitter and sweet waters of the Word and the world come out of you.

Do – Giver – Means

Whatever you are doing right or wrong is giving a part of it – it's planting and sowing into your life – for the better or bitterness – to help you go to Heaven or help you to drive into hell.

There is a high form of betrayal and a low form. The Word of God says against thee and thee only have I sinned and done this evil in thy sight O Lord – lying, cheating, stealing, backbiting, deceiving, unforgiveness is a plant that grows into the tree of betrayal. Then the tree has become the giver of betrayal.

Thinking it, talking about it to long will mostly lead to doing it the Father the seed is planted the deeper it takes root. Then once it has rooted it says (let me out of here) it's time for me to do what was planted inside of you to do good or evil.

The Lord said He created us for His Glory, to show forth His good works, to help others. To lead others to Jesus to show His real love that they never had before. Real love conquers all and that's Jesus on the inside of you. The real Jesus there is only one. Amen.

Thought: So Then How Far Are You and Your Anointing Prepared to Go?

Sub Thought: Do You See It

The Bible says; do not hold back from doing good when it's in your power to do so.

Proverbs 23:7 For as he thinketh in his heart, so *is* he: Eat and drink, saith he to thee; but his heart *is* not with thee.

There are a few things we say when it comes down to helping someone else when we don't want to. Let me share some with you okay:
1. Now What
2. So I Will
3. Let Me See
4. Maybe I Will
5. If I Can
6. As Soon As I
7. I Think I Can
8. Let Me Ask
9. I Will Do It Later
10. It's Not Important
11. They Can Wait
12. You Will Be Fine
13. The Next Time

14. They Don't Really Need It.

John 1:6-13 There was a man sent from God, whose name *was* John. The same came for a witness, to bear witness of the Light, that all *men* through him might believe. He was not that Light, but *was sent* to bear witness of that Light. *That* was the true Light, which lighteth every man that cometh into the world. He was in the world, and the world was made by him, and the world knew him not. He came unto his own, and his own received him not. But as many as received him, to them gave he power to become the sons of God, *even* to them that believe on his name: Which were born, not of blood, nor of the will of the flesh, nor of the will of man, but of God.

The Two Biggest Ones:
1. I Don't Feel Like It
2. Let Me Pray About It

The Lord said it's simply right or wrong. You already know how to do right. I am trying to teach you how to do your wrong that you like.

Ask Yourself

Did Jesus feel like going to the cross to die for your ugly sins that you may live for ever with Him.

Did you pray about doing wrong before you did it?

Thought: God Is Looking for Some Standers

Sub Thought: If You Don't Bow You Won't Bend Then You Won't Burn

1Corinthians 15:57, 58 But thanks *be* to God, which giveth us the victory through our Lord Jesus Christ. Therefore, my beloved brethren, be ye stedfast, unmoveable, always abounding in the work of the Lord, forasmuch as ye know that your labour is not in vain in the Lord.

Daniel 3:15-27 Now if ye be ready that at what time ye hear the sound of the cornet, flute, harp, sackbut, psaltery, and dulcimer, and all kinds of musick, ye fall down and worship the image which I have made; *well:* but if ye worship not, ye shall be cast the same hour into the midst of a burning fiery furnace; and who *is* that God that shall deliver you out of my hands? Shadrach, Meshach, and Abednego, answered and said to the king, O Nebuchadnezzar, we *are* not careful to answer thee in this matter. If it be *so,* our God whom we serve is able to deliver us from the burning fiery furnace, and he will deliver *us* out of thine hand, O king. But if not, be it known unto thee, O king, that we will not serve thy gods, nor

Conforming

worship the golden image which thou hast set up. Then was Nebuchadnezzar full of fury, and the form of his visage was changed against Shadrach, Meshach, and Abednego: *therefore* he spake, and commanded that they should heat the furnace one seven times more than it was wont to be heated. And he commanded the most mighty men that *were* in his army to bind Shadrach, Meshach, and Abednego, *and* to cast *them* into the burning fiery furnace. Then these men were bound in their coats, their hosen, and their hats, and their *other* garments, and were cast into the midst of the burning fiery furnace. Therefore because the king's commandment was urgent, and the furnace exceeding hot, the flame of the fire slew those men that took up Shadrach, Meshach, and Abednego. And these three men, Shadrach, Meshach, and Abednego, fell down bound into the midst of the burning fiery furnace. Then Nebuchadnezzar the king was astonied, and rose up in haste, *and* spake, and said unto his counsellors, Did not we cast three men bound into the midst of the fire? They answered and said unto the king, True, O king. He answered and said, Lo, I see four men loose, walking in the midst of the fire, and they have no hurt; and the form of the fourth is like the Son of God. Then Nebuchadnezzar came near to the mouth of the burning fiery furnace, *and* spake, and said, Shadrach, Meshach, and Abednego, ye servants of the most high God, come forth, and come *hither*. Then Shadrach, Meshach, and Abednego, came forth of the midst of the fire. And the princes, governors, and captains, and the king's counsellors, being gathered together, saw these men, upon whose bodies the fire had no power, nor was an hair of their head singed, neither were their coats changed, nor the smell of fire had passed on them.

Theme: From the Fire to God's Favor

Daniel 3:28-30 *Then* Nebuchadnezzar spake, and said, Blessed *be* the God of Shadrach, Meshach, and Abednego, who hath sent his angel, and delivered his servants that trusted in him, and have changed the king's word, and yielded their bodies, that they might not serve nor worship any god, except their own God. Therefore I make a decree, That every people, nation, and language, which speak any thing amiss against the God of Shadrach, Meshach, and Abednego, shall be cut in pieces, and their houses shall be made a dunghill: because there is no other God that can deliver after this sort. Then the king promoted Shadrach, Meshach, and Abednego, in the province of Babylon.

Front Note: Introduction
Jews God's Chosen People

Daniel 3:12 There are certain Jews whom thou hast set over the affairs of the province of Babylon, Shadrach, Meshach, and Abednego; these men, O king, have not regarded thee: they serve not thy gods, nor worship the golden image which thou hast set up.

My sheep know my voice and a strange voice they will not follow.

Conforming

They will bring you in privately to try to get you to compromise.

They will give one last chance to scare them, before they crucify you.

They will always think about that their god is mightier. Think again.

There can only be one Jesus!

Thought: The Missing Link

Sub Thought: The Piece That Just Couldn't Fit

Mark 8:34 And when he had called the people *unto him* with his disciples also, he said unto them, Whosoever will come after me, let him deny himself, and take up his cross, and follow me.

When you have really done Mark 8:34 you will never fit in anybody's Church but you will fit in your ministry for Jesus and you're not like any body else in the Body of Christ according to these scriptures:

1Peter 2:9 But ye *are* a chosen generation, a royal priesthood, an holy nation, a peculiar people; that ye should shew forth the praises of him who hath called you out of darkness into his marvellous light:

1Corinthinans 1:27 But God hath chosen the foolish things of the world to confound the wise; and God hath chosen the weak things of the world to confound the things which are mighty;

Acts 9:15 But the Lord said unto him, Go thy way: for he is a chosen vessel unto me, to bear

Conforming

my name before the Gentiles, and kings, and the children of Israel:

John 15:16 Ye have not chosen me, but I have chosen you, and ordained you, that ye should go and bring forth fruit, and *that* your fruit should remain: that whatsoever ye shall ask of the Father in my name, he may give it you.

Jesus said in John 15:16 you have no choice, but one when the Master calls. It's either Heaven or Hell. Jesus' way or the wrong way to Hell.

God's Judgment has already been released according to 2 Timothy 3:1-7.

2Timothy 3:1-7 This know also, that in the last days perilous times shall come. For men shall be lovers of their own selves, covetous, boasters, proud, blasphemers, disobedient to parents, unthankful, unholy, Without natural affection, trucebreakers, false accusers, incontinent, fierce, despisers of those that are good, Traitors, heady, highminded, lovers of pleasures more than lovers of God; Having a form of godliness, but denying the power thereof: from such turn away. For of this sort are they which creep into houses, and lead captive silly women laden with sins, led away with divers lusts, Ever learning, and never able to come to the knowledge of the truth.

The Lord said no one knows the day nor the hour when the Son of man will return. He might come for you and leave me are you ready?

Conforming

When we say missing link we often think of someone crazy, but when you have a true walk and life with Jesus. They will call you crazy and beyond the Church folk who don't know Jesus but they know Church. They know the letter but not the Spirit. John 4:24 says that my Jesus is a Spirit, serve me in Spirit and in truth says the Lord. You must be born again; there is no other way in.

John 4:24 God *is* a Spirit: and they that worship him must worship *him* in spirit and in truth.

The wind blows where it wants and you can't tell where it's coming from. So are you, if you are born of Jesus' Spirit.

Remember they will hate you for loving Me says the Lord and count it all joy.

How?

Follow Jesus prescribed way that will endure for-ever, that will never fail if you are living it by faith. Remember faith without works of holiness is dead. You will never really fit in with no-one else but Jesus. Ask Mary they wanted to put her away in the nut house because she was pregnant and had not slept with a man.

They told David he was too little to fight the giant.

They told the three Hebrew boys to walk in the fire and die because they didn't fit in.

Conforming

They told me to die on drugs and that I would never be anything and I would never fit in.

But look at Jesus in me now.

Ps. Call home the Master is waiting.

Conforming

Thought: Praising God on Credit

Sub Thought: Instructions Are Important

Joshua 6:1-21 Now Jericho was straitly shut up because of the children of Israel: none went out, and none came in. And the LORD said unto Joshua, See, I have given into thine hand Jericho, and the king thereof, *and* the mighty men of valour. And ye shall compass the city, all *ye* men of war, *and* go round about the city once. Thus shalt thou do six days. And seven priests shall bear before the ark seven trumpets of rams' horns: and the seventh day ye shall compass the city seven times, and the priests shall blow with the trumpets. And it shall come to pass, that when they make a long *blast* with the ram's horn, *and* when ye hear the sound of the trumpet, all the people shall shout with a great shout; and the wall of the city shall fall down flat, and the people shall ascend up every man straight before him. And Joshua the son of Nun called the priests, and said unto them, Take up the ark of the covenant, and let seven priests bear seven trumpets of rams' horns before the ark of the LORD. And he said unto the people, Pass on, and compass the city, and let him that is armed pass on before the ark of the LORD. And it came to pass, when Joshua had spoken unto the people, that the seven priests bearing the seven trumpets of rams' horns passed on before the LORD, and blew with the trumpets: and the ark of the covenant of the LORD followed them. And the armed men went before the priests that blew with the trumpets, and the rereward came after the ark, *the priests* going on, and blowing with the trumpets. And Joshua had commanded the people, saying, Ye shall not shout, nor make any noise with your voice, neither shall *any* word proceed out of your mouth, until the day I bid you shout; then shall ye shout. So the ark of the LORD compassed the city, going about *it* once: and they came into the camp, and lodged in the camp. And Joshua rose early in the morning, and the priests took up the ark of the LORD. And seven priests bearing seven trumpets of rams' horns before the ark of the LORD went on continually, and blew with the trumpets: and the armed men went before them; but the rereward came after the ark of the LORD, *the priests* going on, and blowing with the trumpets. And the second day they compassed the city once, and returned into the camp: so they did six days. And it came to pass on the seventh day, that they rose early about the dawning of the day, and compassed the city after the same manner seven times: only on that day they compassed the city seven times. And it came to pass at the seventh time, when the priests blew with the trumpets, Joshua said unto the people, Shout; for the LORD hath given you the city. And the city shall be accursed, *even* it, and all that *are* therein, to the LORD: only Rahab the harlot shall live, she

Conforming

and all that *are* with her in the house, because she hid the messengers that we sent. And ye, in any wise keep *yourselves* from the accursed thing, lest ye make *yourselves* accursed, when ye take of the accursed thing, and make the camp of Israel a curse, and trouble it. But all the silver, and gold, and vessels of brass and iron, *are* consecrated unto the LORD: they shall come into the treasury of the LORD. So the people shouted when *the priests* blew with the trumpets: and it came to pass, when the people heard the sound of the trumpet, and the people shouted with a great shout, that the wall fell down flat, so that the people went up into the city, every man straight before him, and they took the city. And they utterly destroyed all that *was* in the city, both man and woman, young and old, and ox, and sheep, and ass, with the edge of the sword.

2Samuel 5:19-25 And David enquired of the LORD, saying, Shall I go up to the Philistines? wilt thou deliver them into mine hand? And the LORD said unto David, Go up: for I will doubtless deliver the Philistines into thine hand. And David came to Baalperazim, and David smote them there, and said, The LORD hath broken forth upon mine enemies before me, as the breach of waters. Therefore he called the name of that place Baalperazim. And there they left their images, and David and his men burned them. And the Philistines came up yet again, and spread themselves in the valley of Rephaim. And when David enquired of the LORD, he said, Thou shalt not go up; *but* fetch a compass behind them, and come upon them

Conforming

over against the mulberry trees. And let it be, when thou hearest the sound of a going in the tops of the mulberry trees, that then thou shalt bestir thyself: for then shall the LORD go out before thee, to smite the host of the Philistines. And David did so, as the LORD had commanded him; and smote the Philistines from Geba until thou come to Gazer.

Theme: God has the victory in His hands but you won't have it until the Lord gives it to you. So wait for it. Amen.

You can't make your own victory it won't work.

6 Points to Make

1. As I was with Moses so shall I be with you Joshua (Put your name there)

2. Time for you to step up Joshua (Put your name there)

3. Whatever land you walk on it's yours

4. Be strong and of good courage, I am with you always even when you can't see me.

5. Follow My Word, My will and My way – there's only one.

6. Don't be afraid, I the Lord thy God is with thee always everywhere

Conforming

The Word

Proverbs 31:1-31 The words of king Lemuel, the prophecy that his mother taught him. What, my son? and what, the son of my womb? and what, the son of my vows? Give not thy strength unto women, nor thy ways to that which destroyeth kings. *It is* not for kings, O Lemuel, *it is* not for kings to drink wine; nor for princes strong drink: Lest they drink, and forget the law, and pervert the judgment of any of the afflicted. Give strong drink unto him that is ready to perish, and wine unto those that be of heavy hearts. Let him drink, and forget his poverty, and remember his misery no more. Open thy mouth for the dumb in the cause of all such as are appointed to destruction. Open thy mouth, judge righteously, and plead the cause of the poor and needy. Who can find a virtuous woman? for her price *is* far above rubies. The heart of her husband doth safely trust in her, so that he shall have no need of spoil. She will do him good and not evil all the days of her life. She seeketh wool, and flax, and worketh willingly with her hands. She is like the merchants' ships; she bringeth her food from afar. She riseth also while it is yet night, and giveth meat to her household, and a portion to her maidens. She considereth a field, and buyeth it: with the fruit of her hands she planteth a vineyard. She girdeth her loins with strength, and strengtheneth her arms. She perceiveth that her merchandise *is* good: her candle goeth not out by night. She layeth her hands to the spindle, and her hands hold the distaff. She stretcheth out her hand to the poor;

yea, she reacheth forth her hands to the needy. She is not afraid of the snow for her household: for all her household *are* clothed with scarlet. She maketh herself coverings of tapestry; her clothing *is* silk and purple. Her husband is known in the gates, when he sitteth among the elders of the land. She maketh fine linen, and selleth *it;* and delivereth girdles unto the merchant. Strength and honour *are* her clothing; and she shall rejoice in time to come. She openeth her mouth with wisdom; and in her tongue *is* the law of kindness. She looketh well to the ways of her household, and eateth not the bread of idleness. Her children arise up, and call her blessed; her husband *also,* and he praiseth her. Many daughters have done virtuously, but thou excellest them all. Favour *is* deceitful, and beauty *is* vain: *but* a woman *that* feareth the LORD, she shall be praised. Give her of the fruit of her hands; and let her own works praise her in the gates.

1Peter 3:7 Likewise, ye husbands, dwell with *them* according to knowledge, giving honour unto the wife, as unto the weaker vessel, and as being heirs together of the grace of life; that your prayers be not hindered.

Jeremiah 31:22 How long wilt thou go about, O thou backsliding daughter? for the LORD hath created a new thing in the earth, A woman shall compass a man.

Proverbs 18:22 *Whoso* findeth a wife findeth a good *thing,* and obtaineth favour of the LORD.

Conforming

1Corinthians 11:7 For a man indeed ought not to cover *his* head, forasmuch as he is the image and glory of God: but the woman is the glory of the man.

Thought: Naked Not Ashamed

Sub Thought: But for Who's Glory

Mark 1:15-32 And saying, The time is fulfilled, and the kingdom of God is at hand: repent ye, and believe the gospel. Now as he walked by the sea of Galilee, he saw Simon and Andrew his brother casting a net into the sea: for they were fishers. And Jesus said unto them, Come ye after me, and I will make you to become fishers of men. And straightway they forsook their nets, and followed him. And when he had gone a little further thence, he saw James the *son* of Zebedee, and John his brother, who also were in the ship mending their nets. And straightway he called them: and they left their father Zebedee in the ship with the hired servants, and went after him. And they went into Capernaum; and straightway on the sabbath day he entered into the synagogue, and taught. And they were astonished at his doctrine: for he taught them as one that had authority, and not as the scribes. And there was in their synagogue a man with an unclean spirit; and he cried out, Saying, Let *us* alone; what have we to do with thee, thou Jesus of Nazareth? art thou come to destroy us? I know thee who thou art, the Holy One of God. And

Conforming

Jesus rebuked him, saying, Hold thy peace, and come out of him. And when the unclean spirit had torn him, and cried with a loud voice, he came out of him. And they were all amazed, insomuch that they questioned among themselves, saying, What thing is this? what new doctrine *is* this? for with authority commandeth he even the unclean spirits, and they do obey him. And immediately his fame spread abroad throughout all the region round about Galilee. And forthwith, when they were come out of the synagogue, they entered into the house of Simon and Andrew, with James and John. But Simon's wife's mother lay sick of a fever, and anon they tell him of her. And he came and took her by the hand, and lifted her up; and immediately the fever left her, and she ministered unto them. And at even, when the sun did set, they brought unto him all that were diseased, and them that were possessed with devils.

Are you alive in Jesus or are you a carbon copy of the devil?

John 1:1-17 In the beginning was the Word, and the Word was with God, and the Word was God. The same was in the beginning with God. All things were made by him; and without him was not any thing made that was made. In him was life; and the life was the light of men. And the light shineth in darkness; and the darkness comprehended it not. There was a man sent from God, whose name *was* John. The same came for a witness, to bear witness of the Light, that all *men* through him might believe. He was

Conforming

not that Light, but *was sent* to bear witness of that Light. *That* was the true Light, which lighteth every man that cometh into the world. He was in the world, and the world was made by him, and the world knew him not. He came unto his own, and his own received him not. But as many as received him, to them gave he power to become the sons of God, *even* to them that believe on his name: Which were born, not of blood, nor of the will of the flesh, nor of the will of man, but of God. And the Word was made flesh, and dwelt among us, (and we beheld his glory, the glory as of the only begotten of the Father,) full of grace and truth. John bare witness of him, and cried, saying, This was he of whom I spake, He that cometh after me is preferred before me: for he was before me. And of his fulness have all we received, and grace for grace. For the law was given by Moses, *but* grace and truth came by Jesus Christ.

Jesus said that the Words I speak are Spirit and they are life.

Spirit Made Alive

Psalms 51:10 Create in me a clean heart, O God; and renew a right spirit within me.

Colossians 2:13 And you, being dead in your sins and the uncircumcision of your flesh, hath he quickened together with him, having forgiven you all trespasses;

Conforming

Matthews 26:41 Watch and pray, that ye enter not into temptation: the spirit indeed *is* willing, but the flesh *is* weak.

1Peter 3:18 For Christ also hath once suffered for sins, the just for the unjust, that he might bring us to God, being put to death in the flesh, but quickened by the Spirit:

Romans 8:16 The Spirit itself beareth witness with our spirit, that we are the children of God:

Ephesians 2:1 And you *hath he quickened,* who were dead in trespasses and sins;

Ephesians 2:5 Even when we were dead in sins, hath quickened us together with Christ, (by grace ye are saved;)

The Carbon Copy

Ephesians 2:2 Wherein in time past ye walked according to the course of this world, according to the prince of the power of the air, the spirit that now worketh in the children of disobedience:

Ephesians 4:18-22 Having the understanding darkened, being alienated from the life of God through the ignorance that is in them, because of the blindness of their heart: Who being past feeling have given themselves over unto lasciviousness, to work all uncleanness with greediness. But ye have not so learned Christ; If so be that ye have heard him, and have been taught by him, as the truth is in Jesus: That ye put off concerning the former conversation the old man, which is corrupt according to the deceitful lusts;

Ephesians 4:25-32 Wherefore putting away lying, speak every man truth with his neighbour: for we are members one of another. Be ye angry, and sin not: let not the sun go down upon your wrath: Neither give place to the devil. Let him that stole steal no more: but rather let him labour, working with *his* hands the thing which is good, that he may have to give to him that needeth. Let no corrupt communication proceed out of your mouth, but that which is good to the use of edifying, that it may minister grace unto the hearers. And grieve not the holy Spirit of God, whereby ye are sealed unto the day of redemption. Let all bitterness, and wrath, and anger, and clamour, and evil speaking, be put away from you, with all malice: And be ye kind one to another, tenderhearted, forgiving one another, even as God for Christ's sake hath forgiven you.

Thought: The Lord Has Made for Me to Do

Sub Thought: What?

1. God prepared a place for man to live and food to eat and everything else we need.

God said let Us make man in Our image after likeness to be just image after Our likeness, to be just like Him in every way high in holiness.

2. Be a creator

3. Be a Provider

4. To love everyone

5. To be a friend to everyone short and long distance

6. To hate evil and sin

7. To let Him do good things through us

8. To learn and teach

9. To walk in the Office He put and ordered us to be in before the world bean.

10. To finish your course

Conforming

Thought: D.N.A.

Focus Verse:
John 3:5-8 Jesus answered, Verily, verily, I say unto thee, Except a man be born of water and *of* the Spirit, he cannot enter into the kingdom of God. That which is born of the flesh is flesh; and that which is born of the Spirit is spirit. Marvel not that I said unto thee, Ye must be born again. The wind bloweth where it listeth, and thou hearest the sound thereof, but canst not tell whence it cometh, and whither it goeth: so is every one that is born of the Spirit.

Jesus said your D.N.A. should be,
D – Devine, Heavenly, Godly
N – Supernatural of the Holy Spirit
A – Agent

John 2:19 Jesus answered and said unto them, Destroy this temple, and in three days I will raise it up.

Acts 1:8 But ye shall receive power, after that the Holy Ghost is come upon you: and ye shall be witnesses unto me both in Jerusalem, and in all Judaea, and in Samaria, and unto the uttermost part of the earth.

Jesus made – spittle to make a man see. He blew on them and they received the Holy Spirit. He laid hands on them and they were healed. He sent His Word and they were healed.

Conforming

The Words I speak are Spirit and they are life.

Agent means – Something that produces or is capable of producing an effect. One that acts or exerts power – One who acts for or in place of another by authority from him – One engaged in under cover activities.

God said agent means – Someone who is filled with the Holy Ghost and His power.

Conforming

Thought: Never Be Without One

Sub Thought: Use What You've Got

Theme: The Holy Spirit, there can only be ONE. God said try the Spirit to see if it be of God.

1Corinthians 10:1-5 Moreover, brethren, I would not that ye should be ignorant, how that all our fathers were under the cloud, and all passed through the sea; And were all baptized unto Moses in the cloud and in the sea; And did all eat the same spiritual meat; And did all drink the same spiritual drink: for they drank of that spiritual Rock that followed them: and that Rock was Christ. But with many of them God was not well pleased: for they were overthrown in the wilderness.

1Corinthians 12:1-18 Now concerning spiritual *gifts,* brethren, I would not have you ignorant. Ye know that ye were Gentiles, carried away unto these dumb idols, even as ye were led. Wherefore I give you to understand, that no man speaking by the Spirit of God calleth Jesus accursed: and *that* no man can say that Jesus is the Lord, but by the Holy Ghost. Now there are diversities of gifts, but the same Spirit. And there are differences of administrations, but the same Lord. And there are diversities of operations, but it is the same God which worketh all in all. But the manifestation of the Spirit is given to every man to profit withal. For to one is given by the Spirit the word of wisdom; to another the word of knowledge by the same Spirit; To another faith by the same Spirit; to another the gifts of healing by the same Spirit; To another the working of miracles; to another prophecy; to another discerning of spirits; to another *divers* kinds of tongues; to another the interpretation of tongues: But all these worketh that one and the selfsame Spirit, dividing to every man severally as he will. For as the body is one, and hath many members, and all the members of that one body, being many, are one body: so also *is* Christ. For by one Spirit are we all baptized into one body, whether *we be* Jews or Gentiles, whether *we be* bond or free; and have been all made to drink into one Spirit. For the body is not one member, but many. If the foot shall say, Because I am not the hand, I am not of the body; is it therefore not of the body? And if the ear shall say, Because I am not the eye, I am not of the body; is it therefore not of the body? If the whole body *were* an eye, where *were* the hearing? If the whole *were* hearing, where *were* the smelling? But now hath God set the members every one of them in the body, as it hath pleased him.

Thought: Holy Ghost Pure Fire

1Thessalonions 5:9-27 For God hath not appointed us to wrath, but to obtain salvation by our Lord Jesus Christ, Who died for us, that, whether we wake or sleep, we should live together with him. Wherefore comfort yourselves together, and edify one another, even as also ye do. And we beseech you, brethren, to know them which labour among you, and are over you in the Lord, and admonish you; And to esteem them very highly in love for their work's sake. *And* be at peace among yourselves. Now we exhort you, brethren, warn them that are unruly, comfort the feebleminded, support the weak, be patient toward all *men*. See that none render evil for evil unto any *man;* but ever follow that which is good, both among yourselves, and to all *men*. Rejoice evermore. Pray without ceasing. In every thing give thanks: for this is the will of God in Christ Jesus concerning you. Quench not the Spirit. Despise not prophesyings. Prove all things; hold fast that which is good. Abstain from all appearance of evil. And the very God of peace sanctify you wholly; and *I pray God* your whole spirit and soul and body be preserved blameless unto the coming of our Lord Jesus Christ. Faithful *is* he that calleth you, who also will do *it*. Brethren, pray for us. Greet all the brethren with an holy kiss. I

Conforming

charge you by the Lord that this epistle be read unto all the holy brethren.

Through the Fire
Through the Rain
Through the Storm
Through the Refiners Fire
Through the Purified Fire
Through the Cutting Fire
Through the Flesh Destroying Fire
Through the Erasing Fire
Through the Gold Making Fire
Through the Steadfast Fire
Through the Abounding in the Word Fire
Through the Cleansing Fire
Through the Separating Fire
Through the Mind Changing Fire
Through the Self Destroying Fire Starting With Me Fire
For Your Glory Fire O Lord
For Your Purpose
For Your Ministry Inside of Me
For Your Souls Every Where
For Your Truth, Thy Word is Truth
Never Leaving You Lord Fire

Thought: The Compelling Kind

Sub Thought: But Some Will Repel to Propel You to Hell

Focus Verse:
Luke 14:16-24 Then said he unto him, A certain man made a great supper, and bade many: And sent his servant at supper time to say to them that were bidden, Come; for all things are now ready. And they all with one *consent* began to make excuse. The first said unto him, I have bought a piece of ground, and I must needs go and see it: I pray thee have me excused. And another said, I have bought five yoke of oxen, and I go to prove them: I pray thee have me excused. And another said, I have married a wife, and therefore I cannot come. So that servant came, and shewed his lord these things. Then the master of the house being angry said to his servant, Go out quickly into the streets and lanes of the city, and bring in hither the poor, and the maimed, and the halt, and the blind. And the servant said, Lord, it is done as thou hast commanded, and yet there is room. And the lord said unto the servant, Go out into the highways and hedges, and compel *them* to come in, that my house may be filled. For I say unto you, That none of those men which were bidden shall taste of my supper.

Conforming

Compel
Repel
Propel

Matthew 28:17-20 And when they saw him, they worshipped him: but some doubted. And Jesus came and spake unto them, saying, All power is given unto me in heaven and in earth. Go ye therefore, and teach all nations, baptizing them in the name of the Father, and of the Son, and of the Holy Ghost: Teaching them to observe all things whatsoever I have commanded you: and, lo, I am with you alway, *even* unto the end of the world. Amen.

Mark 16:14-18 Afterward he appeared unto the eleven as they sat at meat, and upbraided them with their unbelief and hardness of heart, because they believed not them which had seen him after he was risen. And he said unto them, Go ye into all the world, and preach the gospel to every creature. He that believeth and is baptized shall be saved; but he that believeth not shall be damned. And these signs shall follow them that believe; In my name shall they cast out devils; they shall speak with new tongues; They shall take up serpents; and if they drink any deadly thing, it shall not hurt them; they shall lay hands on the sick, and they shall recover.

Luke 24:46-49 And said unto them, Thus it is written, and thus it behoved Christ to suffer, and to rise from the dead the third day: And that repentance and remission of sins should be preached in his name among all nations,

Conforming

beginning at Jerusalem. And ye are witnesses of these things. And, behold, I send the promise of my Father upon you: but tarry ye in the city of Jerusalem, until ye be endued with power from on high.

John 20:20-23 And when he had so said, he shewed unto them *his* hands and his side. Then were the disciples glad, when they saw the Lord. Then said Jesus to them again, Peace *be* unto you: as *my* Father hath sent me, even so send I you. And when he had said this, he breathed on *them,* and saith unto them, Receive ye the Holy Ghost: Whose soever sins ye remit, they are remitted unto them; *and* whose soever *sins* ye retain, they are retained.

Compel Means – to cause one to surrender or bring to submission, to drive or urge forcefully, to cause to do or occur by over whelming pressure.

God said compel means – love always finds a way.

Propel Means – to drive forward or onward by means of force, to urge on.

God said propel means – to be led by the Holy Spirit.

Repel Means – to drive back to turn away to reject to fight against, to discourage.

God said repel means – to lie to people.

Conforming

Thought: My Rock

My Says - Personalized

Redeemer
Ordinance
Correction
Knowledge

Focus Verses:
Isaiah 44:24, 25 Thus saith the LORD, thy redeemer, and he that formed thee from the womb, I *am* the LORD that maketh all *things;* that stretcheth forth the heavens alone; that spreadeth abroad the earth by myself; That frustrateth the tokens of the liars, and maketh diviners mad; that turneth wise *men* backward, and maketh their knowledge foolish;

Jeremiah 50:34 Their Redeemer *is* strong; the LORD of hosts *is* his name: he shall throughly plead their cause, that he may give rest to the land, and disquiet the inhabitants of Babylon.

Job 19:25 For I know *that* my redeemer liveth, and *that* he shall stand at the latter *day* upon the earth:

Redeemer – A person who redeems or buys back, to get or win back, to free from what distresses or harms, to free from captivity by payment or ransom, to release from blame or debt, to restore, to offset the bad effect of the full.

Ordinance – to put in order, a law set forth, something ordained or decreed.

Correction – rebuke, punishment, a bringing into conformity with a standard, something substituted in a place of what is wrong.

Knowledge – the fact or condition of knowing something, the range of one's information or understanding the sum of what is known, the body of truth God's truth not man's facts, facts can be changed God's Word can't.

Title: The Inside Man

Sub Title: He's Omnipresent – Everywhere at once

Theme – Unseen, Yet Always Seen

Main Meat – The Inside Man

2Kings 6:8-23 Then the king of Syria warred against Israel, and took counsel with his servants, saying, In such and such a place *shall be* my camp. And the man of God sent unto the king of Israel, saying, Beware that thou pass not such a place; for thither the Syrians are come down. And the king of Israel sent to the place which the man of God told him and warned him of, and saved himself there, not once nor twice. Therefore the heart of the king of Syria was sore troubled for this thing; and he called his servants, and said unto them, Will ye not shew me which of us *is* for the king of Israel? And one of his servants said, None, my lord, O king: but Elisha, the prophet that *is* in Israel, telleth the king of Israel the words that thou speakest in thy bedchamber. And he said, Go and spy where he *is,* that I may send and fetch him. And it was told him, saying, Behold, *he is* in Dothan. Therefore sent he thither horses, and chariots, and a great host: and they came by night, and compassed the city about. And when the servant of the man of God was risen early, and gone forth, behold, an host compassed the city both with horses and chariots. And his servant said unto him, Alas, my master! how shall we do? And he answered, Fear not: for they that *be* with us *are* more than they that *be* with them. And Elisha prayed, and said, LORD, I pray thee, open his eyes, that he may see. And the LORD opened the eyes of the young man; and he saw: and, behold, the mountain *was* full of horses and chariots of fire round about Elisha. And when they came down to him, Elisha prayed unto the LORD, and said, Smite this people, I pray thee, with blindness. And he smote them with blindness according to the word of Elisha. And Elisha said unto them, This *is* not the way, neither *is* this the city: follow me, and I will bring you to the man whom ye seek. But he led them to Samaria. And it came to pass, when they were come into Samaria, that Elisha said, LORD, open the eyes of these *men,* that they may see. And the LORD opened their eyes, and they saw; and, behold, *they were* in the midst of Samaria. And the king of Israel said unto Elisha, when he saw them, My father, shall I smite *them?* shall I smite *them?* And he answered, Thou shalt not smite *them:* wouldest thou smite those whom thou hast taken captive with thy sword and with thy bow? set bread and water before them, that they may eat and drink, and go to their master. And he prepared great provision for them: and when they had eaten and drunk, he sent them away, and they went to their master. So the bands of Syria came no more into the land of Israel.

Conforming

The inside man will only tell the one who needs to be told and not everyone. He will keep your secret and put the right plan in the right heart to help you. You can only have the inside man on the inside of you, not on the outside. If He's on the outside you're in control - and that's messed up for life here and in your there – and your there won't be where He is. Amen.

Title: Holy Ghost Have Your Own Way

Sub Title: But Listen and Remember One Thing I Won't Move Without You

Theme – The Same Yet Different

Saul Turned Into Paul:
Acts 9:1-22 And Saul, yet breathing out threatenings and slaughter against the disciples of the Lord, went unto the high priest, And desired of him letters to Damascus to the synagogues, that if he found any of this way, whether they were men or women, he might bring them bound unto Jerusalem. And as he journeyed, he came near Damascus: and suddenly there shined round about him a light from heaven: And he fell to the earth, and heard a voice saying unto him, Saul, Saul, why persecutest thou me? And he said, Who art thou, Lord? And the Lord said, I am Jesus whom thou persecutest: *it is* hard for thee to kick against the pricks. And he trembling and astonished said, Lord, what wilt thou have me to do? And the Lord *said* unto him, Arise, and go into the city, and it shall be told thee what thou must do. And the men which journeyed with him stood speechless, hearing a voice, but

Conforming

seeing no man. And Saul arose from the earth; and when his eyes were opened, he saw no man: but they led him by the hand, and brought *him* into Damascus. And he was three days without sight, and neither did eat nor drink. And there was a certain disciple at Damascus, named Ananias; and to him said the Lord in a vision, Ananias. And he said, Behold, I *am here,* Lord. And the Lord *said* unto him, Arise, and go into the street which is called Straight, and enquire in the house of Judas for *one* called Saul, of Tarsus: for, behold, he prayeth, And hath seen in a vision a man named Ananias coming in, and putting *his* hand on him, that he might receive his sight. Then Ananias answered, Lord, I have heard by many of this man, how much evil he hath done to thy saints at Jerusalem: And here he hath authority from the chief priests to bind all that call on thy name. But the Lord said unto him, Go thy way: for he is a chosen vessel unto me, to bear my name before the Gentiles, and kings, and the children of Israel: For I will shew him how great things he must suffer for my name's sake. And Ananias went his way, and entered into the house; and putting his hands on him said, Brother Saul, the Lord, *even* Jesus, that appeared unto thee in the way as thou camest, hath sent me, that thou mightest receive thy sight, and be filled with the Holy Ghost. And immediately there fell from his eyes as it had been scales: and he received sight forthwith, and arose, and was baptized. And when he had received meat, he was strengthened. Then was Saul certain days with the disciples which were at Damascus.

Conforming

And straightway he preached Christ in the synagogues, that he is the Son of God. But all that heard *him* were amazed, and said; Is not this he that destroyed them which called on this name in Jerusalem, and came hither for that intent, that he might bring them bound unto the chief priests? But Saul increased the more in strength, and confounded the Jews which dwelt at Damascus, proving that this is very Christ.

Peter:
Acts 10:1-48 There was a certain man in Caesarea called Cornelius, a centurion of the band called the Italian *band, A* devout *man,* and one that feared God with all his house, which gave much alms to the people, and prayed to God alway. He saw in a vision evidently about the ninth hour of the day an angel of God coming in to him, and saying unto him, Cornelius. And when he looked on him, he was afraid, and said, What is it, Lord? And he said unto him, Thy prayers and thine alms are come up for a memorial before God. And now send men to Joppa, and call for *one* Simon, whose surname is Peter: He lodgeth with one Simon a tanner, whose house is by the sea side: he shall tell thee what thou oughtest to do. And when the angel which spake unto Cornelius was departed, he called two of his household servants, and a devout soldier of them that waited on him continually; And when he had declared all *these* things unto them, he sent them to Joppa. On the morrow, as they went on their journey, and drew nigh unto the city, Peter went up upon the housetop to pray about

Conforming

the sixth hour: And he became very hungry, and would have eaten: but while they made ready, he fell into a trance, And saw heaven opened, and a certain vessel descending unto him, as it had been a great sheet knit at the four corners, and let down to the earth: Wherein were all manner of fourfooted beasts of the earth, and wild beasts, and creeping things, and fowls of the air. And there came a voice to him, Rise, Peter; kill, and eat. But Peter said, Not so, Lord; for I have never eaten any thing that is common or unclean. And the voice *spake* unto him again the second time, What God hath cleansed, *that* call not thou common. This was done thrice: and the vessel was received up again into heaven. Now while Peter doubted in himself what this vision which he had seen should mean, behold, the men which were sent from Cornelius had made enquiry for Simon's house, and stood before the gate, And called, and asked whether Simon, which was surnamed Peter, were lodged there. While Peter thought on the vision, the Spirit said unto him, Behold, three men seek thee. Arise therefore, and get thee down, and go with them, doubting nothing: for I have sent them. Then Peter went down to the men which were sent unto him from Cornelius; and said, Behold, I am he whom ye seek: what *is* the cause wherefore ye are come? And they said, Cornelius the centurion, a just man, and one that feareth God, and of good report among all the nation of the Jews, was warned from God by an holy angel to send for thee into his house, and to hear words of thee. Then called he them in, and lodged *them*. And on the morrow Peter went away with them, and certain brethren from Joppa accompanied him. And the morrow after they entered into Caesarea. And Cornelius waited for them, and had called together his kinsmen and near friends. And as Peter was coming in, Cornelius met him, and fell down at his feet, and worshipped *him*. But Peter took him up, saying, Stand up; I myself also am a man. And as he talked with him, he went in, and found many that were come together. And he said unto them, Ye know how that it is an unlawful thing for a man that is a Jew to keep company, or come unto one of another nation; but God hath shewed me that I should not call any man common or unclean. Therefore came I *unto you* without gainsaying, as soon as I was sent for: I ask therefore for what intent ye have sent for me? And Cornelius said, Four days ago I was fasting until this hour; and at the ninth hour I prayed in my house, and, behold, a man stood before me in bright clothing, And said, Cornelius, thy prayer is heard, and thine alms are had in remembrance in the sight of God. Send therefore to Joppa, and call hither Simon, whose surname is Peter; he is lodged in the house of *one* Simon a tanner by the sea side: who, when he cometh, shall speak unto thee. Immediately therefore I sent to thee; and thou hast well done that thou art come. Now therefore are we all here present before God, to hear all things that are commanded thee of God. Then Peter opened *his* mouth, and said, Of a truth I perceive that God is no respecter of persons: But in every nation he that feareth him, and worketh righteousness, is accepted with him. The word which *God* sent unto the

Conforming

children of Israel, preaching peace by Jesus Christ: (he is Lord of all:) That word, *I say,* ye know, which was published throughout all Judaea, and began from Galilee, after the baptism which John preached; How God anointed Jesus of Nazareth with the Holy Ghost and with power: who went about doing good, and healing all that were oppressed of the devil; for God was with him. And we are witnesses of all things which he did both in the land of the Jews, and in Jerusalem; whom they slew and hanged on a tree: Him God raised up the third day, and shewed him openly; Not to all the people, but unto witnesses chosen before of God, *even* to us, who did eat and drink with him after he rose from the dead. And he commanded us to preach unto the people, and to testify that it is he which was ordained of God *to be* the Judge of quick and dead. To him give all the prophets witness, that through his name whosoever believeth in him shall receive remission of sins. While Peter yet spake these words, the Holy Ghost fell on all them which heard the word. And they of the circumcision which believed were astonished, as many as came with Peter, because that on the Gentiles also was poured out the gift of the Holy Ghost. For they heard them speak with tongues, and magnify God. Then answered Peter, Can any man forbid water, that these should not be baptized, which have received the Holy Ghost as well as we? And he commanded them to be baptized in the name of the Lord. Then prayed they him to tarry certain days.

Conforming

Prophetic Word,
When you tell someone, something or a spirit, to have their way you just gave up control, did you not, when your boss or someone puts you over something or someone and tells you it's in your hands. Handle it then what, what are you prepared to do you expect for them to accept you and be humble to you. What happens if they don't? Have you really been prepared by God to handle it, with His love and long suffering with people. So you say Lord have your own way with me, remember you are giving up all of your control in every area of your life mind, heart, body, soul and spirit. You said Lord create in me a new Spirit like Yours. Born-again in His right. Amen.

Title: Steer Them In

Sub Title: There is No Good Thing That Lies in My Flesh

Theme – Be A Cattleman

Focus Verses:
Matthew 7:15-20 Beware of false prophets, which come to you in sheep's clothing, but inwardly they are ravening wolves. Ye shall know them by their fruits. Do men gather grapes of thorns, or figs of thistles? Even so every good tree bringeth forth good fruit; but a corrupt tree bringeth forth evil fruit. A good tree cannot bring forth evil fruit, neither *can* a corrupt tree bring forth good fruit. Every tree that bringeth not forth good fruit is hewn down, and cast into the fire. Wherefore by their fruits ye shall know them.

John 15:1-7 I am the true vine, and my Father is the husbandman. Every branch in me that beareth not fruit he taketh away: and every *branch* that beareth fruit, he purgeth it, that it may bring forth more fruit. Now ye are clean through the word which I have spoken unto you. Abide in me, and I in you. As the branch cannot bear fruit of itself, except it abide in the vine; no more can ye, except ye abide in me. I am the vine, ye *are* the branches: He that abideth in me, and I in him, the same bringeth

Conforming

forth much fruit: for without me ye can do nothing. If a man abide not in me, he is cast forth as a branch, and is withered; and men gather them, and cast *them* into the fire, and they are burned. If ye abide in me, and my words abide in you, ye shall ask what ye will, and it shall be done unto you.

Steer Means – to direct the course of, to guide, to set and hold to a course, to be subject to guidance, to pursue a course of action.

God said to steer means – the Holy Spirit will lead you and guide you into all truths.

Luke 14:21-24 So that servant came, and shewed his lord these things. Then the master of the house being angry said to his servant, Go out quickly into the streets and lanes of the city, and bring in hither the poor, and the maimed, and the halt, and the blind. And the servant said, Lord, it is done as thou hast commanded, and yet there is room. And the lord said unto the servant, Go out into the highways and hedges, and compel *them* to come in, that my house may be filled. For I say unto you, That none of those men which were bidden shall taste of my supper.

Cattleman Means – someone who tends or raises cattle.

We all need to be taught and raised right, not our right, not by our plans, not by our way of going, doing or thinking about things or people.

Conforming

There is a way that seems right to a man or woman, but in ends in death.

Title: Time Change

Ecclesiastes

Everything on the inside, outside and every area of your life. Everything that's on the outside is subject to change and will. Why? Because it's seen and temporal but the unseen is eternal. The inside will only change two ways for Jesus or for the devil. Time Change – A time for every purpose God's prescribed way for your life, pre-recorded, pre-destined, pre-arranged, pre-laid out for you and me to follow and walk in the way. Jesus said I am the way the truth and the light, if you're coming in, it's only by me only.

God works with man's time but not on man's time. Because some of us are accustom to this time frame and not God's.

God said – get it right, read it right, grab it, hold to it – right means the Word of God forever is my Word settled in Heaven.

Heaven and earth shall pass away but My Word will endure forever, be a doer of the Word and not hearer only deceiving yourself.

Ecclesiastes 3:1-8 To every *thing there is* a season, and a time to every purpose under the heaven: A time to be born, and a time to die; a

Conforming

time to plant, and a time to pluck up *that which is* planted; time to kill, and a time to heal; a time to break down, and a time to build up; A time to weep, and a time to laugh; a time to mourn, and a time to dance; A time to cast away stones, and a time to gather stones together; a time to embrace, and a time to refrain from embracing; A time to get, and a time to lose; a time to keep, and a time to cast away; A time to rend, and a time to sew; a time to keep silence, and a time to speak; A time to love, and a time to hate; a time of war, and a time of peace.

Verse 2: Born of God's Spirit, die to self, plant the Word and pluck out the world.

Verse 3: Kill the flesh, heal the past, breakdown old mindsets and build up your most holy faith.

Verse 4: Weep for life, laugh for death, why? Going to a better place.

Verse 5: Lose your stony heart, build a stone wall against evil, embrace God's love and refrain from hatred.

Verse 6: Gain all that Christ has for you, lose what you think you know - all of it, keep the new you and throw away the old you.

Verse 7: Tear away from whomever and whatever that is holding you back from following Jesus to your fullness. Sow a lot of

Conforming

time with Jesus, when you keep silent Jesus speaks loud for you and speak the Word.

Verse 8: Love conquers all and God is love.

Hate everything that is evil, not people it's the spirit and learn spiritual warfare.

Try to have peace with everyone if they won't, keep yours

If you keep your peace, you will keep your power.

So be strong in the Lord an in the power of His might.

The powers that be are of God. I the Lord created good and evil for my own purpose.

I formed the Heavens and the Earth out of my mouth and the new Earth.

Follow My Word, My will and My way. Time change – everything else will change but I the Lord God can't. In all thy getting, get my understanding when you get my understanding, it won't be standing over you – you will be standing over it. Amen.

Title: Your Flesh is Your Number One Enemy

Sub Title: Jesus Said, But What Have You Done For Me Lately

Galatians 5:17, 18 For the flesh lusteth against the Spirit, and the Spirit against the flesh: and these are contrary the one to the other: so that ye cannot do the things that ye would. But if ye be led of the Spirit, ye are not under the law.

Matthew 26:41 Watch and pray, that ye enter not into temptation: the spirit indeed *is* willing, but the flesh *is* weak.

Focus Verses:
1John 2:15-17 Love not the world, neither the things *that are* in the world. If any man love the world, the love of the Father is not in him. For all that *is* in the world, the lust of the flesh, and the lust of the eyes, and the pride of life, is not of the Father, but is of the world. And the world passeth away, and the lust thereof: but he that doeth the will of God abideth for ever.

Theme: the flesh killeth but My Spirit giveth life.

Conforming

1Peter 3:18-20 For Christ also hath once suffered for sins, the just for the unjust, that he might bring us to God, being put to death in the flesh, but quickened by the Spirit: By which also he went and preached unto the spirits in prison; Which sometime were disobedient, when once the longsuffering of God waited in the days of Noah, while the ark was a preparing, wherein few, that is, eight souls were saved by water.

Matthew 16:17 And Jesus answered and said unto him, Blessed art thou, Simon Barjona: for flesh and blood hath not revealed *it* unto thee, but my Father which is in heaven.

Romans 13:14 But put ye on the Lord Jesus Christ, and make not provision for the flesh, to *fulfil* the lusts *thereof*.

Philippians 3:3 For we are the circumcision, which worship God in the spirit, and rejoice in Christ Jesus, and have no confidence in the flesh.

John 4:24 God *is* a Spirit: and they that worship him must worship *him* in spirit and in truth.

F - Faulty
L - Lustful
E - Excited
S - Shameful
H – Hiding

Title: Start Here

2Corinthians 5:14-18 For the love of Christ constraineth us; because we thus judge, that if one died for all, then were all dead: And *that* he died for all, that they which live should not henceforth live unto themselves, but unto him which died for them, and rose again. Wherefore henceforth know we no man after the flesh: yea, though we have known Christ after the flesh, yet now henceforth know we *him* no more. Therefore if any man *be* in Christ, *he is* a new creature: old things are passed away; behold, all things are become new. And all things *are* of God, who hath reconciled us to himself by Jesus Christ, and hath given to us the ministry of reconciliation;

Living for Christ makes dying to myself look easy.

Lose to Gain:
1Corinthians 9:25-27 And every man that striveth for the mastery is temperate in all things. Now they *do it* to obtain a corruptible crown; but we an incorruptible. I therefore so run, not as uncertainly; so fight I, not as one that beateth the air: But I keep under my body, and bring *it* into subjection: lest that by any means, when I have preached to others, I myself should be a castaway.

Conforming

2Corinthians 4:4-7 In whom the god of this world hath blinded the minds of them which believe not, lest the light of the glorious gospel of Christ, who is the image of God, should shine unto them. For we preach not ourselves, but Christ Jesus the Lord; and ourselves your servants for Jesus' sake. For God, who commanded the light to shine out of darkness, hath shined in our hearts, to *give* the light of the knowledge of the glory of God in the face of Jesus Christ. But we have this treasure in earthen vessels, that the excellency of the power may be of God, and not of us.

Theme: Living

2Corinthians 5:14-18 For the love of Christ constraineth us; because we thus judge, that if one died for all, then were all dead: And *that* he died for all, that they which live should not henceforth live unto themselves, but unto him which died for them, and rose again. Wherefore henceforth know we no man after the flesh: yea, though we have known Christ after the flesh, yet now henceforth know we *him* no more. Therefore if any man *be* in Christ, *he is* a new creature: old things are passed away; behold, all things are become new. And all things *are* of God, who hath reconciled us to himself by Jesus Christ, and hath given to us the ministry of reconciliation;

Recycled Parts by Jesus

PS. Redeemed

Title: It's Feeding Time

Sub Title: You Don't Know What and Who to Feed But I Do Says the Lord.

Theme: I even want you to feed your enemy.

Romans 12:19-21 Dearly beloved, avenge not yourselves, but *rather* give place unto wrath: for it is written, Vengeance *is* mine; I will repay, saith the Lord. Therefore if thine enemy hunger, feed him; if he thirst, give him drink: for in so doing thou shalt heap coals of fire on his head. Be not overcome of evil, but overcome evil with good.

Focus Verse:
John 14:15 If ye love me, keep my commandments.

John 15:1-7 I am the true vine, and my Father is the husbandman. Every branch in me that beareth not fruit he taketh away: and every *branch* that beareth fruit, he purgeth it, that it may bring forth more fruit. Now ye are clean through the word which I have spoken unto you. Abide in me, and I in you. As the branch cannot bear fruit of itself, except it abide in the vine; no more can ye, except ye abide in me. I am the vine, ye *are* the branches: He that

Conforming

abideth in me, and I in him, the same bringeth forth much fruit: for without me ye can do nothing. If a man abide not in me, he is cast forth as a branch, and is withered; and men gather them, and cast *them* into the fire, and they are burned. If ye abide in me, and my words abide in you, ye shall ask what ye will, and it shall be done unto you.

Title: Knowing Your Word

Sub Title: To Know Him is to Love and Obey

John 1:1-14 In the beginning was the Word, and the Word was with God, and the Word was God. The same was in the beginning with God. All things were made by him; and without him was not any thing made that was made. In him was life; and the life was the light of men. And the light shineth in darkness; and the darkness comprehended it not. There was a man sent from God, whose name *was* John. The same came for a witness, to bear witness of the Light, that all *men* through him might believe. He was not that Light, but *was sent* to bear witness of that Light. *That* was the true Light, which lighteth every man that cometh into the world. He was in the world, and the world was made by him, and the world knew him not. He came unto his own, and his own received him not. But as many as received him, to them gave he power to become the sons of God, *even* to them that believe on his name: Which were born, not of blood, nor of the will of the flesh, nor of the will of man, but of God. And the Word was made flesh, and dwelt among us, (and we beheld his glory, the glory as of the only begotten of the Father,) full of grace and truth.

Colossians 3:1-10 If ye then be risen with Christ, seek those things which are above, where Christ sitteth on the right hand of God. Set your affection on things above, not on things on the earth. For ye are dead, and your life is hid with Christ in God. When Christ, *who is* our life, shall appear, then shall ye also appear with him in glory. Mortify therefore your members which are upon the earth; fornication, uncleanness, inordinate affection, evil concupiscence, and covetousness, which is idolatry: For which things' sake the wrath of God cometh on the children of disobedience: In the which ye also walked some time, when ye lived in them. But now ye also put off all these; anger, wrath, malice, blasphemy, filthy communication out of your mouth. Lie not one to another, seeing that ye have put off the old man with his deeds; And have put on the new *man,* which is renewed in knowledge after the image of him that created him:

Colossians 2:1-8 For I would that ye knew what great conflict I have for you, and *for* them at Laodicea, and *for* as many as have not seen my face in the flesh; That their hearts might be comforted, being knit together in love, and unto all riches of the full assurance of understanding, to the acknowledgement of the mystery of God, and of the Father, and of Christ; In whom are hid all the treasures of wisdom and knowledge. And this I say, lest any man should beguile you with enticing words. For though I be absent in the flesh, yet am I with you in the spirit, joying and beholding your order, and the stedfastness of your faith in

Conforming

Christ. As ye have therefore received Christ Jesus the Lord, *so* walk ye in him: Rooted and built up in him, and stablished in the faith, as ye have been taught, abounding therein with thanksgiving. Beware lest any man spoil you through philosophy and vain deceit, after the tradition of men, after the rudiments of the world, and not after Christ.

John 14:15-17 If ye love me, keep my commandments. And I will pray the Father, and he shall give you another Comforter, that he may abide with you for ever; *Even* the Spirit of truth; whom the world cannot receive, because it seeth him not, neither knoweth him: but ye know him; for he dwelleth with you, and shall be in you.

John 14:23, 24 Jesus answered and said unto him, If a man love me, he will keep my words: and my Father will love him, and we will come unto him, and make our abode with him. He that loveth me not keepeth not my sayings: and the word which ye hear is not mine, but the Father's which sent me.

Focus Verse:
Mark 8:17-21 And when Jesus knew *it,* he saith unto them, Why reason ye, because ye have no bread? perceive ye not yet, neither understand? have ye your heart yet hardened? Having eyes, see ye not? and having ears, hear ye not? and do ye not remember? When I brake the five loaves among five thousand, how many baskets full of fragments took ye up? They say unto him, Twelve. And when the seven among four

thousand, how many baskets full of fragments took ye up? And they said, Seven. And he said unto them, How is it that ye do not understand?

Knowing means – to be aware of the truth, to recognize, to have experience with to have an understanding of, to identify with, and to have knowledge with.

Jesus said knowing means – to be born – again of His Spirit, Jesus said to love Him means:
Mark 8:34 And when he had called the people *unto him* with his disciples also, he said unto them, Whosoever will come after me, let him deny himself, and take up his cross, and follow me.

A Word is not what God is, but a Word is what He does. For whatever He says comes to life. The Words I speak are Spirit and they are life.

Are you full of My life or theirs are the Words death. To be led around by every wind of doctrine that means nothing. Apart from Me you can do nothing known or unknown to everyone..... My grace and mercy.

Title: You Did It Lord, Whatever It Is You Did It Lord

Sub Title: Thank You Lord For Your Help Without Me

Focus Verse:
Psalms 51:3 For I acknowledge my transgressions: and my sin *is* ever before me.

Main Meat:
Psalms 51:1-13 To the chief Musician, A Psalm of David, when Nathan the prophet came unto him, after he had gone in to Bathsheba. Have mercy upon me, O God, according to thy lovingkindness: according unto the multitude of thy tender mercies blot out my transgressions. Wash me throughly from mine iniquity, and cleanse me from my sin. For I acknowledge my transgressions: and my sin *is* ever before me. Against thee, thee only, have I sinned, and done *this* evil in thy sight: that thou mightest be justified when thou speakest, *and* be clear when thou judgest. Behold, I was shapen in iniquity; and in sin did my mother conceive me. Behold, thou desirest truth in the inward parts: and in the hidden *part* thou shalt make me to know wisdom. Purge me with hyssop, and I shall be clean: wash me, and I

shall be whiter than snow. Make me to hear joy and gladness; *that* the bones *which* thou hast broken may rejoice. Hide thy face from my sins, and blot out all mine iniquities. Create in me a clean heart, O God; and renew a right spirit within me. Cast me not away from thy presence; and take not thy holy spirit from me. Restore unto me the joy of thy salvation; and uphold me *with thy* free spirit. *Then* will I teach transgressors thy ways; and sinners shall be converted unto thee.

Theme – Jesus is trying to get you out of you.

Mark 8:34-36 And when he had called the people *unto him* with his disciples also, he said unto them, Whosoever will come after me, let him deny himself, and take up his cross, and follow me. For whosoever will save his life shall lose it; but whosoever shall lose his life for my sake and the gospel's, the same shall save it. For what shall it profit a man, if he shall gain the whole world, and lose his own soul?

Title: Say Something before You Can Get Something, Say What the Bible Says the True Word of God

Sub Title: Please Lord Start With This Man In the Mirror, Natural and Spiritual Mirror

Focus Verses:
Exodus 14:15, 16 And the LORD said unto Moses, Wherefore criest thou unto me? speak unto the children of Israel, that they go forward: But lift thou up thy rod, and stretch out thine hand over the sea, and divide it: and the children of Israel shall go on dry *ground* through the midst of the sea.

Title: The Blessing Isn't In What You Lost, It's In What You have Left

Sub Title: What Did I Leave In Your Hands Use It

Focus Verses:
1Samuel 15:22-24 And Samuel said, Hath the LORD *as great* delight in burnt offerings and sacrifices, as in obeying the voice of the LORD? Behold, to obey *is* better than sacrifice, *and* to hearken than the fat of rams. For rebellion *is as* the sin of witchcraft, and stubbornness *is as* iniquity and idolatry. Because thou hast rejected the word of the LORD, he hath also rejected thee from *being* king. And Saul said unto Samuel, I have sinned: for I have transgressed the commandment of the LORD, and thy words: because I feared the people, and obeyed their voice.

Exodus 14:1-4 And the LORD spake unto Moses, saying, Speak unto the children of Israel, that they turn and encamp before Pihahiroth, between Migdol and the sea, over against Baalzephon: before it shall ye encamp by the sea. For Pharaoh will say of the children of Israel, They *are* entangled in the land, the wilderness hath shut them in. And I will

Conforming

harden Pharaoh's heart, that he shall follow after them; and I will be honoured upon Pharaoh, and upon all his host; that the Egyptians may know that I *am* the LORD. And they did so.

Exodus 14:8-14 And the LORD hardened the heart of Pharaoh king of Egypt, and he pursued after the children of Israel: and the children of Israel went out with an high hand. But the Egyptians pursued after them, all the horses *and* chariots of Pharaoh, and his horsemen, and his army, and overtook them encamping by the sea, beside Pihahiroth, before Baalzephon. And when Pharaoh drew nigh, the children of Israel lifted up their eyes, and, behold, the Egyptians marched after them; and they were sore afraid: and the children of Israel cried out unto the LORD. And they said unto Moses, Because *there were* no graves in Egypt, hast thou taken us away to die in the wilderness? wherefore hast thou dealt thus with us, to carry us forth out of Egypt? *Is* not this the word that we did tell thee in Egypt, saying, Let us alone, that we may serve the Egyptians? For *it had been* better for us to serve the Egyptians, than that we should die in the wilderness. And Moses said unto the people, Fear ye not, stand still, and see the salvation of the LORD, which he will shew to you to day: for the Egyptians whom ye have seen to day, ye shall see them again no more for ever. The LORD shall fight for you, and ye shall hold your peace.

Conforming

Exodus 14:17-27 And I, behold, I will harden the hearts of the Egyptians, and they shall follow them: and I will get me honour upon Pharaoh, and upon all his host, upon his chariots, and upon his horsemen. And the Egyptians shall know that I *am* the LORD, when I have gotten me honour upon Pharaoh, upon his chariots, and upon his horsemen. And the angel of God, which went before the camp of Israel, removed and went behind them; and the pillar of the cloud went from before their face, and stood behind them: And it came between the camp of the Egyptians and the camp of Israel; and it was a cloud and darkness *to them,* but it gave light by night *to these:* so that the one came not near the other all the night. And Moses stretched out his hand over the sea; and the LORD caused the sea to go *back* by a strong east wind all that night, and made the sea dry *land,* and the waters were divided. And the children of Israel went into the midst of the sea upon the dry *ground:* and the waters *were* a wall unto them on their right hand, and on their left. And the Egyptians pursued, and went in after them to the midst of the sea, *even* all Pharaoh's horses, his chariots, and his horsemen. And it came to pass, that in the morning watch the LORD looked unto the host of the Egyptians through the pillar of fire and of the cloud, and troubled the host of the Egyptians, And took off their chariot wheels, that they drave them heavily: so that the Egyptians said, Let us flee from the face of Israel; for the LORD fighteth for them against the Egyptians. And the LORD said unto Moses, Stretch out thine hand over the sea, that the

Conforming

waters may come again upon the Egyptians, upon their chariots, and upon their horsemen. And Moses stretched forth his hand over the sea, and the sea returned to his strength when the morning appeared; and the Egyptians fled against it; and the LORD overthrew the Egyptians in the midst of the sea.

Title: Obey or Receive the Sharp Swords

Sub Title: It's a Matter of Life or Death You Choose

2Samuel 2:12-28 And Abner the son of Ner, and the servants of Ishbosheth the son of Saul, went out from Mahanaim to Gibeon. And Joab the son of Zeruiah, and the servants of David, went out, and met together by the pool of Gibeon: and they sat down, the one on the one side of the pool, and the other on the other side of the pool. And Abner said to Joab, Let the young men now arise, and play before us. And Joab said, Let them arise. Then there arose and went over by number twelve of Benjamin, which *pertained* to Ishbosheth the son of Saul, and twelve of the servants of David. And they caught every one his fellow by the head, and *thrust* his sword in his fellow's side; so they fell down together: wherefore that place was called Helkathhazzurim, which *is* in Gibeon. And there was a very sore battle that day; and Abner was beaten, and the men of Israel, before the servants of David. And there were three sons of Zeruiah there, Joab, and Abishai, and Asahel: and Asahel *was as* light of foot as a wild roe. And Asahel pursued after Abner; and in going he turned not to the right hand nor to the left from following Abner. Then Abner looked

Conforming

behind him, and said, *Art* thou Asahel? And he answered, I *am*. And Abner said to him, Turn thee aside to thy right hand or to thy left, and lay thee hold on one of the young men, and take thee his armour. But Asahel would not turn aside from following of him. And Abner said again to Asahel, Turn thee aside from following me: wherefore should I smite thee to the ground? how then should I hold up my face to Joab thy brother? Howbeit he refused to turn aside: wherefore Abner with the hinder end of the spear smote him under the fifth *rib*, that the spear came out behind him; and he fell down there, and died in the same place: and it came to pass, *that* as many as came to the place where Asahel fell down and died stood still. Joab also and Abishai pursued after Abner: and the sun went down when they were come to the hill of Ammah, that *lieth* before Giah by the way of the wilderness of Gibeon. And the children of Benjamin gathered themselves together after Abner, and became one troop, and stood on the top of an hill. Then Abner called to Joab, and said, Shall the sword devour for ever? knowest thou not that it will be bitterness in the latter end? how long shall it be then, ere thou bid the people return from following their brethren? And Joab said, *As* God liveth, unless thou hadst spoken, surely then in the morning the people had gone up every one from following his brother. So Joab blew a trumpet, and all the people stood still, and pursued after Israel no more, neither fought they any more.

Conforming

Thought: God Promised To You, If You Do?

Psalms 91:1-16 He that dwelleth in the secret place of the most High shall abide under the shadow of the Almighty. I will say of the LORD, *He is* my refuge and my fortress: my God; in him will I trust. Surely he shall deliver thee from the snare of the fowler, *and* from the noisome pestilence. He shall cover thee with his feathers, and under his wings shalt thou trust: his truth *shall be thy* shield and buckler. Thou shalt not be afraid for the terror by night; *nor* for the arrow *that* flieth by day; Nor for the pestilence *that* walketh in darkness; *nor* for the destruction *that* wasteth at noonday. A thousand shall fall at thy side, and ten thousand at thy right hand; *but* it shall not come nigh thee. Only with thine eyes shalt thou behold and see the reward of the wicked. Because thou hast made the LORD, *which is* my refuge, *even* the most High, thy habitation; There shall no evil befall thee, neither shall any plague come nigh thy dwelling. For he shall give his angels charge over thee, to keep thee in all thy ways. They shall bear thee up in *their* hands, lest thou dash thy foot against a stone. Thou shalt tread upon the lion and adder: the young lion and the dragon shalt thou trample under feet. Because he hath set his love upon me, therefore will I deliver him: I will set him on high, because he hath known my name. He shall call upon me, and I will answer him: I *will*

Conforming

be with him in trouble; I will deliver him, and honour him. With long life will I satisfy him, and shew him my salvation.

1. He who has moved in, he shall walk in His ways.

2. He is my personal body guard, some trust in chariots and some in horses.

3. Even though I walk through the valley of the shadow of death, I will fear no evil.

4. I am hidden behind the cross, His word is my shield.

5. The Lord did not give me a spirit of fear; but of love, courage and a sound mind.

6. He covers me from seen and unseen danger.

7. The Lord said I will give people for your life.

8. If you keep doing what you are doing right or wrong you will keep getting what you are getting.

9. Because you have ONE God, ONE faith ONE spirit and ONE baptism.

10. When they came they stumbled and fell.

11. In all your ways acknowledge Him and let Him direct you.

12. Even if you get stuck on stupid.

Conforming

13. You shall rule over many Nations stronger and mightier than you.

14. Before I formed you in the womb; I knew you, before you were born I sanctified you, I the Lord ordained you a Prophet to the Nations.

15. I also heard the voice of the Lord saying who can I send who will go for us, then I said O Lord send me.

16. Living in the righteousness of Jesus in obedience to Him, not man.

Conforming

Title: You Don't Know What You Don't Know

Focus Verse:
2Timothy 3:5 Having a form of godliness, but denying the power thereof: from such turn away.

9 Points

1. Come out of you into me says the Lord.

2. Don't serve the position serve me says the Lord.

3. Obey God rather than man, it's better.

4. Learn time with Me says the Lord.

5. Know nothing to learn from Me says the Lord.

6. Have one Lord in your life Me only says the Lord.

7. Your game is over, get real in me says the Lord.

8. If you keep doing what you are doing you will keep getting what you are getting good or evil.

9. Behold I come quickly and I have your reward with me.

2Timothy 3:1-7 This know also, that in the last days perilous times shall come. For men shall be lovers of their own selves, covetous, boasters, proud, blasphemers, disobedient to parents, unthankful, unholy, Without natural affection, trucebreakers, false accusers, incontinent, fierce, despisers of those that are good, Traitors, heady, highminded, lovers of pleasures more than lovers of God; Having a form of godliness, but denying the power thereof: from such turn away. For of this sort are they which creep into houses, and lead captive silly women laden with sins, led away with divers lusts, Ever learning, and never able to come to the knowledge of the truth.

Title: Jesus Has a Need

Sub Title: Will You Fulfill His Need in You – Don't Lie

Focus Verses:
Luke 9:22, 23 Saying, The Son of man must suffer many things, and be rejected of the elders and chief priests and scribes, and be slain, and be raised the third day. And he said to *them* all, If any *man* will come after me, let him deny himself, and take up his cross daily, and follow me.

John 4:1-20 When therefore the Lord knew how the Pharisees had heard that Jesus made and baptized more disciples than John, (Though Jesus himself baptized not, but his disciples,) He left Judaea, and departed again into Galilee. And he must needs go through Samaria. Then cometh he to a city of Samaria, which is called Sychar, near to the parcel of ground that Jacob gave to his son Joseph. Now Jacob's well was there. Jesus therefore, being wearied with *his* journey, sat thus on the well: *and* it was about the sixth hour. There cometh a woman of Samaria to draw water: Jesus saith unto her, Give me to drink. (For his disciples were gone away unto the city to buy meat.) Then saith the woman of Samaria unto him, How is it that thou, being a Jew, askest drink of me, which am a woman of Samaria? for the

Jews have no dealings with the Samaritans. Jesus answered and said unto her, If thou knewest the gift of God, and who it is that saith to thee, Give me to drink; thou wouldest have asked of him, and he would have given thee living water. The woman saith unto him, Sir, thou hast nothing to draw with, and the well is deep: from whence then hast thou that living water? Art thou greater than our father Jacob, which gave us the well, and drank thereof himself, and his children, and his cattle? Jesus answered and said unto her, Whosoever drinketh of this water shall thirst again: But whosoever drinketh of the water that I shall give him shall never thirst; but the water that I shall give him shall be in him a well of water springing up into everlasting life. The woman saith unto him, Sir, give me this water, that I thirst not, neither come hither to draw. Jesus saith unto her, Go, call thy husband, and come hither. The woman answered and said, I have no husband. Jesus said unto her, Thou hast well said, I have no husband: For thou hast had five husbands; and he whom thou now hast is not thy husband: in that saidst thou truly. The woman saith unto him, Sir, I perceive that thou art a prophet. Our fathers worshipped in this mountain; and ye say, that in Jerusalem is the place where men ought to worship.

John 4:23, 24 But the hour cometh, and now is, when the true worshippers shall worship the Father in spirit and in truth: for the Father seeketh such to worship him. God *is* a Spirit: and they that worship him must worship *him* in spirit and in truth.

Conforming

Thought: Trust God When You Can't Trace Him

1Kings 19:11-21 And he said, Go forth, and stand upon the mount before the LORD. And, behold, the LORD passed by, and a great and strong wind rent the mountains, and brake in pieces the rocks before the LORD; *but* the LORD *was* not in the wind: and after the wind an earthquake; *but* the LORD *was* not in the earthquake: And after the earthquake a fire; *but* the LORD *was* not in the fire: and after the fire a still small voice. And it was *so,* when Elijah heard *it,* that he wrapped his face in his mantle, and went out, and stood in the entering in of the cave. And, behold, *there came* a voice unto him, and said, What doest thou here, Elijah? And he said, I have been very jealous for the LORD God of hosts: because the children of Israel have forsaken thy covenant, thrown down thine altars, and slain thy prophets with the sword; and I, *even* I only, am left; and they seek my life, to take it away. And the LORD said unto him, Go, return on thy way to the wilderness of Damascus: and when thou comest, anoint Hazael *to be* king over Syria: And Jehu the son of Nimshi shalt thou anoint *to be* king over Israel: and Elisha the son of Shaphat of Abelmeholah shalt thou anoint *to be* prophet in thy room. And it shall come to pass, *that* him that escapeth the sword of

Conforming

Hazael shall Jehu slay: and him that escapeth from the sword of Jehu shall Elisha slay. Yet I have left *me* seven thousand in Israel, all the knees which have not bowed unto Baal, and every mouth which hath not kissed him. So he departed thence, and found Elisha the son of Shaphat, who *was* plowing *with* twelve yoke *of oxen* before him, and he with the twelfth: and Elijah passed by him, and cast his mantle upon him. And he left the oxen, and ran after Elijah, and said, Let me, I pray thee, kiss my father and my mother, and *then* I will follow thee. And he said unto him, Go back again: for what have I done to thee? And he returned back from him, and took a yoke of oxen, and slew them, and boiled their flesh with the instruments of the oxen, and gave unto the people, and they did eat. Then he arose, and went after Elijah, and ministered unto him.

Rock Means – Hard Headed

Wind Means – Don't be moved by every wind of doctrine

Earth Quake Means – Everything that can and needs to be shaken will be.

Trace Means – Course or path that one follows, a mark or something left behind to show that someone has passed before, a sign or sketch, to track or trail, follow the blueprint of.

God said trace means – live in My image.

Title: Well in the Mean Time, I'll Do This but Not That

Sub Title: Let Me Fix It Says the Lord, You Can't

Focus Verse:
James 1:18-20 Of his own will begat he us with the word of truth, that we should be a kind of firstfruits of his creatures. Wherefore, my beloved brethren, let every man be swift to hear, slow to speak, slow to wrath: For the wrath of man worketh not the righteousness of God.

Theme – The Lord said I don't need your dammed help.

Jamess 1:1-27 James, a servant of God and of the Lord Jesus Christ, to the twelve tribes which are scattered abroad, greeting. My brethren, count it all joy when ye fall into divers temptations; Knowing *this*, that the trying of your faith worketh patience. But let patience have *her* perfect work, that ye may be perfect and entire, wanting nothing. If any of you lack wisdom, let him ask of God, that giveth to all *men* liberally, and upbraideth not; and it shall be given him. But let him ask in

Conforming

faith, nothing wavering. For he that wavereth is like a wave of the sea driven with the wind and tossed. For let not that man think that he shall receive any thing of the Lord. A double minded man *is* unstable in all his ways. Let the brother of low degree rejoice in that he is exalted: But the rich, in that he is made low: because as the flower of the grass he shall pass away. For the sun is no sooner risen with a burning heat, but it withereth the grass, and the flower thereof falleth, and the grace of the fashion of it perisheth: so also shall the rich man fade away in his ways. Blessed *is* the man that endureth temptation: for when he is tried, he shall receive the crown of life, which the Lord hath promised to them that love him. Let no man say when he is tempted, I am tempted of God: for God cannot be tempted with evil, neither tempteth he any man: But every man is tempted, when he is drawn away of his own lust, and enticed. Then when lust hath conceived, it bringeth forth sin: and sin, when it is finished, bringeth forth death. Do not err, my beloved brethren. Every good gift and every perfect gift is from above, and cometh down from the Father of lights, with whom is no variableness, neither shadow of turning. Of his own will begat he us with the word of truth, that we should be a kind of firstfruits of his creatures. Wherefore, my beloved brethren, let every man be swift to hear, slow to speak, slow to wrath: For the wrath of man worketh not the righteousness of God. Wherefore lay apart all filthiness and superfluity of naughtiness, and receive with meekness the engrafted word, which is able to save your souls. But be ye

Conforming

doers of the word, and not hearers only, deceiving your own selves. For if any be a hearer of the word, and not a doer, he is like unto a man beholding his natural face in a glass: For he beholdeth himself, and goeth his way, and straightway forgetteth what manner of man he was. But whoso looketh into the perfect law of liberty, and continueth *therein,* he being not a forgetful hearer, but a doer of the work, this man shall be blessed in his deed. If any man among you seem to be religious, and bridleth not his tongue, but deceiveth his own heart, this man's religion *is* vain. Pure religion and undefiled before God and the Father is this, To visit the fatherless and widows in their affliction, *and* to keep himself unspotted from the world.

Title: The Zebra Standard with a Jackass Mentality

Everything is Not Black and White

Sub Title: Pass it On

Focus Verses:
Revelations 3:15, 16 I know thy works, that thou art neither cold nor hot: I would thou wert cold or hot. So then because thou art lukewarm, and neither cold nor hot, I will spue thee out of my mouth.

8 Standards

1. Standard of Prayer
1Timothy 2:8-11 I will therefore that men pray every where, lifting up holy hands, without wrath and doubting. In like manner also, that women adorn themselves in modest apparel, with shamefacedness and sobriety; not with broided hair, or gold, or pearls, or costly array; But (which becometh women professing godliness) with good works. Let the woman learn in silence with all subjection.

Conforming

2. The Fighting Standard
Isaiah 59:19 So shall they fear the name of the LORD from the west, and his glory from the rising of the sun. When the enemy shall come in like a flood, the Spirit of the LORD shall lift up a standard against him.

3. The Double Standard
James 4:8 Draw nigh to God, and he will draw nigh to you. Cleanse *your* hands, *ye* sinners; and purify *your* hearts, *ye* double minded.

James 1:6-8 But let him ask in faith, nothing wavering. For he that wavereth is like a wave of the sea driven with the wind and tossed. For let not that man think that he shall receive any thing of the Lord. A double minded man *is* unstable in all his ways.

4. The Family Standard
Isaiah 49:22 Thus saith the Lord GOD, Behold, I will lift up mine hand to the Gentiles, and set up my standard to the people: and they shall bring thy sons in *their* arms, and thy daughters shall be carried upon *their* shoulders.

5. The Holy Standard
Isaiah 62:10 Go through, go through the gates; prepare ye the way of the people; cast up, cast up the highway; gather out the stones; lift up a standard for the people.

6. Your False god Standard
Jeremiah 50:2 Declare ye among the nations, and publish, and set up a standard; publish, *and* conceal not: say, Babylon is taken, Bel is

confounded, Merodach is broken in pieces; her idols are confounded, her images are broken in pieces.

7. Battle Standard
Jeremiah 51:12 Set up the standard upon the walls of Babylon, make the watch strong, set up the watchmen, prepare the ambushes: for the LORD hath both devised and done that which he spake against the inhabitants of Babylon.

8. Set Up Your Heavenly Standard, Not Your Earthly
Jeremiah 4:6 Set up the standard toward Zion: retire, stay not: for I will bring evil from the north, and a great destruction.

Heavenly Nugget
Revelations 3:6 He that hath an ear, let him hear what the Spirit saith unto the churches.

Some of us have bigger ears but we still don't hear much and some of us have smaller ears and we still don't do much. So maybe if we all have one ear we can do all in one spirit.

Standard Means – Something set-up and established by authority, Jesus is the best standard that will never be moved or die out and the rest sooner or later.

Title: For Christ Sake

Sub Title: When You're Dead It's Not Hard to Keep on Dyeing for Christ Sake

Acts 13:2-12 As they ministered to the Lord, and fasted, the Holy Ghost said, Separate me Barnabas and Saul for the work whereunto I have called them. And when they had fasted and prayed, and laid *their* hands on them, they sent *them* away. So they, being sent forth by the Holy Ghost, departed unto Seleucia; and from thence they sailed to Cyprus. And when they were at Salamis, they preached the word of God in the synagogues of the Jews: and they had also John to *their* minister. And when they had gone through the isle unto Paphos, they found a certain sorcerer, a false prophet, a Jew, whose name *was* Barjesus: Which was with the deputy of the country, Sergius Paulus, a prudent man; who called for Barnabas and Saul, and desired to hear the word of God. But Elymas the sorcerer (for so is his name by interpretation) withstood them, seeking to turn away the deputy from the faith. Then Saul, (who also *is called* Paul,) filled with the Holy Ghost, set his eyes on him, And said, O full of all subtilty and all mischief, *thou* child of the devil, *thou* enemy of all righteousness, wilt thou not cease to pervert the right ways of the

Lord? And now, behold, the hand of the Lord *is* upon thee, and thou shalt be blind, not seeing the sun for a season. And immediately there fell on him a mist and a darkness; and he went about seeking some to lead him by the hand. Then the deputy, when he saw what was done, believed, being astonished at the doctrine of the Lord.

Focus Verses:
Acts 9:15, 16 But the Lord said unto him, Go thy way: for he is a chosen vessel unto me, to bear my name before the Gentiles, and kings, and the children of Israel: For I will shew him how great things he must suffer for my name's sake.

For Christ Sake

1. Stephen was stoned to death for Christ Sake.

2. The Hebrew boys were thrown into the fire, for Christ sake.

3. Daniel was thrown into the lions den and the lions were hungry for Christ sake.

4. Abraham was willing to kill his only son for Christ sake.

5. Paul and Silas were stomped, beaten, chained up and thrown into prison for Christ sake.

Conforming

6. Read it for yourself Hebrews 11:36-40 for Christ sake.

Hebrews 11:36-40 And others had trial of *cruel* mockings and scourgings, yea, moreover of bonds and imprisonment: They were stoned, they were sawn asunder, were tempted, were slain with the sword: they wandered about in sheepskins and goatskins; being destitute, afflicted, tormented; (Of whom the world was not worthy:) they wandered in deserts, and *in* mountains, and *in* dens and caves of the earth. And these all, having obtained a good report through faith, received not the promise: God having provided some better thing for us, that they without us should not be made perfect.

What are you prepared to do or go through for Christ sake, not for your self righteousness it won't work. Jesus learned to obey through His suffering. He said suffer it to be so, learn to count it all joy.

Title: Click, Click, Click, Click Turn, Click Turn

Sub Title: What is the Name of Your Click Turn?

Job 1:6-12 Now there was a day when the sons of God came to present themselves before the LORD, and Satan came also among them. And the LORD said unto Satan, Whence comest thou? Then Satan answered the LORD, and said, From going to and fro in the earth, and from walking up and down in it. And the LORD said unto Satan, Hast thou considered my servant Job, that *there is* none like him in the earth, a perfect and an upright man, one that feareth God, and escheweth evil? Then Satan answered the LORD, and said, Doth Job fear God for nought? Hast not thou made an hedge about him, and about his house, and about all that he hath on every side? thou hast blessed the work of his hands, and his substance is increased in the land. But put forth thine hand now, and touch all that he hath, and he will curse thee to thy face. And the LORD said unto Satan, Behold, all that he hath *is* in thy power; only upon himself put not forth thine hand. So Satan went forth from the presence of the LORD.

Conforming

Job 2:1-6 Again there was a day when the sons of God came to present themselves before the LORD, and Satan came also among them to present himself before the LORD. And the LORD said unto Satan, From whence comest thou? And Satan answered the LORD, and said, From going to and fro in the earth, and from walking up and down in it. And the LORD said unto Satan, Hast thou considered my servant Job, that *there is* none like him in the earth, a perfect and an upright man, one that feareth God, and escheweth evil? and still he holdeth fast his integrity, although thou movedst me against him, to destroy him without cause. And Satan answered the LORD, and said, Skin for skin, yea, all that a man hath will he give for his life. But put forth thine hand now, and touch his bone and his flesh, and he will curse thee to thy face. And the LORD said unto Satan, Behold, he *is* in thine hand; but save his life.

Focus Verse:
Job 2:11 Now when Job's three friends heard of all this evil that was come upon him, they came every one from his own place; Eliphaz the Temanite, and Bildad the Shuhite, and Zophar the Naamathite: for they had made an appointment together to come to mourn with him and to comfort him.

Theme – Click on Jesus and stay there, you need to repent.

Turns Means – To cause to move around so as to affect a desired end. To affect or alter the function of.

Conforming

God said Turns means – Having a respect of persons. Being a traitor to Him, being in too many peoples mixing bowl.

Conforming

Title: Boarding Time, You Need the Right Pass

Sub Title: Glue Love Plus E

Focus Verse:
Joshua 24:18-24 And the LORD drave out from before us all the people, even the Amorites which dwelt in the land: *therefore* will we also serve the LORD; for he *is* our God. And Joshua said unto the people, Ye cannot serve the LORD: for he *is* an holy God; he *is* a jealous God; he will not forgive your transgressions nor your sins. If ye forsake the LORD, and serve strange gods, then he will turn and do you hurt, and consume you, after that he hath done you good. And the people said unto Joshua, Nay; but we will serve the LORD. And Joshua said unto the people, Ye *are* witnesses against yourselves that ye have chosen you the LORD, to serve him. And they said, *We are* witnesses. Now therefore put away, *said he,* the strange gods which *are* among you, and incline your heart unto the LORD God of Israel. And the people said unto Joshua, The LORD our God will we serve, and his voice will we obey.

1Kings 12:1-16 And Rehoboam went to Shechem: for all Israel were come to Shechem to make him king. And it came to pass, when Jeroboam the son of Nebat, who was yet in Egypt, heard *of it,* (for he was fled from the presence of king Solomon, and Jeroboam dwelt in Egypt;) That they sent and called him. And Jeroboam and all the congregation of Israel came, and spake unto Rehoboam, saying, Thy father made our yoke grievous: now therefore make thou the grievous service of thy father, and his heavy yoke which he put upon us, lighter, and we will serve thee. And he said unto them, Depart yet *for* three days, then come again to me. And the people departed. And king Rehoboam consulted with the old men, that stood before Solomon his father while he yet lived, and said, How do ye advise that I may answer this people? And they spake unto him, saying, If thou wilt be a servant unto this people this day, and wilt serve them, and answer them, and speak good words to them, then they will be thy servants for ever. But he forsook the counsel of the old men, which they had given him, and consulted with the young men that were grown up with him, *and* which stood before him: And he said unto them, What counsel give ye that we may answer this people, who have spoken to me, saying, Make the yoke which thy father did put upon us lighter? And the young men that were grown up with him spake unto him, saying, Thus shalt thou speak unto this people that spake unto thee, saying, Thy father made our yoke heavy, but make thou *it* lighter unto us; thus shalt thou say unto them, My little *finger* shall be thicker than my father's loins. And now whereas my father did lade you with a heavy yoke, I will add to your yoke: my father hath chastised you with whips, but I will chastise you with scorpions. So Jeroboam and all the people came to

Conforming

Rehoboam the third day, as the king had appointed, saying, Come to me again the third day. And the king answered the people roughly, and forsook the old men's counsel that they gave him; And spake to them after the counsel of the young men, saying, My father made your yoke heavy, and I will add to your yoke: my father *also* chastised you with whips, but I will chastise you with scorpions. Wherefore the king hearkened not unto the people; for the cause was from the LORD, that he might perform his saying, which the LORD spake by Ahijah the Shilonite unto Jeroboam the son of Nebat. So when all Israel saw that the king hearkened not unto them, the people answered the king, saying, What portion have we in David? neither *have we* inheritance in the son of Jesse: to your tents, O Israel: now see to thine own house, David. So Israel departed unto their tents.

Focus Verses:
1John 4:7, 8 Beloved, let us love one another: for love is of God; and every one that loveth is born of God, and knoweth God. He that loveth not knoweth not God; for God is love.

Thought:
- G – Give
- L – Love
- U – Unconditionally
- E – Every day
- Plus E – To Every body

Unconditionally Means – Not limited

Conforming

Galatians 5:22, 23 But the fruit of the Spirit is love, joy, peace, longsuffering, gentleness, goodness, faith, Meekness, temperance: against such there is no law.

John 15:16-19 Ye have not chosen me, but I have chosen you, and ordained you, that ye should go and bring forth fruit, and *that* your fruit should remain: that whatsoever ye shall ask of the Father in my name, he may give it you. These things I command you, that ye love one another. If the world hate you, ye know that it hated me before *it hated* you. If ye were of the world, the world would love his own: but because ye are not of the world, but I have chosen you out of the world, therefore the world hateth you.

John 15:12-14 This is my commandment, That ye love one another, as I have loved you. Greater love hath no man than this, that a man lay down his life for his friends. Ye are my friends, if ye do whatsoever I command you.

John 14:15 If ye love me, keep my commandments.

John 14:23-25 Jesus answered and said unto him, If a man love me, he will keep my words: and my Father will love him, and we will come unto him, and make our abode with him. He that loveth me not keepeth not my sayings: and the word which ye hear is not mine, but the Father's which sent me. These things have I spoken unto you, being *yet* present with you.

Conforming

God said love means – to die for, Jesus did it why won't you.

Glue – is a substance that binds things together with one another so that it won't come apart.

Nugget – only Holy Ghost glue can do that.

Title: Working to God Out of Your Substance That Never Ends

Sub Title: First You Have to Learn to Listen and Listen to Learn How to

Focus Verses:
Psalms 34:7, 8 The angel of the LORD encampeth round about them that fear him, and delivereth them. O taste and see that the LORD *is* good: blessed *is* the man *that* trusteth in him.

Psalms 139:1-24 To the chief Musician, A Psalm of David. O LORD, thou hast searched me, and known *me*. Thou knowest my downsitting and mine uprising, thou understandest my thought afar off. Thou compassest my path and my lying down, and art acquainted *with* all my ways. For *there is* not a word in my tongue, *but,* lo, O LORD, thou knowest it altogether. Thou hast beset me behind and before, and laid thine hand upon me. *Such* knowledge *is* too wonderful for me; it is high, I cannot *attain* unto it. Whither shall I go from thy spirit? or whither shall I flee from thy presence? If I ascend up into heaven, thou *art* there: if I make my bed in hell, behold, thou *art there. If* I take the wings of the morning, *and* dwell in the uttermost parts of the sea; Even there shall thy hand lead me, and thy right hand shall hold me. If I say, Surely the darkness shall cover me; even the night shall be light about me. Yea, the darkness hideth not from thee; but the night shineth as the day: the darkness and the light *are* both alike *to thee.* For thou hast possessed my reins: thou hast covered me in my mother's womb. I will praise thee; for I am fearfully *and* wonderfully made: marvellous *are* thy works; and *that* my soul knoweth right well. My substance was not hid from thee, when I was made in secret, *and* curiously wrought in the lowest parts of the earth. Thine eyes did see my substance, yet being unperfect; and in thy book all *my members* were written, *which* in continuance were fashioned, when *as yet there was* none of them. How precious also are thy thoughts unto me, O God! how great is the sum of them! *If* I should count them, they are more in number than the sand: when I awake, I am still with thee. Surely thou wilt slay the wicked, O God: depart from me therefore, ye bloody men. For they speak against thee wickedly, *and* thine enemies take *thy name* in vain. Do not I hate them, O LORD, that hate thee? and am not I grieved with those that rise up against thee? I hate them with perfect hatred: I count them mine enemies. Search me, O God, and know my heart: try me, and know my thoughts: And see if *there be any* wicked way in me, and lead me in the way everlasting.

Title: The Closer Wants to Bring You Closure, So He Can Bring Closure to His Purpose, He's Place on You

Sub Title: Before You Close Down to Close Out Without Him

Focus Verses:
John 4:10 Jesus answered and said unto her, If thou knewest the gift of God, and who it is that saith to thee, Give me to drink; thou wouldest have asked of him, and he would have given thee living water.

John 4:13, 14 Jesus answered and said unto her, Whosoever drinketh of this water shall thirst again: But whosoever drinketh of the water that I shall give him shall never thirst; but the water that I shall give him shall be in him a well of water springing up into everlasting life. I am the vine, ye *are* the branches: He that abideth in me, and I in him, the same bringeth forth much fruit: for without me ye can do nothing.

Conforming

Word Helpers:
Revelations 22:12, 13 And, behold, I come quickly; and my reward *is* with me, to give every man according as his work shall be. I am Alpha and Omega, the beginning and the end, the first and the last.

Revelations 3:19-22 As many as I love, I rebuke and chasten: be zealous therefore, and repent. Behold, I stand at the door, and knock: if any man hear my voice, and open the door, I will come in to him, and will sup with him, and he with me. To him that overcometh will I grant to sit with me in my throne, even as I also overcame, and am set down with my Father in his throne. He that hath an ear, let him hear what the Spirit saith unto the churches.

A closer is the only one who can make sure you finish your God given course.

Close Down Means – to block out any outward view.

Close Out Means – to exclude or terminate.

Title: The Other Side of Me, It Will Come to Pass

Sub Title: The Other Side of Me is My Old Man Trying to Rule Over Me Daily

Focus Verses:
Ezekiel 3:4-10 And he said unto me, Son of man, go, get thee unto the house of Israel, and speak with my words unto them. For thou *art* not sent to a people of a strange speech and of an hard language, *but* to the house of Israel; Not to many people of a strange speech and of an hard language, whose words thou canst not understand. Surely, had I sent thee to them, they would have hearkened unto thee. But the house of Israel will not hearken unto thee; for they will not hearken unto me: for all the house of Israel *are* impudent and hardhearted. Behold, I have made thy face strong against their faces, and thy forehead strong against their foreheads. As an adamant harder than flint have I made thy forehead: fear them not, neither be dismayed at their looks, though they *be* a rebellious house. Moreover he said unto me, Son of man, all my words that I shall speak unto thee receive in thine heart, and hear with thine ears.

Conforming

Theme Turn:
Ezekiel 3:16-24 And it came to pass at the end of seven days, that the word of the LORD came unto me, saying, Son of man, I have made thee a watchman unto the house of Israel: therefore hear the word at my mouth, and give them warning from me. When I say unto the wicked, Thou shalt surely die; and thou givest him not warning, nor speakest to warn the wicked from his wicked way, to save his life; the same wicked *man* shall die in his iniquity; but his blood will I require at thine hand. Yet if thou warn the wicked, and he turn not from his wickedness, nor from his wicked way, he shall die in his iniquity; but thou hast delivered thy soul. Again, When a righteous *man* doth turn from his righteousness, and commit iniquity, and I lay a stumblingblock before him, he shall die: because thou hast not given him warning, he shall die in his sin, and his righteousness which he hath done shall not be remembered; but his blood will I require at thine hand. Nevertheless if thou warn the righteous *man,* that the righteous sin not, and he doth not sin, he shall surely live, because he is warned; also thou hast delivered thy soul. And the hand of the LORD was there upon me; and he said unto me, Arise, go forth into the plain, and I will there talk with thee. Then I arose, and went forth into the plain: and, behold, the glory of the LORD stood there, as the glory which I saw by the river of Chebar: and I fell on my face. Then the spirit entered into me, and set me upon my feet, and spake with me, and said unto me, Go, shut thyself within thine house.

Conforming

The Other Sides of

- Water – Dry
- Daylight – Darkness
- Happy – Sad
- Righteousness – Unrighteousness
- Living for Jesus – Living for the devil
- Humble – Ignorance or Unlearned
- Real – False
- God's Spirit – Serving Flesh
- Love for Souls – Love of Money
- Having the Real Holy Ghost – or Your Own Ghost
- Good – Evil
- Married – Fornication

Title: Same People Different Books

Sub Title: Something Different

Focus Verses:
Jeremiah 10:23, 24 O LORD, I know that the way of man *is* not in himself: *it is* not in man that walketh to direct his steps. O LORD, correct me, but with judgment; not in thine anger, lest thou bring me to nothing.

Your religion will send you to hell. Religion has its own way of serving their God. Christianity and the Word of God teach relationship and oneness with Jesus Christ. Jesus is the only true living God.

John 4:24 God *is* a Spirit: and they that worship him must worship *him* in spirit and in truth.

John 14:6 Jesus saith unto him, I am the way, the truth, and the life: no man cometh unto the Father, but by me.

Let's See the Way to Go

I will Teach You the Way to Go,

Conforming

1Samuel 12:23 Moreover as for me, God forbid that I should sin against the LORD in ceasing to pray for you: but I will teach you the good and the right way:

Teach Me Thy Way O Lord,
Psalms 27:11 Teach me thy way, O LORD, and lead me in a plain path, because of mine enemies.

I have Chosen the Way of Truth,
Psalms 119:30 I have chosen the way of truth: thy judgments have I laid *before me*.

I Hate Every False Way,
Psalms 119:104 Through thy precepts I get understanding: therefore I hate every false way.

He Preserveth the Way of the Saints,
Proverbs 2:8 He keepeth the paths of judgment, and preserveth the way of his saints.

The Way of the Transgressors is Hard,
Proverbs 13:15 Good understanding giveth favour: but the way of transgressors *is* hard.

This is the Way, Walk Ye in it,
Isaiah 30:21 And thine ears shall hear a word behind thee, saying, This *is* the way, walk ye in it, when ye turn to the right hand, and when ye turn to the left.

Conforming

A Way Called Holiness,
Isaiah 35:8 And an highway shall be there, and a way, and it shall be called The way of holiness; the unclean shall not pass over it; but it *shall be* for those: the wayfaring men, though fools, shall not err *therein*.

There is a Way That Seemeth Right to Man, but the End There of is Death,
Proverbs 14:12 There is a way which seemeth right unto a man, but the end thereof *are* the ways of death.

You must and will choose every day whom you will serve Heaven or stay in your hell. You can't play on the devil's play ground and say you serve Jesus, liar.

Title: Love That Becomes a Reflex

Sub Title: When God's Love Really Connects With You, It's Going to Move You to do Things You Never Thought Possible

Focus Verses:
1Corinthians 13:3-8 And though I bestow all my goods to feed *the poor,* and though I give my body to be burned, and have not charity, it profiteth me nothing. Charity suffereth long, *and* is kind; charity envieth not; charity vaunteth not itself, is not puffed up, Doth not behave itself unseemly, seeketh not her own, is not easily provoked, thinketh no evil; Rejoiceth not in iniquity, but rejoiceth in the truth; Beareth all things, believeth all things, hopeth all things, endureth all things. Charity never faileth: but whether *there be* prophecies, they shall fail; whether *there be* tongues, they shall cease; whether *there be* knowledge, it shall vanish away.

There Are 3 Meanings Christ's Love (Main Word Constrain)

Conforming

1. It forces movement in an unnatural manner beyond the norm.

2. It keeps us away from things that were designed to take you out and from throwing your life away.

3. Christ's love keeps you in something. It helps us exactly in the place where He wants us to be.

Reflex Means – An automatic and often inborn response to something. The power of acting or responding with speed fleshly or indiscipline. A way of thinking or behaving.

Conforming

Title: Your Blessing Isn't Here, It's Over There

Focus Verse:
1Kings 18:21 And Elijah came unto all the people, and said, How long halt ye between two opinions? if the LORD *be* God, follow him: but if Baal, *then* follow him. And the people answered him not a word.

1Kings 18:21-40 And Elijah came unto all the people, and said, How long halt ye between two opinions? if the LORD *be* God, follow him: but if Baal, *then* follow him. And the people answered him not a word. Then said Elijah unto the people, I, *even* I only, remain a prophet of the LORD; but Baal's prophets *are* four hundred and fifty men. Let them therefore give us two bullocks; and let them choose one bullock for themselves, and cut it in pieces, and lay *it* on wood, and put no fire *under:* and I will dress the other bullock, and lay *it* on wood, and put no fire *under:* And call ye on the name of your gods, and I will call on the name of the LORD: and the God that answereth by fire, let him be God. And all the people answered and said, It is well spoken. And Elijah said unto the prophets of Baal, Choose you one bullock for yourselves, and dress *it* first; for ye *are* many; and call on the name of your gods, but put no fire *under*. And they took the bullock which was given them, and they dressed *it,* and called on the name of Baal from morning even until

Conforming

noon, saying, O Baal, hear us. But *there was* no voice, nor any that answered. And they leaped upon the altar which was made. And it came to pass at noon, that Elijah mocked them, and said, Cry aloud: for he *is* a god; either he is talking, or he is pursuing, or he is in a journey, *or* peradventure he sleepeth, and must be awaked. And they cried aloud, and cut themselves after their manner with knives and lancets, till the blood gushed out upon them. And it came to pass, when midday was past, and they prophesied until the *time* of the offering of the *evening* sacrifice, that *there was* neither voice, nor any to answer, nor any that regarded. And Elijah said unto all the people, Come near unto me. And all the people came near unto him. And he repaired the altar of the LORD *that was* broken down. And Elijah took twelve stones, according to the number of the tribes of the sons of Jacob, unto whom the word of the LORD came, saying, Israel shall be thy name: And with the stones he built an altar in the name of the LORD: and he made a trench about the altar, as great as would contain two measures of seed. And he put the wood in order, and cut the bullock in pieces, and laid *him* on the wood, and said, Fill four barrels with water, and pour *it* on the burnt sacrifice, and on the wood. And he said, Do *it* the second time. And they did *it* the second time. And he said, Do *it* the third time. And they did *it* the third time. And the water ran round about the altar; and he filled the trench also with water. And it came to pass at *the time of* the offering of the *evening* sacrifice, that Elijah the prophet came near, and said, LORD

God of Abraham, Isaac, and of Israel, let it be known this day that thou *art* God in Israel, and *that* I *am* thy servant, and *that* I have done all these things at thy word. Hear me, O LORD, hear me, that this people may know that thou *art* the LORD God, and *that* thou hast turned their heart back again. Then the fire of the LORD fell, and consumed the burnt sacrifice, and the wood, and the stones, and the dust, and licked up the water that *was* in the trench. And when all the people saw *it,* they fell on their faces: and they said, The LORD, he *is* the God; the LORD, he *is* the God. And Elijah said unto them, Take the prophets of Baal; let not one of them escape. And they took them: and Elijah brought them down to the brook Kishon, and slew them there.

How do We Get There from Here

1. Get to that place of obedience.
2. Do exactly what God tells us to do.
3. Stay there until something happens.
4. Wait on the power of God to fall.
5. Stay there until we change.

Title: Do I Become Domesticated or Do I Be Myself?

Sub Title: I Shot the Sheriff, but I Didn't Shoot the Deputy

Do I become more religious or be that spiritual giant that God has chosen me to be.

1Samuel 17:4-51 And there went out a champion out of the camp of the Philistines, named Goliath, of Gath, whose height *was* six cubits and a span. And *he had* an helmet of brass upon his head, and he *was* armed with a coat of mail; and the weight of the coat *was* five thousand shekels of brass. And *he had* greaves of brass upon his legs, and a target of brass between his shoulders. And the staff of his spear *was* like a weaver's beam; and his spear's head *weighed* six hundred shekels of iron: and one bearing a shield went before him. And he stood and cried unto the armies of Israel, and said unto them, Why are ye come out to set *your* battle in array? *am* not I a Philistine, and ye servants to Saul? choose you a man for you, and let him come down to me. If he be able to fight with me, and to kill me, then will we be your servants: but if I prevail against him, and kill him, then shall ye be our servants, and serve us. And the Philistine said, I defy the armies of Israel this day; give me a man, that we may fight together. When Saul and all Israel heard those words of the Philistine, they were dismayed, and greatly afraid. Now David *was* the son of that Ephrathite of Bethlehemjudah, whose name *was* Jesse; and he had eight sons: and the man went among men *for* an old man in the days of Saul. And the three eldest sons of Jesse went *and* followed Saul to the battle: and the names of his three sons that went to the battle *were* Eliab the firstborn, and next unto him Abinadab, and the third Shammah. And David *was* the youngest: and the three eldest followed Saul. But David went and returned from Saul to feed his father's sheep at Bethlehem. And the Philistine drew near morning and evening, and presented himself forty days. And Jesse said unto David his son, Take now for thy brethren an ephah of this parched *corn,* and these ten loaves, and run to the camp to thy brethren; And carry these ten cheeses unto the captain of *their* thousand, and look how thy brethren fare, and take their pledge. Now Saul, and they, and all the men of Israel, *were* in the valley of Elah, fighting with the Philistines. And David rose up early in the morning, and left the sheep with a keeper, and took, and went, as Jesse had commanded him; and he came to the trench, as the host was going forth to the fight, and shouted for the battle. For Israel and the Philistines had put the battle in array, army against army. And David left his carriage in the hand of the keeper of the carriage, and ran into the army, and

Conforming

came and saluted his brethren. And as he talked with them, behold, there came up the champion, the Philistine of Gath, Goliath by name, out of the armies of the Philistines, and spake according to the same words: and David heard *them*. And all the men of Israel, when they saw the man, fled from him, and were sore afraid. And the men of Israel said, Have ye seen this man that is come up? surely to defy Israel is he come up: and it shall be, *that* the man who killeth him, the king will enrich him with great riches, and will give him his daughter, and make his father's house free in Israel. And David spake to the men that stood by him, saying, What shall be done to the man that killeth this Philistine, and taketh away the reproach from Israel? for who *is* this uncircumcised Philistine, that he should defy the armies of the living God? And the people answered him after this manner, saying, So shall it be done to the man that killeth him. And Eliab his eldest brother heard when he spake unto the men; and Eliab's anger was kindled against David, and he said, Why camest thou down hither? and with whom hast thou left those few sheep in the wilderness? I know thy pride, and the naughtiness of thine heart; for thou art come down that thou mightest see the battle. And David said, What have I now done? *Is there* not a cause? And he turned from him toward another, and spake after the same manner: and the people answered him again after the former manner. And when the words were heard which David spake, they rehearsed *them* before Saul: and he sent for him. And David said to Saul, Let no

Conforming

man's heart fail because of him; thy servant will go and fight with this Philistine. And Saul said to David, Thou art not able to go against this Philistine to fight with him: for thou *art but* a youth, and he a man of war from his youth. And David said unto Saul, Thy servant kept his father's sheep, and there came a lion, and a bear, and took a lamb out of the flock: And I went out after him, and smote him, and delivered *it* out of his mouth: and when he arose against me, I caught *him* by his beard, and smote him, and slew him. Thy servant slew both the lion and the bear: and this uncircumcised Philistine shall be as one of them, seeing he hath defied the armies of the living God. David said moreover, The LORD that delivered me out of the paw of the lion, and out of the paw of the bear, he will deliver me out of the hand of this Philistine. And Saul said unto David, Go, and the LORD be with thee. And Saul armed David with his armour, and he put an helmet of brass upon his head; also he armed him with a coat of mail. And David girded his sword upon his armour, and he assayed to go; for he had not proved *it*. And David said unto Saul, I cannot go with these; for I have not proved *them*. And David put them off him. And he took his staff in his hand, and chose him five smooth stones out of the brook, and put them in a shepherd's bag which he had, even in a scrip; and his sling *was* in his hand: and he drew near to the Philistine. And the Philistine came on and drew near unto David; and the man that bare the shield *went* before him. And when the Philistine looked about, and saw David, he disdained him: for he

Conforming

was *but* a youth, and ruddy, and of a fair countenance. And the Philistine said unto David, *Am* I a dog, that thou comest to me with staves? And the Philistine cursed David by his gods. And the Philistine said to David, Come to me, and I will give thy flesh unto the fowls of the air, and to the beasts of the field. Then said David to the Philistine, Thou comest to me with a sword, and with a spear, and with a shield: but I come to thee in the name of the LORD of hosts, the God of the armies of Israel, whom thou hast defied. This day will the LORD deliver thee into mine hand; and I will smite thee, and take thine head from thee; and I will give the carcases of the host of the Philistines this day unto the fowls of the air, and to the wild beasts of the earth; that all the earth may know that there is a God in Israel. And all this assembly shall know that the LORD saveth not with sword and spear: for the battle *is* the LORD'S, and he will give you into our hands. And it came to pass, when the Philistine arose, and came and drew nigh to meet David, that David hasted, and ran toward the army to meet the Philistine. And David put his hand in his bag, and took thence a stone, and slang *it,* and smote the Philistine in his forehead, that the stone sunk into his forehead; and he fell upon his face to the earth. So David prevailed over the Philistine with a sling and with a stone, and smote the Philistine, and slew him; but *there was* no sword in the hand of David. Therefore David ran, and stood upon the Philistine, and took his sword, and drew it out of the sheath thereof, and slew him, and cut off his head therewith. And when the Philistines saw their champion was dead, they fled.

Title: In the Beginning, the House Without a Home

Sub Title: Created to Create Any and Everything that Pleases the Master

Focus Verses:
John 15:5, 6 I am the vine, ye *are* the branches: He that abideth in me, and I in him, the same bringeth forth much fruit: for without me ye can do nothing. If a man abide not in me, he is cast forth as a branch, and is withered; and men gather them, and cast *them* into the fire, and they are burned.

Revelations 3:14 And unto the angel of the church of the Laodiceans write; These things saith the Amen, the faithful and true witness, the beginning of the creation of God;

Colossians 1:14-19 In whom we have redemption through his blood, *even* the forgiveness of sins: Who is the image of the invisible God, the firstborn of every creature: For by him were all things created, that are in heaven, and that are in earth, visible and invisible, whether *they* *be* thrones, or dominions, or principalities, or powers: all

Conforming

things were created by him, and for him: And he is before all things, and by him all things consist. And he is the head of the body, the church: who is the beginning, the firstborn from the dead; that in all *things* he might have the preeminence. For it pleased *the Father* that in him should all fulness dwell;

Jeremiah 3:14, 15 Turn, O backsliding children, saith the LORD; for I am married unto you: and I will take you one of a city, and two of a family, and I will bring you to Zion: And I will give you pastors according to mine heart, which shall feed you with knowledge and understanding.

1Corinthians 7:32-34 But I would have you without carefulness. He that is unmarried careth for the things that belong to the Lord, how he may please the Lord: But he that is married careth for the things that are of the world, how he may please *his* wife. There is difference *also* between a wife and a virgin. The unmarried woman careth for the things of the Lord, that she may be holy both in body and in spirit: but she that is married careth for the things of the world, how she may please *her* husband.

Main Meat:
Genesis 1:1-31 In the beginning God created the heaven and the earth. And the earth was without form, and void; and darkness *was* upon the face of the deep. And the Spirit of God moved upon the face of the waters. And God said, Let there be light: and there was light.

Conforming

And God saw the light, that *it was* good: and God divided the light from the darkness. And God called the light Day, and the darkness he called Night. And the evening and the morning were the first day. And God said, Let there be a firmament in the midst of the waters, and let it divide the waters from the waters. And God made the firmament, and divided the waters which *were* under the firmament from the waters which *were* above the firmament: and it was so. And God called the firmament Heaven. And the evening and the morning were the second day. And God said, Let the waters under the heaven be gathered together unto one place, and let the dry *land* appear: and it was so. And God called the dry *land* Earth; and the gathering together of the waters called he Seas: and God saw that *it was* good. And God said, Let the earth bring forth grass, the herb yielding seed, *and* the fruit tree yielding fruit after his kind, whose seed *is* in itself, upon the earth: and it was so. And the earth brought forth grass, *and* herb yielding seed after his kind, and the tree yielding fruit, whose seed *was* in itself, after his kind: and God saw that *it was* good. And the evening and the morning were the third day. And God said, Let there be lights in the firmament of the heaven to divide the day from the night; and let them be for signs, and for seasons, and for days, and years: And let them be for lights in the firmament of the heaven to give light upon the earth: and it was so. And God made two great lights; the greater light to rule the day, and the lesser light to rule the night: *he made* the stars also. And God set them in the firmament of the heaven to give light upon the earth, And to rule over the day and over the night, and to divide the light from the darkness: and God saw that *it was* good. And the evening and the morning were the fourth day. And God said, Let the waters bring forth abundantly the moving creature that hath life, and fowl *that* may fly above the earth in the open firmament of heaven. And God created great whales, and every living creature that moveth, which the waters brought forth abundantly, after their kind, and every winged fowl after his kind: and God saw that *it was* good. And God blessed them, saying, Be fruitful, and multiply, and fill the waters in the seas, and let fowl multiply in the earth. And the evening and the morning were the fifth day. And God said, Let the earth bring forth the living creature after his kind, cattle, and creeping thing, and beast of the earth after his kind: and it was so. And God made the beast of the earth after his kind, and cattle after their kind, and every thing that creepeth upon the earth after his kind: and God saw that *it was* good. And God said, Let us make man in our image, after our likeness: and let them have dominion over the fish of the sea, and over the fowl of the air, and over the cattle, and over all the earth, and over every creeping thing that creepeth upon the earth. So God created man in his *own* image, in the image of God created he him; male and female created he them. And God blessed them, and God said unto them, Be fruitful, and multiply, and replenish the earth, and subdue it: and have dominion over the fish of the sea, and over the fowl of the air, and over every living thing that moveth upon the earth.

Conforming

And God said, Behold, I have given you every herb bearing seed, which *is* upon the face of all the earth, and every tree, in the which *is* the fruit of a tree yielding seed; to you it shall be for meat. And to every beast of the earth, and to every fowl of the air, and to every thing that creepeth upon the earth, wherein *there is* life, *I have given* every green herb for meat: and it was so. And God saw every thing that he had made, and, behold, *it was* very good. And the evening and the morning were the sixth day.

The 6 House Nuggets from the Lord

1. If you are born – again this world is not your home.

2. If you're not obedient to God, you are a house without a home.

3. Every house is not your home.

4. The Earth had no home until the Lord put us here.

5. A man or a woman has no home until marriage.

6. A man or a woman has no home until they have fulfilled their God given purpose in life.

Thought: Where There is No Revelation, There is No Vision

Sub Thought: Who or What Gave You Yours?

Focus Verses:
Jeremiah 1:4-9 Then the word of the LORD came unto me, saying, Before I formed thee in the belly I knew thee; and before thou camest forth out of the womb I sanctified thee, *and* I ordained thee a prophet unto the nations. Then said I, Ah, Lord GOD! behold, I cannot speak: for I *am* a child. But the LORD said unto me, Say not, I *am* a child: for thou shalt go to all that I shall send thee, and whatsoever I command thee thou shalt speak. Be not afraid of their faces: for I *am* with thee to deliver thee, saith the LORD. Then the LORD put forth his hand, and touched my mouth. And the LORD said unto me, Behold, I have put my words in thy mouth.

Word Helpers:
Romans 12:2-10 And be not conformed to this world: but be ye transformed by the renewing of your mind, that ye may prove what *is* that good, and acceptable, and perfect, will of God. For I say, through the grace given unto me, to

every man that is among you, not to think *of himself* more highly than he ought to think; but to think soberly, according as God hath dealt to every man the measure of faith. For as we have many members in one body, and all members have not the same office: So we, *being* many, are one body in Christ, and every one members one of another. Having then gifts differing according to the grace that is given to us, whether prophecy, *let us prophesy* according to the proportion of faith; Or ministry, *let us wait* on *our* ministering: or he that teacheth, on teaching; Or he that exhorteth, on exhortation: he that giveth, *let him do it* with simplicity; he that ruleth, with diligence; he that sheweth mercy, with cheerfulness. *Let* love be without dissimulation. Abhor that which is evil; cleave to that which is good. *Be* kindly affected one to another with brotherly love; in honour preferring one another;

Ephesians 4:1-13 I therefore, the prisoner of the Lord, beseech you that ye walk worthy of the vocation wherewith ye are called, With all lowliness and meekness, with longsuffering, forbearing one another in love; Endeavouring to keep the unity of the Spirit in the bond of peace. *There is* one body, and one Spirit, even as ye are called in one hope of your calling; One Lord, one faith, one baptism, One God and Father of all, who *is* above all, and through all, and in you all. But unto every one of us is given grace according to the measure of the gift of Christ. Wherefore he saith, When he ascended up on high, he led captivity captive, and gave gifts unto men. (Now that he ascended, what is

Conforming

it but that he also descended first into the lower parts of the earth? He that descended is the same also that ascended up far above all heavens, that he might fill all things.) And he gave some, apostles; and some, prophets; and some, evangelists; and some, pastors and teachers; For the perfecting of the saints, for the work of the ministry, for the edifying of the body of Christ: Till we all come in the unity of the faith, and of the knowledge of the Son of God, unto a perfect man, unto the measure of the stature of the fulness of Christ:

1Corinthians 12:1-14 Now concerning spiritual *gifts,* brethren, I would not have you ignorant. Ye know that ye were Gentiles, carried away unto these dumb idols, even as ye were led. Wherefore I give you to understand, that no man speaking by the Spirit of God calleth Jesus accursed: and *that* no man can say that Jesus is the Lord, but by the Holy Ghost. Now there are diversities of gifts, but the same Spirit. And there are differences of administrations, but the same Lord. And there are diversities of operations, but it is the same God which worketh all in all. But the manifestation of the Spirit is given to every man to profit withal. For to one is given by the Spirit the word of wisdom; to another the word of knowledge by the same Spirit; To another faith by the same Spirit; to another the gifts of healing by the same Spirit; To another the working of miracles; to another prophecy; to another discerning of spirits; to another *divers* kinds of tongues; to another the interpretation of tongues: But all these worketh that one and the

Conforming

selfsame Spirit, dividing to every man severally as he will. For as the body is one, and hath many members, and all the members of that one body, being many, are one body: so also *is* Christ. For by one Spirit are we all baptized into one body, whether *we be* Jews or Gentiles, whether *we be* bond or free; and have been all made to drink into one Spirit. For the body is not one member, but many.

1Corinthians 14:1 Follow after charity, and desire spiritual *gifts,* but rather that ye may prophesy.

Revelations Means – an act of revealing or communication, divine truth, something that is revealed by God to man.

God said revelation means – the right one from Him or the wrong on from the devil or yours.

Thought: There Can Only Be One

There can only be One Head, you can be appointed to lead, from the head with all control. You don't have full control, if you know it or not. When you think you have full control, you have gotten out of control. Jesus said that the Earth is the Lords and the fullness there of and all that dwells there in and apart from Me there is no other. Jesus said you can do nothing, you can't even breath.

Title: Recognizing Your God Given Love Abilities

Sub Title: An Never Ending Cycle of Victory

Them: Before you do it, you say it.

Focus Verse:
Proverbs 18:21 Death and life *are* in the power of the tongue: and they that love it shall eat the fruit thereof.

Word Helpers:
Genesis 1:26-28 And God said, Let us make man in our image, after our likeness: and let them have dominion over the fish of the sea, and over the fowl of the air, and over the cattle, and over all the earth, and over every creeping thing that creepeth upon the earth. So God created man in his *own* image, in the image of God created he him; male and female created he them. And God blessed them, and God said unto them, Be fruitful, and multiply, and replenish the earth, and subdue it: and have dominion over the fish of the sea, and over the fowl of the air, and over every living thing that moveth upon the earth.

Psalms 116:1, 2 I love the LORD, because he hath heard my voice *and* my supplications.

Because he hath inclined his ear unto me, therefore will I call upon *him* as long as I live.

James 3:2-9 For in many things we offend all. If any man offend not in word, the same *is* a perfect man, *and* able also to bridle the whole body. Behold, we put bits in the horses' mouths, that they may obey us; and we turn about their whole body. Behold also the ships, which though *they be* so great, and *are* driven of fierce winds, yet are they turned about with a very small helm, whithersoever the governor listeth. Even so the tongue is a little member, and boasteth great things. Behold, how great a matter a little fire kindleth! And the tongue *is* a fire, a world of iniquity: so is the tongue among our members, that it defileth the whole body, and setteth on fire the course of nature; and it is set on fire of hell. For every kind of beasts, and of birds, and of serpents, and of things in the sea, is tamed, and hath been tamed of mankind: But the tongue can no man tame; *it is* an unruly evil, full of deadly poison. Therewith bless we God, even the Father; and therewith curse we men, which are made after the similitude of God.

Proverbs 12:19-22 The lip of truth shall be established for ever: but a lying tongue *is* but for a moment. Deceit *is* in the heart of them that imagine evil: but to the counsellors of peace *is* joy. There shall no evil happen to the just: but the wicked shall be filled with mischief. Lying lips *are* abomination to the LORD: but they that deal truly *are* his delight.

Conforming

1Peter 3:10-12 For he that will love life, and see good days, let him refrain his tongue from evil, and his lips that they speak no guile: Let him eschew evil, and do good; let him seek peace, and ensue it. For the eyes of the Lord *are* over the righteous, and his ears *are open* unto their prayers: but the face of the Lord *is* against them that do evil.

Job 20:12, 13 Though wickedness be sweet in his mouth, *though* he hide it under his tongue; *Though* he spare it, and forsake it not; but keep it still within his mouth:

Cycle Means – a course or series of events or operations that reoccur regularly and leads back to the starting point. One complete performance an imaginary circle or orbit in the Heavens.

God said cycle means – getting back on the holiness cycle and staying there.

Heavenly Nugget

If you're not in the right position you will keep on missing whatever you are aiming at, because you are blind. Your ways aren't like mine says the Lord. Your eyes can't see what I see, they are temporal. Get anointed so you can use mine. I the Lord give insight to My chosen ones.

Title: The Transporter – Jonah Chapters 1, 2, 3

Sub Title: Do You Want His 1 or 2 Please Don't Take His 3

Focus Verses:
John 1:6-8 There was a man sent from God, whose name *was* John. The same came for a witness, to bear witness of the Light, that all *men* through him might believe. He was not that Light, but *was sent* to bear witness of that Light.

Ezekiel 3:1-4 Moreover he said unto me, Son of man, eat that thou findest; eat this roll, and go speak unto the house of Israel. So I opened my mouth, and he caused me to eat that roll. And he said unto me, Son of man, cause thy belly to eat, and fill thy bowels with this roll that I give thee. Then did I eat *it;* and it was in my mouth as honey for sweetness. And he said unto me, Son of man, go, get thee unto the house of Israel, and speak with my words unto them.

7 Points to Make to the Transporter
1. When you run from the Lord you keep going down.
2. Even others know who you are.

Conforming

3. Jesus will make everyone know that He's God and your God.
4. Prayer, giving and wickedness – these things go up before the Lord.
5. The Lord will shake you out of you.
6. He always the God of another chance, forgiving.
7. With God there is always something to learn about you.

Transporter Means – a messenger or carrier, someone who delivers something or someone from one place to another. (Note not all transporters are sent by God.)

Let's Look at Some Transporters

Big, little, heavy, light, old, new, known, or unknown, smelly, stinky, dirty, holy, unholy, true, false, acceptable, unacceptable, life and death.

Trans – to get across, beyond through, also to change, as to the other side.

Porter – A person who carries burdens or baggage that belongs to someone else, a person who cleans different places.

Title: The Place of Cutting You Out of the Way

Sub Title: You Need to Go to the Place of Cutting

Theme – Bearing the Marks of Change

Focus Verses:
Colossians 2:11-16 In whom also ye are circumcised with the circumcision made without hands, in putting off the body of the sins of the flesh by the circumcision of Christ: Buried with him in baptism, wherein also ye are risen with *him* through the faith of the operation of God, who hath raised him from the dead. And you, being dead in your sins and the uncircumcision of your flesh, hath he quickened together with him, having forgiven you all trespasses; Blotting out the handwriting of ordinances that was against us, which was contrary to us, and took it out of the way, nailing it to his cross; *And* having spoiled principalities and powers, he made a shew of them openly, triumphing over them in it. Let no man therefore judge you in meat, or in drink, or in respect of an holyday, or of the new moon, or of the sabbath *days:*

Conforming

1Kings 17:1-24 And Elijah the Tishbite, *who was* of the inhabitants of Gilead, said unto Ahab, *As* the LORD God of Israel liveth, before whom I stand, there shall not be dew nor rain these years, but according to my word. And the word of the LORD came unto him, saying, Get thee hence, and turn thee eastward, and hide thyself by the brook Cherith, that *is* before Jordan. And it shall be, *that* thou shalt drink of the brook; and I have commanded the ravens to feed thee there. So he went and did according unto the word of the LORD: for he went and dwelt by the brook Cherith, that *is* before Jordan. And the ravens brought him bread and flesh in the morning, and bread and flesh in the evening; and he drank of the brook. And it came to pass after a while, that the brook dried up, because there had been no rain in the land. And the word of the LORD came unto him, saying, Arise, get thee to Zarephath, which *belongeth* to Zidon, and dwell there: behold, I have commanded a widow woman there to sustain thee. So he arose and went to Zarephath. And when he came to the gate of the city, behold, the widow woman *was* there gathering of sticks: and he called to her, and said, Fetch me, I pray thee, a little water in a vessel, that I may drink. And as she was going to fetch *it,* he called to her, and said, Bring me, I pray thee, a morsel of bread in thine hand. And she said, *As* the LORD thy God liveth, I have not a cake, but an handful of meal in a barrel, and a little oil in a cruse: and, behold, I *am* gathering two sticks, that I may go in and dress it for me and my son, that we may eat it, and die. And Elijah said unto her, Fear not; go

Conforming

and do as thou hast said: but make me thereof a little cake first, and bring *it* unto me, and after make for thee and for thy son. For thus saith the LORD God of Israel, The barrel of meal shall not waste, neither shall the cruse of oil fail, until the day *that* the LORD sendeth rain upon the earth. And she went and did according to the saying of Elijah: and she, and he, and her house, did eat *many* days. *And* the barrel of meal wasted not, neither did the cruse of oil fail, according to the word of the LORD, which he spake by Elijah. And it came to pass after these things, *that* the son of the woman, the mistress of the house, fell sick; and his sickness was so sore, that there was no breath left in him. And she said unto Elijah, What have I to do with thee, O thou man of God? art thou come unto me to call my sin to remembrance, and to slay my son? And he said unto her, Give me thy son. And he took him out of her bosom, and carried him up into a loft, where he abode, and laid him upon his own bed. And he cried unto the LORD, and said, O LORD my God, hast thou also brought evil upon the widow with whom I sojourn, by slaying her son? And he stretched himself upon the child three times, and cried unto the LORD, and said, O LORD my God, I pray thee, let this child's soul come into him again. And the LORD heard the voice of Elijah; and the soul of the child came into him again, and he revived. And Elijah took the child, and brought him down out of the chamber into the house, and delivered him unto his mother: and Elijah said, See, thy son liveth. And the woman said to Elijah, Now by this I know that thou *art* a man

Conforming

of God, *and* that the word of the LORD in thy mouth *is* truth.

The Circumcision of the heart is two – fold. God's part Deuteronomy 30:6, 7 – Your part Jeremiah 4:4. God's part is you to conform to Him – Your part is to be ye transformed, from your old to His new.

Deuteronomy 30:6, 7 And the LORD thy God will circumcise thine heart, and the heart of thy seed, to love the LORD thy God with all thine heart, and with all thy soul, that thou mayest live. And the LORD thy God will put all these curses upon thine enemies, and on them that hate thee, which persecuted thee.

Jeremiah 4:4 Circumcise yourselves to the LORD, and take away the foreskins of your heart, ye men of Judah and inhabitants of Jerusalem: lest my fury come forth like fire, and burn that none can quench *it,* because of the evil of your doings.

9 Cutting Points

1. The Word came
2. Instructions came
3. Where and what to do came
4. The need was met
5. Obedience – the promotion came
6. Put not in your own time limit on what God is doing
7. After a while you will find out there is only one way, the Lord's
8. Your waiting is never wasted it is invested

Conforming

9. You have to go to and then through the prison before you can get to the place

Title: Producing the Proof

Sub Title: You Are a Product of What You Are Producing

Theme – And It Came to Pass After These Things, After What Things

After You

Give Me your dead marriage
Give Me your dead Ministry
Give Me your impossible situation
Give Me your broken heart
Give Me your bitterness, anger, gossiping, hatred and your unforgiveness.

Heavenly Nuggets

1. You have to put the icing on the cake for it to work.
2. Without the inner court, there will be no outer court manifestations.
3. You will do new things

2Corinthian 5:17 Therefore if any man *be* in Christ, *he is* a new creature: old things are

Conforming

passed away; behold, all things are become new.

Hebrews 10:19, 20 Having therefore, brethren, boldness to enter into the holiest by the blood of Jesus, By a new and living way, which he hath consecrated for us, through the veil, that is to say, his flesh;

Ezekiel 36:26, 27 A new heart also will I give you, and a new spirit will I put within you: and I will take away the stony heart out of your flesh, and I will give you an heart of flesh. And I will put my spirit within you, and cause you to walk in my statutes, and ye shall keep my judgments, and do *them*.

Colossians 3:10 And have put on the new *man*, which is renewed in knowledge after the image of him that created him:

Isaiah 55:8, 9 For my thoughts *are* not your thoughts, neither *are* your ways my ways, saith the LORD. For *as* the heavens are higher than the earth, so are my ways higher than your ways, and my thoughts than your thoughts.

Psalms 33:3 Sing unto him a new song; play skilfully with a loud noise.

Luke 18:27 And he said, The things which are impossible with men are possible with God.

Under the Law you couldn't touch the dead, but under Christ you can.

Conforming

Leviticus 21:1-24 And the LORD said unto Moses, Speak unto the priests the sons of Aaron, and say unto them, There shall none be defiled for the dead among his people: But for his kin, that is near unto him, *that is,* for his mother, and for his father, and for his son, and for his daughter, and for his brother, And for his sister a virgin, that is nigh unto him, which hath had no husband; for her may he be defiled. *But* he shall not defile himself, *being* a chief man among his people, to profane himself. They shall not make baldness upon their head, neither shall they shave off the corner of their beard, nor make any cuttings in their flesh. They shall be holy unto their God, and not profane the name of their God: for the offerings of the LORD made by fire, *and* the bread of their God, they do offer: therefore they shall be holy. They shall not take a wife *that is* a whore, or profane; neither shall they take a woman put away from her husband: for he *is* holy unto his God. Thou shalt sanctify him therefore; for he offereth the bread of thy God: he shall be holy unto thee: for I the LORD, which sanctify you, *am* holy. And the daughter of any priest, if she profane herself by playing the whore, she profaneth her father: she shall be burnt with fire. And *he that is* the high priest among his brethren, upon whose head the anointing oil was poured, and that is consecrated to put on the garments, shall not uncover his head, nor rend his clothes; Neither shall he go in to any dead body, nor defile himself for his father, or for his mother; Neither shall he go out of the sanctuary, nor profane the sanctuary of his God; for the crown

Conforming

of the anointing oil of his God *is* upon him: I *am* the LORD. And he shall take a wife in her virginity. A widow, or a divorced woman, or profane, *or* an harlot, these shall he not take: but he shall take a virgin of his own people to wife. Neither shall he profane his seed among his people: for I the LORD do sanctify him. And the LORD spake unto Moses, saying, Speak unto Aaron, saying, Whosoever *he be* of thy seed in their generations that hath *any* blemish, let him not approach to offer the bread of his God. For whatsoever man *he be* that hath a blemish, he shall not approach: a blind man, or a lame, or he that hath a flat nose, or any thing superfluous, Or a man that is brokenfooted, or brokenhanded, Or crookbackt, or a dwarf, or that hath a blemish in his eye, or be scurvy, or scabbed, or hath his stones broken; No man that hath a blemish of the seed of Aaron the priest shall come nigh to offer the offerings of the LORD made by fire: he hath a blemish; he shall not come nigh to offer the bread of his God. He shall eat the bread of his God, *both* of the most holy, and of the holy. Only he shall not go in unto the vail, nor come nigh unto the altar, because he hath a blemish; that he profane not my sanctuaries: for I the LORD do sanctify them. And Moses told *it* unto Aaron, and to his sons, and unto all the children of Israel.

Jesus respected their law and He called Lazarus from the dead and did not touch him.

Title: When I Truly Die Then I Can Speak, Never the Less Not I but Christ

Sub Title: Being Dead, Yet He Speaks

Focus Verses:
John 3:30 He must increase, but I *must* decrease.

2Kings 13:14 Now Elisha was fallen sick of his sickness whereof he died. And Joash the king of Israel came down unto him, and wept over his face, and said, O my father, my father, the chariot of Israel, and the horsemen thereof.

2Kings 13:20, 21 And Elisha died, and they buried him. And the bands of the Moabites invaded the land at the coming in of the year. And it came to pass, as they were burying a man, that, behold, they spied a band *of men;* and they cast the man into the sepulchre of Elisha: and when the man was let down, and touched the bones of Elisha, he revived, and stood up on his feet.

Hebrews 11:4 By faith Abel offered unto God a more excellent sacrifice than Cain, by which he obtained witness that he was righteous, God testifying of his gifts: and by it he being dead yet speaketh.

There Are Two Types of Deaths

1. Premature Deaths – When you are turned over for the destruction of your flesh, so your soul might be saved.

1Corinthians 5:4, 5 In the name of our Lord Jesus Christ, when ye are gathered together, and my spirit, with the power of our Lord Jesus Christ, To deliver such an one unto Satan for the destruction of the flesh, that the spirit may be saved in the day of the Lord Jesus.

2. Every man has a appointed time to die.

Ecc 3:2 A time to be born, and a time to die; a time to plant, and a time to pluck up *that which is* planted;

Title: Go Again Seven Times, Don't Give Up

Sub Title: It's a Right – Now Time

Focus Verses:
Hebrews 11:1-3 Now faith is the substance of things hoped for, the evidence of things not seen. For by it the elders obtained a good report. Through faith we understand that the worlds were framed by the word of God, so that things which are seen were not made of things which do appear.

2Kings 5:1-16 Now Naaman, captain of the host of the king of Syria, was a great man with his master, and honourable, because by him the LORD had given deliverance unto Syria: he was also a mighty man in valour, *but he was* a leper. And the Syrians had gone out by companies, and had brought away captive out of the land of Israel a little maid; and she waited on Naaman's wife. And she said unto her mistress, Would God my lord *were* with the prophet that *is* in Samaria! for he would recover him of his leprosy. And *one* went in, and told his lord, saying, Thus and thus said the maid that *is* of the land of Israel. And the king of Syria said, Go to, go, and I will send a letter unto the king of Israel. And he departed,

Conforming

and took with him ten talents of silver, and six thousand *pieces* of gold, and ten changes of raiment. And he brought the letter to the king of Israel, saying, Now when this letter is come unto thee, behold, I have *therewith* sent Naaman my servant to thee, that thou mayest recover him of his leprosy. And it came to pass, when the king of Israel had read the letter, that he rent his clothes, and said, *Am* I God, to kill and to make alive, that this man doth send unto me to recover a man of his leprosy? wherefore consider, I pray you, and see how he seeketh a quarrel against me. And it was *so,* when Elisha the man of God had heard that the king of Israel had rent his clothes, that he sent to the king, saying, Wherefore hast thou rent thy clothes? let him come now to me, and he shall know that there is a prophet in Israel. So Naaman came with his horses and with his chariot, and stood at the door of the house of Elisha. And Elisha sent a messenger unto him, saying, Go and wash in Jordan seven times, and thy flesh shall come again to thee, and thou shalt be clean. But Naaman was wroth, and went away, and said, Behold, I thought, He will surely come out to me, and stand, and call on the name of the LORD his God, and strike his hand over the place, and recover the leper. *Are* not Abana and Pharpar, rivers of Damascus, better than all the waters of Israel? may I not wash in them, and be clean? So he turned and went away in a rage. And his servants came near, and spake unto him, and said, My father, *if* the prophet had bid thee *do some* great thing, wouldest thou not have done *it?* how much rather then, when he saith to thee, Wash, and

Conforming

be clean? Then went he down, and dipped himself seven times in Jordan, according to the saying of the man of God: and his flesh came again like unto the flesh of a little child, and he was clean. And he returned to the man of God, he and all his company, and came, and stood before him: and he said, Behold, now I know that *there is* no God in all the earth, but in Israel: now therefore, I pray thee, take a blessing of thy servant. But he said, *As* the LORD liveth, before whom I stand, I will receive none. And he urged him to take *it;* but he refused.

Luke 18:1-8 And he spake a parable unto them *to this end,* that men ought always to pray, and not to faint; Saying, There was in a city a judge, which feared not God, neither regarded man: And there was a widow in that city; and she came unto him, saying, Avenge me of mine adversary. And he would not for a while: but afterward he said within himself, Though I fear not God, nor regard man; Yet because this widow troubleth me, I will avenge her, lest by her continual coming she weary me. And the Lord said, Hear what the unjust judge saith. And shall not God avenge his own elect, which cry day and night unto him, though he bear long with them? I tell you that he will avenge them speedily. Nevertheless when the Son of man cometh, shall he find faith on the earth?

1Kings 18:41-46 And Elijah said unto Ahab, Get thee up, eat and drink; for *there is* a sound of abundance of rain. So Ahab went up to eat and to drink. And Elijah went up to the top of

Conforming

Carmel; and he cast himself down upon the earth, and put his face between his knees, And said to his servant, Go up now, look toward the sea. And he went up, and looked, and said, *There is* nothing. And he said, Go again seven times. And it came to pass at the seventh time, that he said, Behold, there ariseth a little cloud out of the sea, like a man's hand. And he said, Go up, say unto Ahab, Prepare *thy chariot,* and get thee down, that the rain stop thee not. And it came to pass in the mean while, that the heaven was black with clouds and wind, and there was a great rain. And Ahab rode, and went to Jezreel. And the hand of the LORD was on Elijah; and he girded up his loins, and ran before Ahab to the entrance of Jezreel.

7 Points Made

1. Against hope believe in hope
2. Press their way, even though it looked unseen
3. It's beginning to rain
4. Faith rain
5. Follow the Lord's mouth instruction
6. They got a faith reaction
7. Faith pleases God to move for you

Title: Poison Needs an Antidote the Holy Ghost

Sub Title:
1 – For the Money
2 – For the Show
3 – To Get Ready
4 – To Go Straight to Hell

Focus Verses:
Mark 16:12-20 After that he appeared in another form unto two of them, as they walked, and went into the country. And they went and told *it* unto the residue: neither believed they them. Afterward he appeared unto the eleven as they sat at meat, and upbraided them with their unbelief and hardness of heart, because they believed not them which had seen him after he was risen. And he said unto them, Go ye into all the world, and preach the gospel to every creature. He that believeth and is baptized shall be saved; but he that believeth not shall be damned. And these signs shall follow them that believe; In my name shall they cast out devils; they shall speak with new tongues; They shall take up serpents; and if they drink any deadly thing, it shall not hurt them; they shall lay hands on the sick, and they shall recover. So then after the Lord had

Conforming

spoken unto them, he was received up into heaven, and sat on the right hand of God. And they went forth, and preached every where, the Lord working with *them,* and confirming the word with signs following. Amen.

Malachi 3:8-12 Will a man rob God? Yet ye have robbed me. But ye say, Wherein have we robbed thee? In tithes and offerings. Ye *are* cursed with a curse: for ye have robbed me, *even* this whole nation. Bring ye all the tithes into the storehouse, that there may be meat in mine house, and prove me now herewith, saith the LORD of hosts, if I will not open you the windows of heaven, and pour you out a blessing, that *there shall* not *be room* enough *to receive it.* And I will rebuke the devourer for your sakes, and he shall not destroy the fruits of your ground; neither shall your vine cast her fruit before the time in the field, saith the LORD of hosts. And all nations shall call you blessed: for ye shall be a delightsome land, saith the LORD of hosts.

Acts 5:1-15 But a certain man named Ananias, with Sapphira his wife, sold a possession, And kept back *part* of the price, his wife also being privy *to it,* and brought a certain part, and laid *it* at the apostles' feet. But Peter said, Ananias, why hath Satan filled thine heart to lie to the Holy Ghost, and to keep back *part* of the price of the land? Whiles it remained, was it not thine own? and after it was sold, was it not in thine own power? why hast thou conceived this thing in thine heart? thou hast not lied unto men, but unto God. And Ananias hearing these

Conforming

words fell down, and gave up the ghost: and great fear came on all them that heard these things. And the young men arose, wound him up, and carried *him* out, and buried *him*. And it was about the space of three hours after, when his wife, not knowing what was done, came in. And Peter answered unto her, Tell me whether ye sold the land for so much? And she said, Yea, for so much. Then Peter said unto her, How is it that ye have agreed together to tempt the Spirit of the Lord? behold, the feet of them which have buried thy husband *are* at the door, and shall carry thee out. Then fell she down straightway at his feet, and yielded up the ghost: and the young men came in, and found her dead, and, carrying *her* forth, buried *her* by her husband. And great fear came upon all the church, and upon as many as heard these things. And by the hands of the apostles were many signs and wonders wrought among the people; (and they were all with one accord in Solomon's porch. And of the rest durst no man join himself to them: but the people magnified them. And believers were the more added to the Lord, multitudes both of men and women.) Insomuch that they brought forth the sick into the streets, and laid *them* on beds and couches, that at the least the shadow of Peter passing by might overshadow some of them.

Antidote Means – A remedy to counteract the effects of poison. Something that relieves prevents or counteracts.

Conforming

Poison Means – A substance that through its chemical action kills injures or impairs an organism, some thing destructive or harmful.

The thief comes not but for to kill, steal and destroy.

The devil comes also to blind you so that you will fall into destruction or harms way.

Title: Filling My Empty Vessels

Sub Title: I Put My Treasure in You, Learn How to Use it Correctly, No Matter Who You Think You Are

Theme – Somebody, Somewhere Needs to be Filled Will You Help?

Focus Verses:
Luke 14:22-24 And the servant said, Lord, it is done as thou hast commanded, and yet there is room. And the lord said unto the servant, Go out into the highways and hedges, and compel *them* to come in, that my house may be filled. For I say unto you, That none of those men which were bidden shall taste of my supper.

2Kings 4:1-7 Now there cried a certain woman of the wives of the sons of the prophets unto Elisha, saying, Thy servant my husband is dead; and thou knowest that thy servant did fear the LORD: and the creditor is come to take unto him my two sons to be bondmen. And Elisha said unto her, What shall I do for thee? tell me, what hast thou in the house? And she said, Thine handmaid hath not any thing in the house, save a pot of oil. Then he said, Go,

Conforming

borrow thee vessels abroad of all thy neighbours, *even* empty vessels; borrow not a few. And when thou art come in, thou shalt shut the door upon thee and upon thy sons, and shalt pour out into all those vessels, and thou shalt set aside that which is full. So she went from him, and shut the door upon her and upon her sons, who brought *the vessels* to her; and she poured out. And it came to pass, when the vessels were full, that she said unto her son, Bring me yet a vessel. And he said unto her, *There is* not a vessel more. And the oil stayed. Then she came and told the man of God. And he said, Go, sell the oil, and pay thy debt, and live thou and thy children of the rest.

Note – God's power will accomplish God's purpose.

Note:
Genesis 2:7 And the LORD God formed man *of* the dust of the ground, and breathed into his nostrils the breath of life; and man became a living soul.

Genesis 1:27-29 So God created man in his *own* image, in the image of God created he him; male and female created he them. And God blessed them, and God said unto them, Be fruitful, and multiply, and replenish the earth, and subdue it: and have dominion over the fish of the sea, and over the fowl of the air, and over every living thing that moveth upon the earth. And God said, Behold, I have given you every herb bearing seed, which *is* upon the face of all the earth, and every tree, in the which *is* the

Conforming

fruit of a tree yielding seed; to you it shall be for meat.

Genesis 5:1-4 This *is* the book of the generations of Adam. In the day that God created man, in the likeness of God made he him; Male and female created he them; and blessed them, and called their name Adam, in the day when they were created. And Adam lived an hundred and thirty years, and begat *a son* in his own likeness, after his image; and called his name Seth: And the days of Adam after he had begotten Seth were eight hundred years: and he begat sons and daughters:

Note – Everything earthly comes from the dust.

Genesis 2:1-25 Thus the heavens and the earth were finished, and all the host of them. And on the seventh day God ended his work which he had made; and he rested on the seventh day from all his work which he had made. And God blessed the seventh day, and sanctified it: because that in it he had rested from all his work which God created and made. These *are* the generations of the heavens and of the earth when they were created, in the day that the LORD God made the earth and the heavens, And every plant of the field before it was in the earth, and every herb of the field before it grew: for the LORD God had not caused it to rain upon the earth, and *there was* not a man to till the ground. But there went up a mist from the earth, and watered the whole face of the ground. And the LORD God formed man *of* the dust of the ground, and breathed into his nostrils the breath of life; and man became a living soul. And the LORD God planted a garden eastward in Eden; and there he put the man whom he had formed. And out of the ground made the LORD God to grow every tree that is pleasant to the sight, and good for food; the tree of life also in the midst of the garden, and the tree of knowledge of good and evil. And a river went out of Eden to water the garden; and from thence it was parted, and became into four heads. The name of the first *is* Pison: that *is* it which compasseth the whole land of Havilah, where *there is* gold; And the gold of that land *is* good: there *is* bdellium and the onyx stone. And the name of the second river *is* Gihon: the same *is* it that compasseth the whole land of Ethiopia. And the name of the third river *is* Hiddekel: that *is* it which goeth toward the east of Assyria. And the fourth river *is* Euphrates. And the LORD God took the man, and put him into the garden of Eden to dress it and to keep it. And the LORD God commanded the man, saying, Of every tree of the garden thou mayest freely eat: But of the tree of the knowledge of good and evil, thou shalt not eat of it: for in the day that thou eatest thereof thou shalt surely die. And the LORD God said, *It is* not good that the man should be alone; I will make him an help meet for him. And out of the ground the LORD God formed every beast of the field, and every fowl of the air; and brought *them* unto Adam to see what he would call them: and whatsoever Adam called every living creature, that *was* the name thereof. And Adam gave names to all cattle, and to the fowl of the air, and to every beast of the field; but for

Conforming

Adam there was not found an help meet for him. And the LORD God caused a deep sleep to fall upon Adam, and he slept: and he took one of his ribs, and closed up the flesh instead thereof; And the rib, which the LORD God had taken from man, made he a woman, and brought her unto the man. And Adam said, This *is* now bone of my bones, and flesh of my flesh: she shall be called Woman, because she was taken out of Man. Therefore shall a man leave his father and his mother, and shall cleave unto his wife: and they shall be one flesh. And they were both naked, the man and his wife, and were not ashamed.

Title: God Said You Are Divinely Designed For His Purpose

Sub Title: God Planned You for His Pleasure, Formed You for His Family and Shaped You for His Service

Ephesians 1:4, 5 According as he hath chosen us in him before the foundation of the world, that we should be holy and without blame before him in love: Having predestinated us unto the adoption of children by Jesus Christ to himself, according to the good pleasure of his will,

Romans 12:5 So we, *being* many, are one body in Christ, and every one members one of another.

Ephesians 2:10 For we are his workmanship, created in Christ Jesus unto good works, which God hath before ordained that we should walk in them.

It Begins in Your Heart

Conforming

Matthew 12:34 O generation of vipers, how can ye, being evil, speak good things? for out of the abundance of the heart the mouth speaketh.

Luke 6:45 A good man out of the good treasure of his heart bringeth forth that which is good; and an evil man out of the evil treasure of his heart bringeth forth that which is evil: for of the abundance of the heart his mouth speaketh.

Word Helpers

Job 33:6 Behold, I *am* according to thy wish in God's stead: I also am formed out of the clay.

Jeremiah 1:4, 5 Then the word of the LORD came unto me, saying, Before I formed thee in the belly I knew thee; and before thou camest forth out of the womb I sanctified thee, *and* I ordained thee a prophet unto the nations.

Isaiah 45:9-13 Woe unto him that striveth with his Maker! *Let* the potsherd *strive* with the potsherds of the earth. Shall the clay say to him that fashioneth it, What makest thou? or thy work, He hath no hands? Woe unto him that saith unto *his* father, What begettest thou? or to the woman, What hast thou brought forth? Thus saith the LORD, the Holy One of Israel, and his Maker, Ask me of things to come concerning my sons, and concerning the work of my hands command ye me. I have made the earth, and created man upon it: I, *even* my hands, have stretched out the heavens, and all their host have I commanded. I have raised him up in righteousness, and I will direct all his

Conforming

ways: he shall build my city, and he shall let go my captives, not for price nor reward, saith the LORD of hosts.

Isaiah 64:8, 9 But now, O LORD, thou *art* our father; we *are* the clay, and thou our potter; and we all *are* the work of thy hand. Be not wroth very sore, O LORD, neither remember iniquity for ever: behold, see, we beseech thee, we *are* all thy people.

Jeremiah 18:6-12 O house of Israel, cannot I do with you as this potter? saith the LORD. Behold, as the clay *is* in the potter's hand, so *are* ye in mine hand, O house of Israel. *At what* instant I shall speak concerning a nation, and concerning a kingdom, to pluck up, and to pull down, and to destroy *it;* If that nation, against whom I have pronounced, turn from their evil, I will repent of the evil that I thought to do unto them. And *at what* instant I shall speak concerning a nation, and concerning a kingdom, to build and to plant *it;* If it do evil in my sight, that it obey not my voice, then I will repent of the good, wherewith I said I would benefit them. Now therefore go to, speak to the men of Judah, and to the inhabitants of Jerusalem, saying, Thus saith the LORD; Behold, I frame evil against you, and devise a device against you: return ye now every one from his evil way, and make your ways and your doings good. And they said, There is no hope: but we will walk after our own devices, and we will every one do the imagination of his evil heart.

Romans 9:20-24 Nay but, O man, who art thou that repliest against God? Shall the thing formed say to him that formed *it,* Why hast thou made me thus? Hath not the potter power over the clay, of the same lump to make one vessel unto honour, and another unto dishonour? *What* if God, willing to shew *his* wrath, and to make his power known, endured with much longsuffering the vessels of wrath fitted to destruction: And that he might make known the riches of his glory on the vessels of mercy, which he had afore prepared unto glory, Even us, whom he hath called, not of the Jews only, but also of the Gentiles?

John 9:6, 7 When he had thus spoken, he spat on the ground, and made clay of the spittle, and he anointed the eyes of the blind man with the clay, And said unto him, Go, wash in the pool of Siloam, (which is by interpretation, Sent.) He went his way therefore, and washed, and came seeing.

Title: Discerning the Nature of False Doctrine, Jesus Only Brought His

Focus Verses:
1John 3:23, 24 And this is his commandment, That we should believe on the name of his Son Jesus Christ, and love one another, as he gave us commandment. And he that keepeth his commandments dwelleth in him, and he in him. And hereby we know that he abideth in us, by the Spirit which he hath given us.

1John 4:1-3 Beloved, believe not every spirit, but try the spirits whether they are of God: because many false prophets are gone out into the world. Hereby know ye the Spirit of God: Every spirit that confesseth that Jesus Christ is come in the flesh is of God: And every spirit that confesseth not that Jesus Christ is come in the flesh is not of God: and this is that *spirit* of antichrist, whereof ye have heard that it should come; and even now already is it in the world.

1John 4:5-8 They are of the world: therefore speak they of the world, and the world heareth them. We are of God: he that knoweth God heareth us; he that is not of God heareth not us. Hereby know we the spirit of truth, and the spirit of error. Beloved, let us love one another:

Conforming

for love is of God; and every one that loveth is born of God, and knoweth God. He that loveth not knoweth not God; for God is love.

1John 4:13 Hereby know we that we dwell in him, and he in us, because he hath given us of his Spirit.

Discerning

Hebrews 5:11-14 Of whom we have many things to say, and hard to be uttered, seeing ye are dull of hearing. For when for the time ye ought to be teachers, ye have need that one teach you again which *be* the first principles of the oracles of God; and are become such as have need of milk, and not of strong meat. For every one that useth milk *is* unskilful in the word of righteousness: for he is a babe. But strong meat belongeth to them that are of full age, *even* those who by reason of use have their senses exercised to discern both good and evil.

Hebrews 4:12-16 For the word of God *is* quick, and powerful, and sharper than any twoedged sword, piercing even to the dividing asunder of soul and spirit, and of the joints and marrow, and *is* a discerner of the thoughts and intents of the heart. Neither is there any creature that is not manifest in his sight: but all things *are* naked and opened unto the eyes of him with whom we have to do. Seeing then that we have a great high priest, that is passed into the heavens, Jesus the Son of God, let us hold fast *our* profession. For we have not an high priest which cannot be touched with the feeling of our infirmities; but was in all points tempted like as *we are, yet* without sin. Let us therefore come boldly unto the throne of grace, that we may obtain mercy, and find grace to help in time of need.

1Corinthians 2:9-16 But as it is written, Eye hath not seen, nor ear heard, neither have entered into the heart of man, the things which God hath prepared for them that love him. But God hath revealed *them* unto us by his Spirit: for the Spirit searcheth all things, yea, the deep things of God. For what man knoweth the things of a man, save the spirit of man which is in him? even so the things of God knoweth no man, but the Spirit of God. Now we have received, not the spirit of the world, but the spirit which is of God; that we might know the things that are freely given to us of God. Which things also we speak, not in the words which man's wisdom teacheth, but which the Holy Ghost teacheth; comparing spiritual things with spiritual. But the natural man receiveth not the things of the Spirit of God: for they are foolishness unto him: neither can he know *them,* because they are spiritually discerned. But he that is spiritual judgeth all things, yet he himself is judged of no man. For who hath known the mind of the Lord, that he may instruct him? But we have the mind of Christ.

Malachi 3:15-18 And now we call the proud happy; yea, they that work wickedness are set up; yea, *they that* tempt God are even delivered. Then they that feared the LORD spake often one to another: and the LORD

Conforming

hearkened, and heard *it,* and a book of remembrance was written before him for them that feared the LORD, and that thought upon his name. And they shall be mine, saith the LORD of hosts, in that day when I make up my jewels; and I will spare them, as a man spareth his own son that serveth him. Then shall ye return, and discern between the righteous and the wicked, between him that serveth God and him that serveth him not.

Discern – to separate, to understand the difference between. To detect with another senses than vision, to discriminate against the devil, revealing in sight and understanding to the hidden, good and evil.

Note

Know no man by the flesh but by the Spirit. Try the spirit to see whether it be of God, many spirits have went out. Having a form of Godliness but denying His power.

Romans 6:17 But God be thanked, that ye were the servants of sin, but ye have obeyed from the heart that form of doctrine which was delivered you.

Doctrine:
Ephesians 4:14 That we *henceforth* be no more children, tossed to and fro, and carried about with every wind of doctrine, by the sleight of men, *and* cunning craftiness, whereby they lie in wait to deceive;

Conforming

Ephesians 4:17-32 This I say therefore, and testify in the Lord, that ye henceforth walk not as other Gentiles walk, in the vanity of their mind, Having the understanding darkened, being alienated from the life of God through the ignorance that is in them, because of the blindness of their heart: Who being past feeling have given themselves over unto lasciviousness, to work all uncleanness with greediness. But ye have not so learned Christ; If so be that ye have heard him, and have been taught by him, as the truth is in Jesus: That ye put off concerning the former conversation the old man, which is corrupt according to the deceitful lusts; And be renewed in the spirit of your mind; And that ye put on the new man, which after God is created in righteousness and true holiness. Wherefore putting away lying, speak every man truth with his neighbour: for we are members one of another. Be ye angry, and sin not: let not the sun go down upon your wrath: Neither give place to the devil. Let him that stole steal no more: but rather let him labour, working with *his* hands the thing which is good, that he may have to give to him that needeth. Let no corrupt communication proceed out of your mouth, but that which is good to the use of edifying, that it may minister grace unto the hearers. And grieve not the holy Spirit of God, whereby ye are sealed unto the day of redemption. Let all bitterness, and wrath, and anger, and clamour, and evil speaking, be put away from you, with all malice: And be ye kind one to another, tenderhearted, forgiving one another, even as God for Christ's sake hath forgiven you.

2John 1:9-11 Whosoever transgresseth, and abideth not in the doctrine of Christ, hath not God. He that abideth in the doctrine of Christ, he hath both the Father and the Son. If there come any unto you, and bring not this doctrine, receive him not into *your* house, neither bid him God speed: For he that biddeth him God speed is partaker of his evil deeds.

Deuteronomy 32:2 My doctrine shall drop as the rain, my speech shall distil as the dew, as the small rain upon the tender herb, and as the showers upon the grass:

Job 11:1-10 Then answered Zophar the Naamathite, and said, Should not the multitude of words be answered? and should a man full of talk be justified? Should thy lies make men hold their peace? and when thou mockest, shall no man make thee ashamed? For thou hast said, My doctrine *is* pure, and I am clean in thine eyes. But oh that God would speak, and open his lips against thee; And that he would shew thee the secrets of wisdom, that *they are* double to that which is! Know therefore that God exacteth of thee *less* than thine iniquity *deserveth*. Canst thou by searching find out God? canst thou find out the Almighty unto perfection? *It is* as high as heaven; what canst thou do? deeper than hell; what canst thou know? The measure thereof *is* longer than the earth, and broader than the sea. If he cut off, and shut up, or gather together, then who can hinder him?

Conforming

John 7:17 If any man will do his will, he shall know of the doctrine, whether it be of God, or *whether* I speak of myself.

Romans 16:17 Now I beseech you, brethren, mark them which cause divisions and offences contrary to the doctrine which ye have learned; and avoid them.

2Timothy 4:3-5 For the time will come when they will not endure sound doctrine; but after their own lusts shall they heap to themselves teachers, having itching ears; And they shall turn away *their* ears from the truth, and shall be turned unto fables. But watch thou in all things, endure afflictions, do the work of an evangelist, make full proof of thy ministry.

1Timothy 4:1-5 Now the Spirit speaketh expressly, that in the latter times some shall depart from the faith, giving heed to seducing spirits, and doctrines of devils; Speaking lies in hypocrisy; having their conscience seared with a hot iron; Forbidding to marry, *and commanding* to abstain from meats, which God hath created to be received with thanksgiving of them which believe and know the truth. For every creature of God *is* good, and nothing to be refused, if it be received with thanksgiving: For it is sanctified by the word of God and prayer.

Has your feast day of the Holy Spirit fully come yet?

Conforming

Acts 2:1 And when the day of Pentecost was fully come, they were all with one accord in one place.

Conforming

Title: My Plans – Empty Plans

Note – Your ways are not my ways say the Lord.

Focus Verses:
Jeremiah 10:23, 24 O LORD, I know that the way of man *is* not in himself: *it is* not in man that walketh to direct his steps. O LORD, correct me, but with judgment; not in thine anger, lest thou bring me to nothing.

Jeremiah 32:39, 40 And I will give them one heart, and one way, that they may fear me for ever, for the good of them, and of their children after them: And I will make an everlasting covenant with them, that I will not turn away from them, to do them good; but I will put my fear in their hearts, that they shall not depart from me.

1 – John 14:6 Jesus saith unto him, I am the way, the truth, and the life: no man cometh unto the Father, but by me.

2 – Psalms 10:3-7 For the wicked boasteth of his heart's desire, and blesseth the covetous, *whom* the LORD abhorreth. The wicked, through the pride of his countenance, will not seek *after God:* God *is* not in all his thoughts. His ways are always grievous; thy judgments *are* far above out of his sight: *as*

Conforming

for all his enemies, he puffeth at them. He hath said in his heart, I shall not be moved: for *I shall* never *be* in adversity. His mouth is full of cursing and deceit and fraud: under his tongue *is* mischief and vanity.

3 – Psalms 25:4 Shew me thy ways, O LORD; teach me thy paths.

4 – Psalms 119:30 I have chosen the way of truth: thy judgments have I laid *before me*.

5 – Proverbs 16:7 When a man's ways please the LORD, he maketh even his enemies to be at peace with him.

6 – Proverbs 16:25 There is a way that seemeth right unto a man, but the end thereof *are* the ways of death.

7 – Proverbs 14:12 There is a way which seemeth right unto a man, but the end thereof *are* the ways of death.

8 – Isaiah 30:21 And thine ears shall hear a word behind thee, saying, This *is* the way, walk ye in it, when ye turn to the right hand, and when ye turn to the left.

9 – Isaiah 35:8 And an highway shall be there, and a way, and it shall be called The way of holiness; the unclean shall not pass over it; but it *shall be* for those: the wayfaring men, though fools, shall not err *therein*.

10 – Isaiah 43:19 Behold, I will do a new thing; now it shall spring forth; shall ye not know

Conforming

it? I will even make a way in the wilderness, *and* rivers in the desert.

11 – Psalms 119:168 I have kept thy precepts and thy testimonies: for all my ways *are* before thee.

12 – 1Samuel 12:23 Moreover as for me, God forbid that I should sin against the LORD in ceasing to pray for you: but I will teach you the good and the right way:

13 – Matthew 7:14 Because strait *is* the gate, and narrow *is* the way, which leadeth unto life, and few there be that find it.

Plans Means – To have in mind, to devise a way or course of doing something, to attain an end, to lay a foundation, a design, plot, scheme or project or method.

Empty Means – Without containing nothing lacking reality or substance or value, void of sense, foolish, hungry, having no purpose or result of real life or comfort, blank, vacant, void.

Foot note – There was something so powerful that when Jesus walked by and said follow me. Matthew the tax collector left his position. Peter, James and John left their fishing business. There is something so powerful about the mantle, that is coming upon you that it will cause you to leave everything in order to follow the destiny of God has for you.

Conforming

1Kings 19:19, 20 So he departed thence, and found Elisha the son of Shaphat, who *was* plowing *with* twelve yoke *of oxen* before him, and he with the twelfth: and Elijah passed by him, and cast his mantle upon him. And he left the oxen, and ran after Elijah, and said, Let me, I pray thee, kiss my father and my mother, and *then* I will follow thee. And he said unto him, Go back again: for what have I done to thee?

Title: A Passing On of the Mantle On Your Head to Mine

Sub Title: That's Enough, Do As I'm Told

Focus Verses:
1Corinthians 3:10-15 According to the grace of God which is given unto me, as a wise masterbuilder, I have laid the foundation, and another buildeth thereon. But let every man take heed how he buildeth thereupon. For other foundation can no man lay than that is laid, which is Jesus Christ. Now if any man build upon this foundation gold, silver, precious stones, wood, hay, stubble; Every man's work shall be made manifest: for the day shall declare it, because it shall be revealed by fire; and the fire shall try every man's work of what sort it is. If any man's work abide which he hath built thereupon, he shall receive a reward. If any man's work shall be burned, he shall suffer loss: but he himself shall be saved; yet so as by fire.

Hebrews 6:1-3 Therefore leaving the principles of the doctrine of Christ, let us go on unto perfection; not laying again the foundation of repentance from dead works, and of faith

Conforming

toward God, Of the doctrine of baptisms, and of laying on of hands, and of resurrection of the dead, and of eternal judgment. And this will we do, if God permit.

1Kings 19:19-21 So he departed thence, and found Elisha the son of Shaphat, who *was* plowing *with* twelve yoke *of oxen* before him, and he with the twelfth: and Elijah passed by him, and cast his mantle upon him. And he left the oxen, and ran after Elijah, and said, Let me, I pray thee, kiss my father and my mother, and *then* I will follow thee. And he said unto him, Go back again: for what have I done to thee? And he returned back from him, and took a yoke of oxen, and slew them, and boiled their flesh with the instruments of the oxen, and gave unto the people, and they did eat. Then he arose, and went after Elijah, and ministered unto him.

2Kings 2:1-12 And it came to pass, when the LORD would take up Elijah into heaven by a whirlwind, that Elijah went with Elisha from Gilgal. And Elijah said unto Elisha, Tarry here, I pray thee; for the LORD hath sent me to Bethel. And Elisha said *unto him, As* the LORD liveth, and *as* thy soul liveth, I will not leave thee. So they went down to Bethel. And the sons of the prophets that *were* at Bethel came forth to Elisha, and said unto him, Knowest thou that the LORD will take away thy master from thy head to day? And he said, Yea, I know *it;* hold ye your peace. And Elijah said unto him, Elisha, tarry here, I pray thee; for the LORD hath sent me to Jericho. And he said, *As*

Conforming

the LORD liveth, and *as* thy soul liveth, I will not leave thee. So they came to Jericho. And the sons of the prophets that *were* at Jericho came to Elisha, and said unto him, Knowest thou that the LORD will take away thy master from thy head to day? And he answered, Yea, I know *it;* hold ye your peace. And Elijah said unto him, Tarry, I pray thee, here; for the LORD hath sent me to Jordan. And he said, *As* the LORD liveth, and *as* thy soul liveth, I will not leave thee. And they two went on. And fifty men of the sons of the prophets went, and stood to view afar off: and they two stood by Jordan. And Elijah took his mantle, and wrapped *it* together, and smote the waters, and they were divided hither and thither, so that they two went over on dry ground. And it came to pass, when they were gone over, that Elijah said unto Elisha, Ask what I shall do for thee, before I be taken away from thee. And Elisha said, I pray thee, let a double portion of thy spirit be upon me. And he said, Thou hast asked a hard thing: *nevertheless,* if thou see me *when I am* taken from thee, it shall be so unto thee; but if not, it shall not be *so*. And it came to pass, as they still went on, and talked, that, behold, *there appeared* a chariot of fire, and horses of fire, and parted them both asunder; and Elijah went up by a whirlwind into heaven. And Elisha saw *it,* and he cried, My father, my father, the chariot of Israel, and the horsemen thereof. And he saw him no more: and he took hold of his own clothes, and rent them in two pieces.

Conforming

The Mantle

1. It's a mantle of divine intimacy.
John 14:16 And I will pray the Father, and he shall give you another Comforter, that he may abide with you for ever;

2. It's a mantle of a supernatural calling.
John 20:21 Then said Jesus to them again, Peace *be* unto you: as *my* Father hath sent me, even so send I you.

3. It's a mantle of invested authority.
Luke 9:1, 2 Then he called his twelve disciples together, and gave them power and authority over all devils, and to cure diseases. And he sent them to preach the kingdom of God, and to heal the sick.

Luke 24:49-53 And, behold, I send the promise of my Father upon you: but tarry ye in the city of Jerusalem, until ye be endued with power from on high. And he led them out as far as to Bethany, and he lifted up his hands, and blessed them. And it came to pass, while he blessed them, he was parted from them, and carried up into heaven. And they worshipped him, and returned to Jerusalem with great joy: And were continually in the temple, praising and blessing God. Amen.

Acts 1:8 But ye shall receive power, after that the Holy Ghost is come upon you: and ye shall be witnesses unto me both in Jerusalem, and in all Judaea, and in Samaria, and unto the uttermost part of the earth.

Conforming

Luke 10:19 Behold, I give unto you power to tread on serpents and scorpions, and over all the power of the enemy: and nothing shall by any means hurt you.

Many are called but few are chosen. Many prophets followed them but only a few got it.

Only a few of the called will make it said the Lord - why? Because the Lord knows the end from the beginning and you don't.

Title: There is Someone in the Oven and the Lord Has Commanded Them to Come Out.

Sub Title: It's Better to Die Now Than Later

Focus Verses:
Philippians 1:20, 21 According to my earnest expectation and *my* hope, that in nothing I shall be ashamed, but *that* with all boldness, as always, *so* now also Christ shall be magnified in my body, whether *it be* by life, or by death. For to me to live *is* Christ, and to die *is* gain.

Meat:
Deuteronomy 4:20 But the LORD hath taken you, and brought you forth out of the iron furnace, *even* out of Egypt, to be unto him a people of inheritance, as *ye are* this day.

Deuteronomy 4:5, 6 Behold, I have taught you statutes and judgments, even as the LORD my God commanded me, that ye should do so in the land whither ye go to possess it. Keep therefore and do *them;* for this *is* your wisdom and your understanding in the sight of the nations, which shall hear all these statutes, and

Conforming

say, Surely this great nation *is* a wise and understanding people.

Main Meat:
Daniel 3:4-20 Then an herald cried aloud, To you it is commanded, O people, nations, and languages, *That* at what time ye hear the sound of the cornet, flute, harp, sackbut, psaltery, dulcimer, and all kinds of musick, ye fall down and worship the golden image that Nebuchadnezzar the king hath set up: And whoso falleth not down and worshippeth shall the same hour be cast into the midst of a burning fiery furnace. Therefore at that time, when all the people heard the sound of the cornet, flute, harp, sackbut, psaltery, and all kinds of musick, all the people, the nations, and the languages, fell down *and* worshipped the golden image that Nebuchadnezzar the king had set up. Wherefore at that time certain Chaldeans came near, and accused the Jews. They spake and said to the king Nebuchadnezzar, O king, live for ever. Thou, O king, hast made a decree, that every man that shall hear the sound of the cornet, flute, harp, sackbut, psaltery, and dulcimer, and all kinds of musick, shall fall down and worship the golden image: And whoso falleth not down and worshippeth, *that* he should be cast into the midst of a burning fiery furnace. There are certain Jews whom thou hast set over the affairs of the province of Babylon, Shadrach, Meshach, and Abednego; these men, O king, have not regarded thee: they serve not thy gods, nor worship the golden image which thou hast set up. Then Nebuchadnezzar in *his* rage

and fury commanded to bring Shadrach, Meshach, and Abednego. Then they brought these men before the king. Nebuchadnezzar spake and said unto them, *Is it* true, O Shadrach, Meshach, and Abednego, do not ye serve my gods, nor worship the golden image which I have set up? Now if ye be ready that at what time ye hear the sound of the cornet, flute, harp, sackbut, psaltery, and dulcimer, and all kinds of musick, ye fall down and worship the image which I have made; *well:* but if ye worship not, ye shall be cast the same hour into the midst of a burning fiery furnace; and who *is* that God that shall deliver you out of my hands? Shadrach, Meshach, and Abednego, answered and said to the king, O Nebuchadnezzar, we *are* not careful to answer thee in this matter. If it be *so,* our God whom we serve is able to deliver us from the burning fiery furnace, and he will deliver *us* out of thine hand, O king. But if not, be it known unto thee, O king, that we will not serve thy gods, nor worship the golden image which thou hast set up. Then was Nebuchadnezzar full of fury, and the form of his visage was changed against Shadrach, Meshach, and Abednego: *therefore* he spake, and commanded that they should heat the furnace one seven times more than it was wont to be heated. And he commanded the most mighty men that *were* in his army to bind Shadrach, Meshach, and Abednego, *and* to cast *them* into the burning fiery furnace.

Conforming

Focus **Verses**:
Ecclesiastes 7:17 Be not over much wicked, neither be thou foolish: why shouldest thou die before thy time?

Matthew 13:41, 42 The Son of man shall send forth his angels, and they shall gather out of his kingdom all things that offend, and them which do iniquity; And shall cast them into a furnace of fire: there shall be wailing and gnashing of teeth.

John 11:1-11 Now a certain *man* was sick, *named* Lazarus, of Bethany, the town of Mary and her sister Martha. (It was *that* Mary which anointed the Lord with ointment, and wiped his feet with her hair, whose brother Lazarus was sick.) Therefore his sisters sent unto him, saying, Lord, behold, he whom thou lovest is sick. When Jesus heard *that,* he said, This sickness is not unto death, but for the glory of God, that the Son of God might be glorified thereby. Now Jesus loved Martha, and her sister, and Lazarus. When he had heard therefore that he was sick, he abode two days still in the same place where he was. Then after that saith he to *his* disciples, Let us go into Judaea again. *His* disciples say unto him, Master, the Jews of late sought to stone thee; and goest thou thither again? Jesus answered, Are there not twelve hours in the day? If any man walk in the day, he stumbleth not, because he seeth the light of this world. But if a man walk in the night, he stumbleth, because there is no light in him. These things said he: and after that he saith unto them, Our friend

Lazarus sleepeth; but I go, that I may awake him out of sleep.

John 11:14, 15 Then said Jesus unto them plainly, Lazarus is dead. And I am glad for your sakes that I was not there, to the intent ye may believe; nevertheless let us go unto him.

John 11:33, 34 When Jesus therefore saw her weeping, and the Jews also weeping which came with her, he groaned in the spirit, and was troubled, And said, Where have ye laid him? They said unto him, Lord, come and see.

John 11:39-44 Jesus said, Take ye away the stone. Martha, the sister of him that was dead, saith unto him, Lord, by this time he stinketh: for he hath been *dead* four days. Jesus saith unto her, Said I not unto thee, that, if thou wouldest believe, thou shouldest see the glory of God? Then they took away the stone *from the place* where the dead was laid. And Jesus lifted up *his* eyes, and said, Father, I thank thee that thou hast heard me. And I knew that thou hearest me always: but because of the people which stand by I said *it,* that they may believe that thou hast sent me. And when he thus had spoken, he cried with a loud voice, Lazarus, come forth. And he that was dead came forth, bound hand and foot with graveclothes: and his face was bound about with a napkin. Jesus saith unto them, Loose him, and let him go.

Conforming

Oven Means – Those Who,
O – Overcome
V – Have Victory
E – Have Eternal Life
N – Now

Focus Verses:
John 16:28 I came forth from the Father, and am come into the world: again, I leave the world, and go to the Father.

Genesis 18:17 And the LORD said, Shall I hide from Abraham that thing which I do;

Thought – Things to Know
No risk - no reward, no stepping out - no victory, no turning to - no life, no walking away from self - no entry, no submission - no acceptance, no saying no to the devil - no yes to the Lord Jesus, no to she, he or me - no separation, no relationship - no love, no love - no Heaven.

Matthew left his tax business and followed Me. How?

Mark 8:34 And when he had called the people *unto him* with his disciples also, he said unto them, Whosoever will come after me, let him deny himself, and take up his cross, and follow me.

Matthew 4:17-22 From that time Jesus began to preach, and to say, Repent: for the kingdom of heaven is at hand. And Jesus, walking by the sea of Galilee, saw two brethren, Simon called

Peter, and Andrew his brother, casting a net into the sea: for they were fishers. And he saith unto them, Follow me, and I will make you fishers of men. And they straightway left *their* nets, and followed him. And going on from thence, he saw other two brethren, James *the son* of Zebedee, and John his brother, in a ship with Zebedee their father, mending their nets; and he called them. And they immediately left the ship and their father, and followed him.

John 1:43-51 The day following Jesus would go forth into Galilee, and findeth Philip, and saith unto him, Follow me. Now Philip was of Bethsaida, the city of Andrew and Peter. Philip findeth Nathanael, and saith unto him, We have found him, of whom Moses in the law, and the prophets, did write, Jesus of Nazareth, the son of Joseph. And Nathanael said unto him, Can there any good thing come out of Nazareth? Philip saith unto him, Come and see. Jesus saw Nathanael coming to him, and saith of him, Behold an Israelite indeed, in whom is no guile! Nathanael saith unto him, Whence knowest thou me? Jesus answered and said unto him, Before that Philip called thee, when thou wast under the fig tree, I saw thee. Nathanael answered and saith unto him, Rabbi, thou art the Son of God; thou art the King of Israel. Jesus answered and said unto him, Because I said unto thee, I saw thee under the fig tree, believest thou? thou shalt see greater things than these. And he saith unto him, Verily, verily, I say unto you, Hereafter ye shall see heaven open, and the angels of God

Conforming

ascending and descending upon the Son of man.

Luke 5:27, 28 And after these things he went forth, and saw a publican, named Levi, sitting at the receipt of custom: and he said unto him, Follow me. And he left all, rose up, and followed him.

Genesis 12:1-4 Now the LORD had said unto Abram, Get thee out of thy country, and from thy kindred, and from thy father's house, unto a land that I will shew thee: And I will make of thee a great nation, and I will bless thee, and make thy name great; and thou shalt be a blessing: And I will bless them that bless thee, and curse him that curseth thee: and in thee shall all families of the earth be blessed. So Abram departed, as the LORD had spoken unto him; and Lot went with him: and Abram *was* seventy and five years old when he departed out of Haran.

Genesis 2:21-25 And the LORD God caused a deep sleep to fall upon Adam, and he slept: and he took one of his ribs, and closed up the flesh instead thereof; And the rib, which the LORD God had taken from man, made he a woman, and brought her unto the man. And Adam said, This *is* now bone of my bones, and flesh of my flesh: she shall be called Woman, because she was taken out of Man. Therefore shall a man leave his father and his mother, and shall cleave unto his wife: and they shall be one flesh. And they were both naked, the man and his wife, and were not ashamed.

Conforming

Matthew 19:4-6 And he answered and said unto them, Have ye not read, that he which made *them* at the beginning made them male and female, And said, For this cause shall a man leave father and mother, and shall cleave to his wife: and they twain shall be one flesh? Wherefore they are no more twain, but one flesh. What therefore God hath joined together, let not man put asunder.

Conforming

Title: And I Will Dwell in the House of the Lord Forever

John 15:1-5 I am the true vine, and my Father is the husbandman. Every branch in me that beareth not fruit he taketh away: and every *branch* that beareth fruit, he purgeth it, that it may bring forth more fruit. Now ye are clean through the word which I have spoken unto you. Abide in me, and I in you. As the branch cannot bear fruit of itself, except it abide in the vine; no more can ye, except ye abide in me. I am the vine, ye *are* the branches: He that abideth in me, and I in him, the same bringeth forth much fruit: for without me ye can do nothing.

Focus Verses:
Psalms 91:1 He that dwelleth in the secret place of the most High shall abide under the shadow of the Almighty.

Psalms 91:16 With long life will I satisfy him, and shew him my salvation.

Psalms 34:8 O taste and see that the LORD *is* good: blessed *is* the man *that* trusteth in him.

There Are 12 and I Will Dwell In

1. and I will abide in

Conforming

2. and I will His Word in
3. and I will obey in
4. and I will walk in
5. and I will speak in
6. and I will show in
7. and I will keep His integrity in
8. and I will do unto others in
9. and I will pray in
10. and I will fast in
11. and I will be humble in
12. and I will not fight back in

From a caterpillar to a butterfly – from a tadpole into a frog.

Tadpole – A frog or toad that has a rounded body, with a long tail, bordered by fins and external gills soon replaced by internal gills. Then under goes a metamorphosis to an adult caterpillar –a warm like larva of a butterfly or moth, that goes through a change.

Larva – a larva is the early form of an animal, a babe, before adulthood you will never out grow Jesus dummy.

Conforming

Title: My God is Jesus

Sub Title: You Will Act Like Whom or What You Serve, On the Inside

Focus Verses:
Matthew 7:21-23 Not every one that saith unto me, Lord, Lord, shall enter into the kingdom of heaven; but he that doeth the will of my Father which is in heaven. Many will say to me in that day, Lord, Lord, have we not prophesied in thy name? and in thy name have cast out devils? and in thy name done many wonderful works? And then will I profess unto them, I never knew you: depart from me, ye that work iniquity.

Exodus 3:14, 15 And God said unto Moses, I AM THAT I AM: and he said, Thus shalt thou say unto the children of Israel, I AM hath sent me unto you. And God said moreover unto Moses, Thus shalt thou say unto the children of Israel, The LORD God of your fathers, the God of Abraham, the God of Isaac, and the God of Jacob, hath sent me unto you: this *is* my name for ever, and this *is* my memorial unto all generations.

Matthew 6:23, 24 But if thine eye be evil, thy whole body shall be full of darkness. If therefore the light that is in thee be darkness, how great *is* that darkness! No man can serve two masters: for either he will hate the one, and love the other; or else he will hold to the one, and despise the other. Ye cannot serve God and mammon.

Proverbs 10:16 The labour of the righteous *tendeth* to life: the fruit of the wicked to sin.

Proverbs 12:14 A man shall be satisfied with good by the fruit of *his* mouth: and the recompence of a man's hands shall be rendered unto him.

Proverbs 18:20 A man's belly shall be satisfied with the fruit of his mouth; *and* with the increase of his lips shall he be filled.

Matthew 3:10 And now also the axe is laid unto the root of the trees: therefore every tree which bringeth not forth good fruit is hewn down, and cast into the fire.

Matthew 12:33 Either make the tree good, and his fruit good; or else make the tree corrupt, and his fruit corrupt: for the tree is known by *his* fruit.

Matthew 7:16-23 Ye shall know them by their fruits. Do men gather grapes of thorns, or figs of thistles? Even so every good tree bringeth forth good fruit; but a corrupt tree bringeth forth evil fruit. A good tree cannot bring forth evil fruit, neither *can* a corrupt tree bring forth good fruit. Every tree that bringeth not forth good fruit is hewn down, and cast into the fire. Wherefore by their fruits ye shall know them. Not every one that saith unto me, Lord, Lord, shall enter into the kingdom of heaven; but he that doeth the will of my Father which is in heaven. Many will say to me in that day, Lord, Lord, have we not prophesied in thy name? and in thy name have cast out devils? and in thy name done many wonderful works? And then will I profess unto them, I never knew you: depart from me, ye that work iniquity.

4 Things to Know According to Colossians 4:17
Colossians 4:17 And say to Archippus, Take heed to the ministry which thou hast received in the Lord, that thou fulfil it.

1. To be successful, a ministry must be received from God, not achieved through academic excellence or natural abilities or talents. Talents without God's anointing, is using your own wisdom – fleshly.

2. Today man believers are resting in their caves of comfort and materialism. There are multitudes that are afraid to step forward boldly and declare God's Word. They don't risk their lives or reputations.

3. Aligning yourself with God's purpose, material things should not be your focus practical should not be your mission.

4. The Lord said do His purpose with His power and His authority, in all thy ways

acknowledge Him and He will direct you everyday.

Matthew 7:28, 29 And it came to pass, when Jesus had ended these sayings, the people were astonished at his doctrine: For he taught them as *one* having authority, and not as the scribes.

My God is Jesus

We are representatives of the living God and we are called to do battle with satanic forces for the souls of men and nations.

Conforming

Title: Masked Murder

Sub Title: Lies Kill People – Spiritually Then Naturally

Theme – No Longer Ashamed

John 10:10 The thief cometh not, but for to steal, and to kill, and to destroy: I am come that they might have life, and that they might have *it* more abundantly.

2Corinthians 5:17, 18 Therefore if any man *be* in Christ, *he is* a new creature: old things are passed away; behold, all things are become new. And all things *are* of God, who hath reconciled us to himself by Jesus Christ, and hath given to us the ministry of reconciliation;

Things to Know

1. Half truths kill people
2. What you think can kill people
3. What you don't know can kill people

Let's Take an Inside Look

1. Some pain go's deeper than just the physical. Our only God can take the scars away.

Conforming

2. Hope for healing – call on the greatest physician.

3. Let it go – self pity

4. Erasing the scars of the past – shame

5. Seeing myself as God see's me – old things have passed away.

6. God's unconditional acceptance – His love that surpasses all love.

7. That day I caught the revelation that God loved me unconditionally no matter what.

1Peter 2:21-25 For even hereunto were ye called: because Christ also suffered for us, leaving us an example, that ye should follow his steps: Who did no sin, neither was guile found in his mouth: Who, when he was reviled, reviled not again; when he suffered, he threatened not; but committed *himself* to him that judgeth righteously: Who his own self bare our sins in his own body on the tree, that we, being dead to sins, should live unto righteousness: by whose stripes ye were healed. For ye were as sheep going astray; but are now returned unto the Shepherd and Bishop of your souls.

It freed me up to see this new lease on life that He made possible just for me when no one else would or could. Show me such great and everlasting love, for GOD'S LOVE.

Conforming

Title: The Mirror Man

Sub Title: Who is This Mirror Man

Theme – We All Have One!

Focus Verses:
1Peter 2:21-25 For even hereunto were ye called: because Christ also suffered for us, leaving us an example, that ye should follow his steps: Who did no sin, neither was guile found in his mouth: Who, when he was reviled, reviled not again; when he suffered, he threatened not; but committed *himself* to him that judgeth righteously: Who his own self bare our sins in his own body on the tree, that we, being dead to sins, should live unto righteousness: by whose stripes ye were healed. For ye were as sheep going astray; but are now returned unto the Shepherd and Bishop of your souls.

Genesis 1:26-28 And God said, Let us make man in our image, after our likeness: and let them have dominion over the fish of the sea, and over the fowl of the air, and over the cattle, and over all the earth, and over every creeping thing that creepeth upon the earth. So God created man in his *own* image, in the image of God created he him; male and female created he them. And God blessed them, and God said unto them, Be fruitful, and multiply, and replenish the earth, and subdue it: and have dominion over the fish of the sea, and over the fowl of the air, and over every living thing that moveth upon the earth.

The Mirror Man See's All,
Knows All and Hears All

And can do all with one key – Jesus Christ

Your extra – the mirror man is not real but the man is.

Proverbs 15:3 The eyes of the LORD *are* in every place, beholding the evil and the good.

2Peter 3:11 *Seeing* then *that* all these things shall be dissolved, what manner *of persons* ought ye to be in *all* holy conversation and godliness,

Revelations 2:7 He that hath an ear, let him hear what the Spirit saith unto the churches; To him that overcometh will I give to eat of the tree of life, which is in the midst of the paradise of God.

Revelations 2:11 He that hath an ear, let him hear what the Spirit saith unto the churches; He that overcometh shall not be hurt of the second death.

Revelations 2:17 He that hath an ear, let him hear what the Spirit saith unto the churches; To him that overcometh will I give to eat of the

Conforming

hidden manna, and will give him a white stone, and in the stone a new name written, which no man knoweth saving he that receiveth *it*.

Title: The Dove, the Rock and the Water

From the Dove we get our Focus Verses:
Matthew 10:16-20 Behold, I send you forth as sheep in the midst of wolves: be ye therefore wise as serpents, and harmless as doves. But beware of men: for they will deliver you up to the councils, and they will scourge you in their synagogues; And ye shall be brought before governors and kings for my sake, for a testimony against them and the Gentiles. But when they deliver you up, take no thought how or what ye shall speak: for it shall be given you in that same hour what ye shall speak. For it is not ye that speak, but the Spirit of your Father which speaketh in you.

From the Dove we get – the Eagle and the Hawk. The Eagle will protect or defend, the Hawk will attack.

From the Rock we get – steadfastness and being fixed in place.
Romans 9:33 As it is written, Behold, I lay in Sion a stumblingstone and rock of offence: and whosoever believeth on him shall not be ashamed.

Matthew 16:18 And I say also unto thee, That thou art Peter, and upon this rock I will build

Conforming

my church; and the gates of hell shall not prevail against it.

Deuteronomy 32:4-12 *is* the Rock, his work *is* perfect: for all his ways *are* judgment: a God of truth and without iniquity, just and right *is* he. They have corrupted themselves, their spot *is* not *the spot* of his children: *they are* a perverse and crooked generation. Do ye thus requite the LORD, O foolish people and unwise? *is* not he thy father *that* hath bought thee? hath he not made thee, and established thee? Remember the days of old, consider the years of many generations: ask thy father, and he will shew thee; thy elders, and they will tell thee. When the most High divided to the nations their inheritance, when he separated the sons of Adam, he set the bounds of the people according to the number of the children of Israel. For the LORD'S portion *is* his people; Jacob *is* the lot of his inheritance. He found him in a desert land, and in the waste howling wilderness; he led him about, he instructed him, he kept him as the apple of his eye. As an eagle stirreth up her nest, fluttereth over her young, spreadeth abroad her wings, taketh them, beareth them on her wings: *So* the LORD alone did lead him, and *there was* no strange god with him.

Deuteronomy 32:31-33 For their rock *is* not as our Rock, even our enemies themselves *being* judges. For their vine *is* of the vine of Sodom, and of the fields of Gomorrah: their grapes *are* grapes of gall, their clusters *are* bitter: Their wine *is* the poison of dragons, and the cruel venom of asps.

Psalms 61:2, 3 From the end of the earth will I cry unto thee, when my heart is overwhelmed: lead me to the rock *that* is higher than I. For thou hast been a shelter for me, *and* a strong tower from the enemy.

Psalms 27:5 For in the time of trouble he shall hide me in his pavilion: in the secret of his tabernacle shall he hide me; he shall set me up upon a rock.

Psalms 40:2, 3 He brought me up also out of an horrible pit, out of the miry clay, and set my feet upon a rock, *and* established my goings. And he hath put a new song in my mouth, *even* praise unto our God: many shall see *it,* and fear, and shall trust in the LORD.

Psalms 31:3 For thou *art* my rock and my fortress; therefore for thy name's sake lead me, and guide me.

Psalms 71:3 Be thou my strong habitation, whereunto I may continually resort: thou hast given commandment to save me; for thou *art* my rock and my fortress.

Psalms 94:22, 23 But the LORD is my defence; and my God *is* the rock of my refuge. And he shall bring upon them their own iniquity, and shall cut them off in their own wickedness; *yea,* the LORD our God shall cut them off.

Conforming

From the Water we get – deliverance of Water, because some of us have unstable water from sin.

Genesis 49:4 Unstable as water, thou shalt not excel; because thou wentest up to thy father's bed; then defiledst thou *it:* he went up to my couch.

So we have to make our waters sure according to,

Isaiah 33:16 He shall dwell on high: his place of defence *shall be* the munitions of rocks: bread shall be given him; his waters *shall be* sure.

John 4:10 Jesus answered and said unto her, If thou knewest the gift of God, and who it is that saith to thee, Give me to drink; thou wouldest have asked of him, and he would have given thee living water.

John 7:37, 38 In the last day, that great *day* of the feast, Jesus stood and cried, saying, If any man thirst, let him come unto me, and drink. He that believeth on me, as the scripture hath said, out of his belly shall flow rivers of living water.

Because you can't do both according to,
James 3:12-18 Can the fig tree, my brethren, bear olive berries? either a vine, figs? so *can* no fountain both yield salt water and fresh. Who *is* a wise man and endued with knowledge among you? let him shew out of a good conversation his works with meekness of wisdom. But if ye

Conforming

have bitter envying and strife in your hearts, glory not, and lie not against the truth. This wisdom descendeth not from above, but *is* earthly, sensual, devilish. For where envying and strife *is,* there *is* confusion and every evil work. But the wisdom that is from above is first pure, then peaceable, gentle, *and* easy to be intreated, full of mercy and good fruits, without partiality, and without hypocrisy. And the fruit of righteousness is sown in peace of them that make peace.

1John 5:8-12 And there are three that bear witness in earth, the Spirit, and the water, and the blood: and these three agree in one. If we receive the witness of men, the witness of God is greater: for this is the witness of God which he hath testified of his Son. He that believeth on the Son of God hath the witness in himself: he that believeth not God hath made him a liar; because he believeth not the record that God gave of his Son. And this is the record, that God hath given to us eternal life, and this life is in his Son. He that hath the Son hath life; *and* he that hath not the Son of God hath not life.

Focus Verses:
2Corinthians 3:2-6 Ye are our epistle written in our hearts, known and read of all men: *Forasmuch as ye are* manifestly declared to be the epistle of Christ ministered by us, written not with ink, but with the Spirit of the living God; not in tables of stone, but in fleshy tables of the heart. And such trust have we through Christ to God-ward: Not that we are sufficient of ourselves to think any thing as of ourselves;

Conforming

but our sufficiency *is* of God; Who also hath made us able ministers of the new testament; not of the letter, but of the spirit: for the letter killeth, but the spirit giveth life.

Things to Know

1. People see you before you do. They take you for what they see in you, not for what you say. For they see and not hear the real you. Do you see?

2. Are you worth more than many sparrows?

3. Believe me for the work sake.

4. If it be good or evil.

Meat Time

Title: Delivering Face Value, It's About Your New Nature

Sub Title: If You Have Allowed Christ to Give You ONE His

Matthew 10:30, 31 But the very hairs of your head are all numbered. Fear ye not therefore, ye are of more value than many sparrows.

Job 28:16 It cannot be valued with the gold of Ophir, with the precious onyx, or the sapphire.

Job 28:19 The topaz of Ethiopia shall not equal it, neither shall it be valued with pure gold.

Matthew 27:3 Then Judas, which had betrayed him, when he saw that he was condemned, repented himself, and brought again the thirty pieces of silver to the chief priests and elders, Saying, I have sinned in that I have betrayed the innocent blood. And they said, What *is that* to us? see thou *to that*. And he cast down the pieces of silver in the temple, and departed, and went and hanged himself. And the chief priests took the silver pieces, and said, It is not lawful for to put them into the treasury, because it is the price of blood. And they took

Conforming

counsel, and bought with them the potter's field, to bury strangers in. Wherefore that field was called, The field of blood, unto this day. Then was fulfilled that which was spoken by Jeremy the prophet, saying, And they took the thirty pieces of silver, the price of him that was valued, whom they of the children of Israel did value; And gave them for the potter's field, as the Lord appointed me. And Jesus stood before the governor: and the governor asked him, saying, Art thou the King of the Jews? And Jesus said unto him, Thou sayest.

Romans 1:15-32 So, as much as in me is, I am ready to preach the gospel to you that are at Rome also. For I am not ashamed of the gospel of Christ: for it is the power of God unto salvation to every one that believeth; to the Jew first, and also to the Greek. For therein is the righteousness of God revealed from faith to faith: as it is written, The just shall live by faith. For the wrath of God is revealed from heaven against all ungodliness and unrighteousness of men, who hold the truth in unrighteousness; Because that which may be known of God is manifest in them; for God hath shewed *it* unto them. For the invisible things of him from the creation of the world are clearly seen, being understood by the things that are made, *even* his eternal power and Godhead; so that they are without excuse: Because that, when they knew God, they glorified *him* not as God, neither were thankful; but became vain in their imaginations, and their foolish heart was darkened. Professing themselves to be wise, they became fools, And changed the glory of the uncorruptible God into an image made like to corruptible man, and to birds, and fourfooted beasts, and creeping things. Wherefore God also gave them up to uncleanness through the lusts of their own hearts, to dishonour their own bodies between themselves: Who changed the truth of God into a lie, and worshipped and served the creature more than the Creator, who is blessed for ever. Amen. For this cause God gave them up unto vile affections: for even their women did change the natural use into that which is against nature: And likewise also the men, leaving the natural use of the woman, burned in their lust one toward another; men with men working that which is unseemly, and receiving in themselves that recompence of their error which was meet. And even as they did not like to retain God in *their* knowledge, God gave them over to a reprobate mind, to do those things which are not convenient; Being filled with all unrighteousness, fornication, wickedness, covetousness, maliciousness; full of envy, murder, debate, deceit, malignity; whisperers, Backbiters, haters of God, despiteful, proud, boasters, inventors of evil things, disobedient to parents, Without understanding, covenantbreakers, without natural affection, implacable, unmerciful: Who knowing the judgment of God, that they which commit such things are worthy of death, not only do the same, but have pleasure in them that do them.

Title: Learning to Walk in a No Account Kind of Love

Sub Title: Touchy, Touchy ONE DAY You Will Need Someone to Touch You

Focus Verses:
2Peter 3:3 Knowing this first, that there shall come in the last days scoffers, walking after their own lusts,

Jude 1:16-19 These are murmurers, complainers, walking after their own lusts; and their mouth speaketh great swelling *words,* having men's persons in admiration because of advantage. But, beloved, remember ye the words which were spoken before of the apostles of our Lord Jesus Christ; How that they told you there should be mockers in the last time, who should walk after their own ungodly lusts. These be they who separate themselves, sensual, having not the Spirit.

2Corinthians 4:2, 3 But have renounced the hidden things of dishonesty, not walking in craftiness, nor handling the word of God deceitfully; but by manifestation of the truth commending ourselves to every man's conscience in the sight of God. But if our gospel be hid, it is hid to them that are lost:

Word Helpers

1Corinthians 13:1-13 Though I speak with the tongues of men and of angels, and have not charity, I am become *as* sounding brass, or a tinkling cymbal. And though I have *the gift of* prophecy, and understand all mysteries, and all knowledge; and though I have all faith, so that I could remove mountains, and have not charity, I am nothing. And though I bestow all my goods to feed *the poor,* and though I give my body to be burned, and have not charity, it profiteth me nothing. Charity suffereth long, *and* is kind; charity envieth not; charity vaunteth not itself, is not puffed up, Doth not behave itself unseemly, seeketh not her own, is not easily provoked, thinketh no evil; Rejoiceth not in iniquity, but rejoiceth in the truth; Beareth all things, believeth all things, hopeth all things, endureth all things. Charity never faileth: but whether *there be* prophecies, they shall fail; whether *there be* tongues, they shall cease; whether *there be* knowledge, it shall vanish away. For we know in part, and we prophesy in part. But when that which is perfect is come, then that which is in part shall be done away. When I was a child, I spake as a child, I understood as a child, I thought as a child: but when I became a man, I put away childish things. For now we see through a glass, darkly; but then face to face: now I know in part; but then shall I know even as also I am

Conforming

known. And now abideth faith, hope, charity, these three; but the greatest of these *is* charity.

Genesis 3:8, 9 And they heard the voice of the LORD God walking in the garden in the cool of the day: and Adam and his wife hid themselves from the presence of the LORD God amongst the trees of the garden. And the LORD God called unto Adam, and said unto him, Where *art* thou?

Daniel 3:25 He answered and said, Lo, I see four men loose, walking in the midst of the fire, and they have no hurt; and the form of the fourth is like the Son of God.

Luke 1:15-17 For he shall be great in the sight of the Lord, and shall drink neither wine nor strong drink; and he shall be filled with the Holy Ghost, even from his mother's womb. And many of the children of Israel shall he turn to the Lord their God. And he shall go before him in the spirit and power of Elias, to turn the hearts of the fathers to the children, and the disobedient to the wisdom of the just; to make ready a people prepared for the Lord.

2John 1:4 I rejoiced greatly that I found of thy children walking in truth, as we have received a commandment from the Father.

Acts 9:31 Then had the churches rest throughout all Judaea and Galilee and Samaria, and were edified; and walking in the fear of the Lord, and in the comfort of the Holy Ghost, were multiplied.

Conforming

Romans 5:5 And hope maketh not ashamed; because the love of God is shed abroad in our hearts by the Holy Ghost which is given unto us.

1 Corinthians Chapter 13 Breakdown

1. Talking Loud and saying nothing
2. Vain
3. Religious
4. Humble
5. Godly
6. Deliverance
7. Long Suffered
8. Walk by faith, not by sight
9. Know your place
10. Jesus fully comes
11. When I became a child of God
12. When I start seeing through the eyes of God
13. Christ on the inside in the fullness

Conforming

Title: The Lord Said Let Me Introduce You to My Knife

Sub Title: It Cuts You Going in and Pull it Cuts You Coming Out – Two Edge

Focus Verses:
Matthew 5:30 And if thy right hand offend thee, cut it off, and cast *it* from thee: for it is profitable for thee that one of thy members should perish, and not *that* thy whole body should be cast into hell.

Matthew 18:8 Wherefore if thy hand or thy foot offend thee, cut them off, and cast *them* from thee: it is better for thee to enter into life halt or maimed, rather than having two hands or two feet to be cast into everlasting fire.

Mark 9:43 And if thy hand offend thee, cut it off: it is better for thee to enter into life maimed, than having two hands to go into hell, into the fire that never shall be quenched:

Job 8:13 -15 So *are* the paths of all that forget God; and the hypocrite's hope shall perish: Whose hope shall be cut off, and whose trust *shall be* a spider's web. He shall lean upon his house, but it shall not stand: he shall hold it fast, but it shall not endure.

Psalms 37:9, 10 For evildoers shall be cut off: but those that wait upon the LORD, they shall inherit the earth. For yet a little while, and the wicked *shall* not *be:* yea, thou shalt diligently consider his place, and it *shall* not *be.*

Proverbs 2:21, 22 For the upright shall dwell in the land, and the perfect shall remain in it. But the wicked shall be cut off from the earth, and the transgressors shall be rooted out of it.

Ephesians 6:17 And take the helmet of salvation, and the sword of the Spirit, which is the word of God:

Hebrews 4:12 For the word of God *is* quick, and powerful, and sharper than any twoedged sword, piercing even to the dividing asunder of soul and spirit, and of the joints and marrow, and *is* a discerner of the thoughts and intents of the heart.

Introducing God's Knives

1. Prep or utility knife – get you ready
2. Boning knife – cutting the flesh
3. Carving knife – to leave His holy mark
4. Paring knife – getting anything that's left behind
5. Steak knife – getting you ready to receive His best
6. Boring knife – releasing the old

Conforming

7. Bread knife – receiving His new bread of life
8. Chiefs knife – ready for the Master's cut

Title: Wonder Working Blood

Sub Title: No Additives Needed

Romans 5:8, 9 But God commendeth his love toward us, in that, while we were yet sinners, Christ died for us. Much more then, being now justified by his blood, we shall be saved from wrath through him.

Isaiah 59:7, 8 Their feet run to evil, and they make haste to shed innocent blood: their thoughts *are* thoughts of iniquity; wasting and destruction *are* in their paths. The way of peace they know not; and *there is* no judgment in their goings: they have made them crooked paths: whosoever goeth therein shall not know peace.

10 Heavenly Nuggets About the Blood

1. Every drop went some where
Luke 22:20 Likewise also the cup after supper, saying, This cup *is* the new testament in my blood, which is shed for you.

Conforming

Mark 14:24 And he said unto them, This is my blood of the new testament, which is shed for many.

1Corinthians 11:25 After the same manner also *he took* the cup, when he had supped, saying, This cup is the new testament in my blood: this do ye, as oft as ye drink *it,* in remembrance of me.

2. Cleansing blood
1John 1:7 But if we walk in the light, as he is in the light, we have fellowship one with another, and the blood of Jesus Christ his Son cleanseth us from all sin.

Revelations 7:14 And I said unto him, Sir, thou knowest. And he said to me, These are they which came out of great tribulation, and have washed their robes, and made them white in the blood of the Lamb.

3. New life was introduced
Hebrews 10:16-21 This *is* the covenant that I will make with them after those days, saith the Lord, I will put my laws into their hearts, and in their minds will I write them; And their sins and iniquities will I remember no more. Now where remission of these *is, there is* no more offering for sin. Having therefore, brethren, boldness to enter into the holiest by the blood of Jesus, By a new and living way, which he hath consecrated for us, through the veil, that is to say, his flesh; And *having* an high priest over the house of God;

4. Delivering and deliverance blood
Colossians 1:16-21 For by him were all things created, that are in heaven, and that are in earth, visible and invisible, whether *they be* thrones, or dominions, or principalities, or powers: all things were created by him, and for him: And he is before all things, and by him all things consist. And he is the head of the body, the church: who is the beginning, the firstborn from the dead; that in all *things* he might have the preeminence. For it pleased *the Father* that in him should all fulness dwell; And, having made peace through the blood of his cross, by him to reconcile all things unto himself; by him, *I say,* whether *they be* things in earth, or things in heaven. And you, that were sometime alienated and enemies in *your* mind by wicked works, yet now hath he reconciled

5. Power packing blood
1Peter 1:2 Elect according to the foreknowledge of God the Father, through sanctification of the Spirit, unto obedience and sprinkling of the blood of Jesus Christ: Grace unto you, and peace, be multiplied.

6. Yoke destroying blood
Ephesians 2:11-16 Wherefore remember, that ye *being* in time past Gentiles in the flesh, who are called Uncircumcision by that which is called the Circumcision in the flesh made by hands; That at that time ye were without Christ, being aliens from the commonwealth of Israel, and strangers from the covenants of promise, having no hope, and without God in the world: But now in Christ Jesus ye who

Conforming

sometimes were far off are made nigh by the blood of Christ. For he is our peace, who hath made both one, and hath broken down the middle wall of partition *between us;* Having abolished in his flesh the enmity, *even* the law of commandments *contained* in ordinances; for to make in himself of twain one new man, *so* making peace; And that he might reconcile both unto God in one body by the cross, having slain the enmity thereby:

7. Blind eyes were open blood
8. Deaf ears were open blood
9. The dumb mute spoke blood
10. Complete forgiveness was given blood

Ephesians 1:7 In whom we have redemption through his blood, the forgiveness of sins, according to the riches of his grace;

Heavenly Nugget About Me

Hebrews 9:2-22 For there was a tabernacle made; the first, wherein *was* the candlestick, and the table, and the shewbread; which is called the sanctuary. And after the second veil, the tabernacle which is called the Holiest of all; Which had the golden censer, and the ark of the covenant overlaid round about with gold, wherein *was* the golden pot that had manna, and Aaron's rod that budded, and the tables of the covenant; And over it the cherubims of glory shadowing the mercyseat; of which we cannot now speak particularly. Now when these things were thus ordained, the priests went always into the first tabernacle, accomplishing the service *of God*. But into the second *went* the high priest alone once every year, not without blood, which he offered for himself, and *for* the errors of the people: The Holy Ghost this signifying, that the way into the holiest of all was not yet made manifest, while as the first tabernacle was yet standing: Which *was* a figure for the time then present, in which were offered both gifts and sacrifices, that could not make him that did the service perfect, as pertaining to the conscience; W*hich stood* only in meats and drinks, and divers washings, and carnal ordinances, imposed *on them* until the time of reformation. But Christ being come an high priest of good things to come, by a greater and more perfect tabernacle, not made with hands, that is to say, not of this building; Neither by the blood of goats and calves, but by his own blood he entered in once into the holy place, having obtained eternal redemption *for us.* For if the blood of bulls and of goats, and the ashes of an heifer sprinkling the unclean, sanctifieth to the purifying of the flesh: How much more shall the blood of Christ, who through the eternal Spirit offered himself without spot to God, purge your conscience from dead works to serve the living God? And for this cause he is the mediator of the new testament, that by means of death, for the redemption of the transgressions *that were* under the first testament, they which are called might receive the promise of eternal inheritance. For where a testament *is,* there must also of necessity be the death of the testator. For a testament *is* of force after men are dead: otherwise it is of no strength at all while the testator liveth. Whereupon neither

Conforming

the first *testament* was dedicated without blood. For when Moses had spoken every precept to all the people according to the law, he took the blood of calves and of goats, with water, and scarlet wool, and hyssop, and sprinkled both the book, and all the people, Saying, This *is* the blood of the testament which God hath enjoined unto you. Moreover he sprinkled with blood both the tabernacle, and all the vessels of the ministry. And almost all things are by the law purged with blood; and without shedding of blood is no remission.

From wonder – we get miracle
From miracle – we get supernatural
From supernatural – we get Jesus
No one else can work or create miracles but Jesus.

Conforming

Title: What Kind of Leader Are You from the Inside Out

Sub Title: The Foundation of Character

Main Meat:
Psalms 139:19-24 Surely thou wilt slay the wicked, O God: depart from me therefore, ye bloody men. For they speak against thee wickedly, *and* thine enemies take *thy name* in vain. Do not I hate them, O LORD, that hate thee? and am not I grieved with those that rise up against thee? I hate them with perfect hatred: I count them mine enemies. Search me, O God, and know my heart: try me, and know my thoughts: And see if *there be any* wicked way in me, and lead me in the way everlasting.

Psalms 34:9 O fear the LORD, ye his saints: for *there is* no want to them that fear him.

Psalms 40:1-4 To the chief Musician, A Psalm of David. I waited patiently for the LORD; and he inclined unto me, and heard my cry. He brought me up also out of an horrible pit, out of the miry clay, and set my feet upon a rock, *and* established my goings. And he hath put a new song in my mouth, *even* praise unto our God:

Conforming

many shall see *it,* and fear, and shall trust in the LORD. Blessed *is* that man that maketh the LORD his trust, and respecteth not the proud, nor such as turn aside to lies.

Psalms 32:7-9 Thou *art* my hiding place; thou shalt preserve me from trouble; thou shalt compass me about with songs of deliverance. Selah. I will instruct thee and teach thee in the way which thou shalt go: I will guide thee with mine eye. Be ye not as the horse, *or* as the mule, *which* have no understanding: whose mouth must be held in with bit and bridle, lest they come near unto thee.

Psalms 42:1-4 To the chief Musician, Maschil, for the sons of Korah. As the hart panteth after the water brooks, so panteth my soul after thee, O God. My soul thirsteth for God, for the living God: when shall I come and appear before God? My tears have been my meat day and night, while they continually say unto me, Where *is* thy God? When I remember these *things,* I pour out my soul in me: for I had gone with the multitude, I went with them to the house of God, with the voice of joy and praise, with a multitude that kept holyday.

Psalms 25:1-5 *A Psalm* of David. Unto thee, O LORD, do I lift up my soul. O my God, I trust in thee: let me not be ashamed, let not mine enemies triumph over me. Yea, let none that wait on thee be ashamed: let them be ashamed which transgress without cause. Shew me thy ways, O LORD; teach me thy paths. Lead me in

Conforming

thy truth, and teach me: for thou *art* the God of my salvation; on thee do I wait all the day.

1. Truth and trust
2. Real ship and relationship
3. Intelligence and integrity
4. Assurance and Action
5. Character is a choice you make
6. Your actions are inspirable from your character
7. What's eating away at your character?
8. We must keep an eye on our patterns of our behavior
9. Wrong behavior wrong spirit
10. Check regular for any weakness that remains
11. We must always use the tune-up tool, to keep the inside motor running properly with oil of the Holy Ghost, giving its flow.
12. To be a Godly leader, I believe must stay teachable and pliable in God's hands, so we help others.

Conforming

Title: How Many gods do You Preach, Teach or Serve

Focus Verses:
Philippians 2:4-11 Look not every man on his own things, but every man also on the things of others. Let this mind be in you, which was also in Christ Jesus: Who, being in the form of God, thought it not robbery to be equal with God: But made himself of no reputation, and took upon him the form of a servant, and was made in the likeness of men: And being found in fashion as a man, he humbled himself, and became obedient unto death, even the death of the cross. Wherefore God also hath highly exalted him, and given him a name which is above every name: That at the name of Jesus every knee should bow, of *things* in heaven, and *things* in earth, and *things* under the earth; And *that* every tongue should confess that Jesus Christ *is* Lord, to the glory of God the Father.

Ephesians 1:18-23 The eyes of your understanding being enlightened; that ye may know what is the hope of his calling, and what the riches of the glory of his inheritance in the saints, And what *is* the exceeding greatness of his power to us-ward who believe, according to the working of his mighty power, Which he wrought in Christ, when he raised him from the dead, and set *him* at his own right hand in the heavenly *places,* Far above all principality, and power, and might, and dominion, and every name that is named, not only in this world, but also in that which is to come: And hath put all *things* under his feet, and gave him *to be* the head over all *things* to the church, Which is his body, the fulness of him that filleth all in all.

The Bible says there is only ONE GOD, ONE SPIRIT, ONE FAITH and ONE BAPTISM.

1. God is Creation
Revelations 3:13, 14 He that hath an ear, let him hear what the Spirit saith unto the churches. And unto the angel of the church of the Laodiceans write; These things saith the Amen, the faithful and true witness, the beginning of the creation of God;

Colossians 1:13-22 Who hath delivered us from the power of darkness, and hath translated *us* into the kingdom of his dear Son: In whom we have redemption through his blood, *even* the forgiveness of sins: Who is the image of the invisible God, the firstborn of every creature: For by him were all things created, that are in heaven, and that are in earth, visible and invisible, whether *they be* thrones, or dominions, or principalities, or powers: all things were created by him, and for him: And he is before all things, and by him all things consist. And he is the head of the body, the church: who is the beginning, the firstborn from the dead; that in all *things* he might have the preeminence. For it pleased *the Father* that in him should all fulness dwell; And, having made peace through the blood of his cross, by him to reconcile all things unto himself; by him, *I say,* whether *they be* things in earth, or things in heaven. And you, that were sometime alienated and enemies in *your* mind by wicked works, yet now hath he reconciled In the body of his flesh through death, to present you holy and unblameable and unreproveable in his sight:

2. Son in Redemption
Acts 2:38 Then Peter said unto them, Repent, and be baptized every one of you in the name of Jesus Christ for the remission of sins, and ye shall receive the gift of the Holy Ghost.

Acts 4:12 Neither is there salvation in any other: for there is none other name under heaven given among men, whereby we must be saved.

3. Holy Ghost Indwelling
John 14:3, 4 And if I go and prepare a place for you, I will come again, and receive you unto myself; that where I am, *there* ye may be also. And whither I go ye know, and the way ye know.

John 14:16-19 And I will pray the Father, and he shall give you another Comforter, that he may abide with you for ever; *Even* the Spirit of truth; whom the world cannot receive, because it seeth him not, neither knoweth him: but ye know him; for he dwelleth with you, and shall be in you. I will not leave you comfortless: I will come to you. Yet a little while, and the world seeth me no more; but ye see me: because I live, ye shall live also.

John 14:26 But the Comforter, *which is* the Holy Ghost, whom the Father will send in my name, he shall teach you all things, and bring all things to your remembrance, whatsoever I have said unto you.

John 14:24 He that loveth me not keepeth not my sayings: and the word which ye hear is not mine, but the Father's which sent me.

Isaiah 44:24 Thus saith the LORD, thy redeemer, and he that formed thee from the womb, I *am* the LORD that maketh all *things;* that stretcheth forth the heavens alone; that spreadeth abroad the earth by myself;

Isaiah 45:11 Thus saith the LORD, the Holy One of Israel, and his Maker, Ask me of things to come concerning my sons, and concerning the work of my hands command ye me.

Isaiah 44:6 Thus saith the LORD the King of Israel, and his redeemer the LORD of hosts; I *am* the first, and I *am* the last; and beside me *there is* no God.

Isaiah 44:1, 2 Yet now hear, O Jacob my servant; and Israel, whom I have chosen: Thus saith the LORD that made thee, and formed thee from the womb, *which* will help thee; Fear not, O Jacob, my servant; and thou, Jesurun, whom I have chosen.

Conforming

Isaiah 43:3, 4 For I *am* the LORD thy God, the Holy One of Israel, thy Saviour: I gave Egypt *for* thy ransom, Ethiopia and Seba for thee. Since thou wast precious in my sight, thou hast been honourable, and I have loved thee: therefore will I give men for thee, and people for thy life.

Isaiah 43:10, 11 Ye *are* my witnesses, saith the LORD, and my servant whom I have chosen: that ye may know and believe me, and understand that I *am* he: before me there was no God formed, neither shall there be after me. I, *even* I, *am* the LORD; and beside me *there is* no saviour.

Isaiah 43:14, 15 Thus saith the LORD, your redeemer, the Holy One of Israel; For your sake I have sent to Babylon, and have brought down all their nobles, and the Chaldeans, whose cry *is* in the ships. I *am* the LORD, your Holy One, the creator of Israel, your King.

Title: Give Me Water Says the Lord, the Same I Gave You to Drink, Living Water

Sub Title: No Deposit, No Return

Focus Verse:
James 3:12 Can the fig tree, my brethren, bear olive berries? either a vine, figs? so *can* no fountain both yield salt water and fresh.

W – Walking
A – Always
T – Towards
E – The Eternal
R – Realm

Word Helpers

Jeremiah 2:13 For my people have committed two evils; they have forsaken me the fountain of living waters, *and* hewed them out cisterns, broken cisterns, that can hold no water.

Conforming

1Peter 3:17-20 For *it is* better, if the will of God be so, that ye suffer for well doing, than for evil doing. For Christ also hath once suffered for sins, the just for the unjust, that he might bring us to God, being put to death in the flesh, but quickened by the Spirit: By which also he went and preached unto the spirits in prison; Which sometime were disobedient, when once the longsuffering of God waited in the days of Noah, while the ark was a preparing, wherein few, that is, eight souls were saved by water.

John 7:37, 38 In the last day, that great *day* of the feast, Jesus stood and cried, saying, If any man thirst, let him come unto me, and drink. He that believeth on me, as the scripture hath said, out of his belly shall flow rivers of living water.

Revelations 22:17, 18 And the Spirit and the bride say, Come. And let him that heareth say, Come. And let him that is athirst come. And whosoever will, let him take the water of life freely. For I testify unto every man that heareth the words of the prophecy of this book, If any man shall add unto these things, God shall add unto him the plagues that are written in this book:

Main Meat:
John 4:5-18 Then cometh he to a city of Samaria, which is called Sychar, near to the parcel of ground that Jacob gave to his son Joseph. Now Jacob's well was there. Jesus therefore, being wearied with *his* journey, sat thus on the well: *and* it was about the sixth

hour. There cometh a woman of Samaria to draw water: Jesus saith unto her, Give me to drink. (For his disciples were gone away unto the city to buy meat.) Then saith the woman of Samaria unto him, How is it that thou, being a Jew, askest drink of me, which am a woman of Samaria? for the Jews have no dealings with the Samaritans. Jesus answered and said unto her, If thou knewest the gift of God, and who it is that saith to thee, Give me to drink; thou wouldest have asked of him, and he would have given thee living water. The woman saith unto him, Sir, thou hast nothing to draw with, and the well is deep: from whence then hast thou that living water? Art thou greater than our father Jacob, which gave us the well, and drank thereof himself, and his children, and his cattle? Jesus answered and said unto her, Whosoever drinketh of this water shall thirst again: But whosoever drinketh of the water that I shall give him shall never thirst; but the water that I shall give him shall be in him a well of water springing up into everlasting life. The woman saith unto him, Sir, give me this water, that I thirst not, neither come hither to draw. Jesus saith unto her, Go, call thy husband, and come hither. The woman answered and said, I have no husband. Jesus said unto her, Thou hast well said, I have no husband: For thou hast had five husbands; and he whom thou now hast is not thy husband: in that saidst thou truly.

Isaiah 33:16 He shall dwell on high: his place of defence *shall be* the munitions of rocks: bread shall be given him; his waters *shall be* sure.

Conforming

Isaiah 27:3 I the LORD do keep it; I will water it every moment: lest *any* hurt it, I will keep it night and day.

Isaiah 44:2, 3 Thus saith the LORD that made thee, and formed thee from the womb, *which* will help thee; Fear not, O Jacob, my servant; and thou, Jesurun, whom I have chosen. For I will pour water upon him that is thirsty, and floods upon the dry ground: I will pour my spirit upon thy seed, and my blessing upon thine offspring:

Isaiah 43:19-22 Behold, I will do a new thing; now it shall spring forth; shall ye not know it? I will even make a way in the wilderness, *and* rivers in the desert. The beast of the field shall honour me, the dragons and the owls: because I give waters in the wilderness, *and* rivers in the desert, to give drink to my people, my chosen. This people have I formed for myself; they shall shew forth my praise. But thou hast not called upon me, O Jacob; but thou hast been weary of me, O Israel.

1John 5:8 And there are three that bear witness in earth, the Spirit, and the water, and the blood: and these three agree in one.

Title: Drawing Power, Using the Jesus Kind

Sub Title: Enemies of the Truth

Word Helpers

2Timothy 2:1-26 Thou therefore, my son, be strong in the grace that is in Christ Jesus. And the things that thou hast heard of me among many witnesses, the same commit thou to faithful men, who shall be able to teach others also. Thou therefore endure hardness, as a good soldier of Jesus Christ. No man that warreth entangleth himself with the affairs of *this* life; that he may please him who hath chosen him to be a soldier. And if a man also strive for masteries, *yet* is he not crowned, except he strive lawfully. The husbandman that laboureth must be first partaker of the fruits. Consider what I say; and the Lord give thee understanding in all things. Remember that Jesus Christ of the seed of David was raised from the dead according to my gospel: Wherein I suffer trouble, as an evil doer, *even* unto bonds; but the word of God is not bound. Therefore I endure all things for the elect's sakes, that they may also obtain the salvation which is in Christ Jesus with eternal glory. *It is* a faithful saying: For if we be dead with *him*,

Conforming

we shall also live with *him:* If we suffer, we shall also reign with *him:* if we deny *him,* he also will deny us: If we believe not, *yet* he abideth faithful: he cannot deny himself. Of these things put *them* in remembrance, charging *them* before the Lord that they strive not about words to no profit, *but* to the subverting of the hearers. Study to shew thyself approved unto God, a workman that needeth not to be ashamed, rightly dividing the word of truth. But shun profane *and* vain babblings: for they will increase unto more ungodliness. And their word will eat as doth a canker: of whom is Hymenaeus and Philetus; Who concerning the truth have erred, saying that the resurrection is past already; and overthrow the faith of some. Nevertheless the foundation of God standeth sure, having this seal, The Lord knoweth them that are his. And, Let every one that nameth the name of Christ depart from iniquity. But in a great house there are not only vessels of gold and of silver, but also of wood and of earth; and some to honour, and some to dishonour. If a man therefore purge himself from these, he shall be a vessel unto honour, sanctified, and meet for the master's use, *and* prepared unto every good work. Flee also youthful lusts: but follow righteousness, faith, charity, peace, with them that call on the Lord out of a pure heart. But foolish and unlearned questions avoid, knowing that they do gender strifes. And the servant of the Lord must not strive; but be gentle unto all *men,* apt to teach, patient, In meekness instructing those that oppose themselves; if God peradventure will give them repentance to the acknowledging of the truth;

And *that* they may recover themselves out of the snare of the devil, who are taken captive by him at his will.

Matthew 18:1-9 At the same time came the disciples unto Jesus, saying, Who is the greatest in the kingdom of heaven? And Jesus called a little child unto him, and set him in the midst of them, And said, Verily I say unto you, Except ye be converted, and become as little children, ye shall not enter into the kingdom of heaven. Whosoever therefore shall humble himself as this little child, the same is greatest in the kingdom of heaven. And whoso shall receive one such little child in my name receiveth me. But whoso shall offend one of these little ones which believe in me, it were better for him that a millstone were hanged about his neck, and *that* he were drowned in the depth of the sea. Woe unto the world because of offences! for it must needs be that offences come; but woe to that man by whom the offence cometh! Wherefore if thy hand or thy foot offend thee, cut them off, and cast *them* from thee: it is better for thee to enter into life halt or maimed, rather than having two hands or two feet to be cast into everlasting fire. And if thine eye offend thee, pluck it out, and cast *it* from thee: it is better for thee to enter into life with one eye, rather than having two eyes to be cast into hell fire.

John 17:2-4 As thou hast given him power over all flesh, that he should give eternal life to as many as thou hast given him. And this is life eternal, that they might know thee the only

Conforming

true God, and Jesus Christ, whom thou hast sent. I have glorified thee on the earth: I have finished the work which thou gavest me to do.

Romans 13:1, 2 Let every soul be subject unto the higher powers. For there is no power but of God: the powers that be are ordained of God. Whosoever therefore resisteth the power, resisteth the ordinance of God: and they that resist shall receive to themselves damnation.

Matthew 6:13 And lead us not into temptation, but deliver us from evil: For thine is the kingdom, and the power, and the glory, for ever. Amen.

1Chronicles 29:11-13 Thine, O LORD, *is* the greatness, and the power, and the glory, and the victory, and the majesty: for all *that is* in the heaven and in the earth *is thine;* thine *is* the kingdom, O LORD, and thou art exalted as head above all. Both riches and honour *come* of thee, and thou reignest over all; and in thine hand *is* power and might; and in thine hand *it is* to make great, and to give strength unto all. Now therefore, our God, we thank thee, and praise thy glorious name.

It takes power to do everything you do; spiritual, mental or physical. To get up or lay down, to spit, to lie, cheat or steal. It all takes some effort and that takes power. It takes power to talk, walk, to do good or evil.

To help someone or to harm it all takes Jesus' power. Through Him we live, move and have

Conforming

our being. But some of us like to and some of us still tap into the demonic realm, the devil's worship of doing things. All power is in my hands good or evil. There are still a lot of us who still have a form of Godliness, but denying the power that saved their rotten butts.

2Timothy 3:1-10 This know also, that in the last days perilous times shall come. For men shall be lovers of their own selves, covetous, boasters, proud, blasphemers, disobedient to parents, unthankful, unholy, Without natural affection, trucebreakers, false accusers, incontinent, fierce, despisers of those that are good, Traitors, heady, highminded, lovers of pleasures more than lovers of God; Having a form of godliness, but denying the power thereof: from such turn away. For of this sort are they which creep into houses, and lead captive silly women laden with sins, led away with divers lusts, Ever learning, and never able to come to the knowledge of the truth. Now as Jannes and Jambres withstood Moses, so do these also resist the truth: men of corrupt minds, reprobate concerning the faith. But they shall proceed no further: for their folly shall be manifest unto all *men,* as theirs also was. But thou hast fully known my doctrine, manner of life, purpose, faith, longsuffering, charity, patience,

Conforming

Word Helpers – the Downside

Luke 4:6 And the devil said unto him, All this power will I give thee, and the glory of them: for that is delivered unto me; and to whomsoever I will I give it.

Leviticus 26:19 And I will break the pride of your power; and I will make your heaven as iron, and your earth as brass:

Acts 26:15-18 And I said, Who art thou, Lord? And he said, I am Jesus whom thou persecutest. But rise, and stand upon thy feet: for I have appeared unto thee for this purpose, to make thee a minister and a witness both of these things which thou hast seen, and of those things in the which I will appear unto thee; Delivering thee from the people, and *from* the Gentiles, unto whom now I send thee, To open their eyes, *and* to turn *them* from darkness to light, and *from* the power of Satan unto God, that they may receive forgiveness of sins, and inheritance among them which are sanctified by faith that is in me.

Acts 1:7, 8 And he said unto them, It is not for you to know the times or the seasons, which the Father hath put in his own power. But ye shall receive power, after that the Holy Ghost is come upon you: and ye shall be witnesses unto me both in Jerusalem, and in all Judaea, and in Samaria, and unto the uttermost part of the earth.

Conforming

1Peter 3:17-19 For *it is* better, if the will of God be so, that ye suffer for well doing, than for evil doing. For Christ also hath once suffered for sins, the just for the unjust, that he might bring us to God, being put to death in the flesh, but quickened by the Spirit: By which also he went and preached unto the spirits in prison;

Ephesians 2:5 Even when we were dead in sins, hath quickened us together with Christ, (by grace ye are saved;)

Colossians 2:13 And you, being dead in your sins and the uncircumcision of your flesh, hath he quickened together with him, having forgiven you all trespasses;

A New Heart and a New Spirit I Will Give You

Focus Verse:
Ezekiel 18:31 Cast away from you all your transgressions, whereby ye have transgressed; and make you a new heart and a new spirit: for why will ye die, O house of Israel?

Some follow their own spirit.
Ezekiel 13:3 Thus saith the Lord GOD; Woe unto the foolish prophets, that follow their own spirit, and have seen nothing!

God wants to give us His excellent Spirit.
Daniel 5:12 Forasmuch as an excellent spirit, and knowledge, and understanding, interpreting of dreams, and shewing of hard sentences, and dissolving of doubts, were found in the same Daniel, whom the king

named Belteshazzar: now let Daniel be called, and he will shew the interpretation.

God's Spirit searcheth all things.
1Corinthians 2:10 But God hath revealed *them* unto us by his Spirit: for the Spirit searcheth all things, yea, the deep things of God.

God said beloved believe not every spirit.
1John 4:1 Beloved, believe not every spirit, but try the spirits whether they are of God: because many false prophets are gone out into the world.

Title: Show the Study, Study to Show for it

Sub Title: It Shows if You've Studied Your Mind or Christ's Mind

Heavenly Nuggets

If there is no divine revelation there is no understanding. For out of the abundance of your heart, your mouth will speak. But the Holy Ghost speaks through you, even when you don't know it, to tell the truth. No Holy Ghost no holiness just flesh which leads to corruptness which leads to damnation which leads to hell. Are you going there?

Focus Verses:
Proverbs 3:4-7 So shalt thou find favour and good understanding in the sight of God and man. Trust in the LORD with all thine heart; and lean not unto thine own understanding. In all thy ways acknowledge him, and he shall direct thy paths. Be not wise in thine own eyes: fear the LORD, and depart from evil.

Proverbs 3:11, 12 My son, despise not the chastening of the LORD; neither be weary of his correction: For whom the LORD loveth he

Conforming

correcteth; even as a father the son *in whom* he delighteth.

John 14:16 And I will pray the Father, and he shall give you another Comforter, that he may abide with you for ever;

Something you need to know – God is the planner and He has to be yours.

Planner Means – to be two dimensional in quality and God's Spirit in you working with Him.

Plan Means – the foundation, fix in place, a method for achieve an end. A way of doing something or going.

Title: People With a Plan

Sub Title: God's Plan Will Fit Your Hand

My ways are not your ways says the Lord. As far as the east is from the west, as far as Heaven is from hell, yet each one of you could be there, in a twinkling of an eye.

The Right Planned Way

Proverbs 16:7 When a man's ways please the LORD, he maketh even his enemies to be at peace with him.

1Samuel 12:23 Moreover as for me, God forbid that I should sin against the LORD in ceasing to pray for you: but I will teach you the good and the right way:

Psalms 27:11 Teach me thy way, O LORD, and lead me in a plain path, because of mine enemies.

Psalms 86:11 Teach me thy way, O LORD; I will walk in thy truth: unite my heart to fear thy name.

Conforming

Psalms 119:30 I have chosen the way of truth: thy judgments have I laid *before me.*
Psalms 119:104 Through thy precepts I get understanding: therefore I hate every false way.

Psalms 119:128 Therefore I esteem all *thy* precepts *concerning* all *things to be* right; *and* I hate every false way.

Isaiah 30:21 And thine ears shall hear a word behind thee, saying, This *is* the way, walk ye in it, when ye turn to the right hand, and when ye turn to the left.

Isaiah 35:8 And an highway shall be there, and a way, and it shall be called The way of holiness; the unclean shall not pass over it; but it *shall be* for those: the wayfaring men, though fools, shall not err *therein.*

Direction – Steps – Way

Psalms 37:23 The steps of a *good* man are ordered by the LORD: and he delighteth in his way.

Psalms 37:31, 32 The law of his God *is* in his heart; none of his steps shall slide. The wicked watcheth the righteous, and seeketh to slay him.

Psalms 119:133 Order my steps in thy word: and let not any iniquity have dominion over me.

Conforming

Proverbs 16:9 A man's heart deviseth his way: but the LORD directeth his steps.

Jeremiah 10:23-25 O LORD, I know that the way of man *is* not in himself: *it is* not in man that walketh to direct his steps. O LORD, correct me, but with judgment; not in thine anger, lest thou bring me to nothing. Pour out thy fury upon the heathen that know thee not, and upon the families that call not on thy name: for they have eaten up Jacob, and devoured him, and consumed him, and have made his habitation desolate.

Title: Everybody Knows That There is a God but Few Know the One and Only True, Living God – Jesus Christ

Sub Title: Let's Find Out What We Need to Know

Focus Verses:
John 4:24 God *is* a Spirit: and they that worship him must worship *him* in spirit and in truth.

John 3:1-11 There was a man of the Pharisees, named Nicodemus, a ruler of the Jews: The same came to Jesus by night, and said unto him, Rabbi, we know that thou art a teacher come from God: for no man can do these miracles that thou doest, except God be with him. Jesus answered and said unto him, Verily, verily, I say unto thee, Except a man be born again, he cannot see the kingdom of God. Nicodemus saith unto him, How can a man be born when he is old? can he enter the second time into his mother's womb, and be born? Jesus answered, Verily, verily, I say unto thee, Except a man be born of water and *of* the

Conforming

Spirit, he cannot enter into the kingdom of God. That which is born of the flesh is flesh; and that which is born of the Spirit is spirit. Marvel not that I said unto thee, Ye must be born again. The wind bloweth where it listeth, and thou hearest the sound thereof, but canst not tell whence it cometh, and whither it goeth: so is every one that is born of the Spirit. Nicodemus answered and said unto him, How can these things be? Jesus answered and said unto him, Art thou a master of Israel, and knowest not these things? Verily, verily, I say unto thee, We speak that we do know, and testify that we have seen; and ye receive not our witness.

2Corinthians 10:12-18 For we dare not make ourselves of the number, or compare ourselves with some that commend themselves: but they measuring themselves by themselves, and comparing themselves among themselves, are not wise. But we will not boast of things without *our* measure, but according to the measure of the rule which God hath distributed to us, a measure to reach even unto you. For we stretch not ourselves beyond *our measure,* as though we reached not unto you: for we are come as far as to you also in *preaching* the gospel of Christ: Not boasting of things without *our* measure, *that is,* of other men's labours; but having hope, when your faith is increased, that we shall be enlarged by you according to our rule abundantly, To preach the gospel in the *regions* beyond you, *and* not to boast in another man's line of things made ready to our hand. But he that glorieth, let him glory in the

Conforming

Lord. For not he that commendeth himself is approved, but whom the Lord commendeth.

Foundation Verses

Ezekiel 1:26 And above the firmament that *was* over their heads *was* the likeness of a throne, as the appearance of a sapphire stone: and upon the likeness of the throne *was* the likeness as the appearance of a man above upon it.

Colossians 1:13-19 Who hath delivered us from the power of darkness, and hath translated *us* into the kingdom of his dear Son: In whom we have redemption through his blood, *even* the forgiveness of sins: Who is the image of the invisible God, the firstborn of every creature: For by him were all things created, that are in heaven, and that are in earth, visible and invisible, whether *they be* thrones, or dominions, or principalities, or powers: all things were created by him, and for him: And he is before all things, and by him all things consist. And he is the head of the body, the church: who is the beginning, the firstborn from the dead; that in all *things* he might have the preeminence. For it pleased *the Father* that in him should all fulness dwell;

Revelations 3:13, 14 He that hath an ear, let him hear what the Spirit saith unto the churches. And unto the angel of the church of the Laodiceans write; These things saith the Amen, the faithful and true witness, the beginning of the creation of God;

Conforming

Main Meat:
John 1:1-14 In the beginning was the Word, and the Word was with God, and the Word was God. The same was in the beginning with God. All things were made by him; and without him was not any thing made that was made. In him was life; and the life was the light of men. And the light shineth in darkness; and the darkness comprehended it not. There was a man sent from God, whose name *was* John. The same came for a witness, to bear witness of the Light, that all *men* through him might believe. He was not that Light, but *was sent* to bear witness of that Light. *That* was the true Light, which lighteth every man that cometh into the world. He was in the world, and the world was made by him, and the world knew him not. He came unto his own, and his own received him not. But as many as received him, to them gave he power to become the sons of God, *even* to them that believe on his name: Which were born, not of blood, nor of the will of the flesh, nor of the will of man, but of God. And the Word was made flesh, and dwelt among us, (and we beheld his glory, the glory as of the only begotten of the Father,) full of grace and truth.

Romans 12:1-5 I beseech you therefore, brethren, by the mercies of God, that ye present your bodies a living sacrifice, holy, acceptable unto God, *which is* your reasonable service. And be not conformed to this world: but be ye transformed by the renewing of your mind, that ye may prove what *is* that good, and acceptable, and perfect, will of God. For I say, through the grace given unto me, to every man

Conforming

that is among you, not to think *of himself* more highly than he ought to think; but to think soberly, according as God hath dealt to every man the measure of faith. For as we have many members in one body, and all members have not the same office: So we, *being* many, are one body in Christ, and every one members one of another.

Ephesians 4:1-10 I therefore, the prisoner of the Lord, beseech you that ye walk worthy of the vocation wherewith ye are called, With all lowliness and meekness, with longsuffering, forbearing one another in love; Endeavouring to keep the unity of the Spirit in the bond of peace. *There is* one body, and one Spirit, even as ye are called in one hope of your calling; One Lord, one faith, one baptism, One God and Father of all, who *is* above all, and through all, and in you all. But unto every one of us is given grace according to the measure of the gift of Christ. Wherefore he saith, When he ascended up on high, he led captivity captive, and gave gifts unto men. (Now that he ascended, what is it but that he also descended first into the lower parts of the earth? He that descended is the same also that ascended up far above all heavens, that he might fill all things.)

1John 4:1 Beloved, believe not every spirit, but try the spirits whether they are of God: because many false prophets are gone out into the world.

Know no man by the flesh, but by the Spirit.

True Reflections Come from Within

Sub Title: Rules of Engagement

Jude 1:6 And the angels which kept not their first estate, but left their own habitation, he hath reserved in everlasting chains under darkness unto the judgment of the great day.

Jude 1:14-19 And Enoch also, the seventh from Adam, prophesied of these, saying, Behold, the Lord cometh with ten thousands of his saints, To execute judgment upon all, and to convince all that are ungodly among them of all their ungodly deeds which they have ungodly committed, and of all their hard *speeches* which ungodly sinners have spoken against him. These are murmurers, complainers, walking after their own lusts; and their mouth speaketh great swelling *words,* having men's persons in admiration because of advantage. But, beloved, remember ye the words which were spoken before of the apostles of our Lord Jesus Christ; How that they told you there should be mockers in the last time, who should walk after their own ungodly lusts. These be they who separate themselves, sensual, having not the Spirit.

Conforming

2Timothy 3:1-7 This know also, that in the last days perilous times shall come. For men shall be lovers of their own selves, covetous, boasters, proud, blasphemers, disobedient to parents, unthankful, unholy, Without natural affection, trucebreakers, false accusers, incontinent, fierce, despisers of those that are good, Traitors, heady, highminded, lovers of pleasures more than lovers of God; Having a form of godliness, but denying the power thereof: from such turn away. For of this sort are they which creep into houses, and lead captive silly women laden with sins, led away with divers lusts, Ever learning, and never able to come to the knowledge of the truth.

Rules of Engagement

1. Joshua 24:15 And if it seem evil unto you to serve the LORD, choose you this day whom ye will serve; whether the gods which your fathers served that *were* on the other side of the flood, or the gods of the Amorites, in whose land ye dwell: but as for me and my house, we will serve the LORD.

2. Be ye Holy for I am Holy
   Leviticus 20:7 Sanctify yourselves therefore, and be ye holy: for I *am* the LORD your God.

3. Matthew 7:13, 14 Enter ye in at the strait gate: for wide *is* the gate, and broad *is* the way, that leadeth to destruction, and many there be which go in thereat: Because strait *is* the gate, and narrow *is* the way, which

leadeth unto life, and few there be that find it.

4. 1Thessalonions 4:11 And that ye study to be quiet, and to do your own business, and to work with your own hands, as we commanded you;

2Timothy 2:15, 16 Study to shew thyself approved unto God, a workman that needeth not to be ashamed, rightly dividing the word of truth. But shun profane *and* vain babblings: for they will increase unto more ungodliness.

5. Matthew 6:21 For where your treasure is, there will your heart be also.

Matthew 6:31-34 Therefore take no thought, saying, What shall we eat? or, What shall we drink? or, Wherewithal shall we be clothed? (For after all these things do the Gentiles seek:) for your heavenly Father knoweth that ye have need of all these things. But seek ye first the kingdom of God, and his righteousness; and all these things shall be added unto you. Take therefore no thought for the morrow: for the morrow shall take thought for the things of itself. Sufficient unto the day *is* the evil thereof.

Everybody is searching for someone or something to believe in real or false. Jesus said believe me for the work sake because there is no other help but me.

Conforming

Psalms 121:1-8 A Song of degrees. I will lift up mine eyes unto the hills, from whence cometh my help. My help *cometh* from the LORD, which made heaven and earth. He will not suffer thy foot to be moved: he that keepeth thee will not slumber. Behold, he that keepeth Israel shall neither slumber nor sleep. The LORD *is* thy keeper: the LORD *is* thy shade upon thy right hand. The sun shall not smite thee by day, nor the moon by night. The LORD shall preserve thee from all evil: he shall preserve thy soul. The LORD shall preserve thy going out and thy coming in from this time forth, and even for evermore.

Psalms 120:1-3 A Song of degrees. In my distress I cried unto the LORD, and he heard me. Deliver my soul, O LORD, from lying lips, *and* from a deceitful tongue. What shall be given unto thee? or what shall be done unto thee, thou false tongue?

Psalms 124:1-6 A Song of degrees of David. If *it had not been* the LORD who was on our side, now may Israel say; If *it had not been* the LORD who was on our side, when men rose up against us: Then they had swallowed us up quick, when their wrath was kindled against us: Then the waters had overwhelmed us, the stream had gone over our soul: Then the proud waters had gone over our soul. Blessed *be* the LORD, who hath not given us *as* a prey to their teeth.

Title Multiplied 1 ½ X 2 ½ = 4

Sub Title: Everything Multiplied the Good, the Evil and the Ugly

Focus Verses:
John 6:5-15 When Jesus then lifted up *his* eyes, and saw a great company come unto him, he saith unto Philip, Whence shall we buy bread, that these may eat? And this he said to prove him: for he himself knew what he would do. Philip answered him, Two hundred pennyworth of bread is not sufficient for them, that every one of them may take a little. One of his disciples, Andrew, Simon Peter's brother, saith unto him, There is a lad here, which hath five barley loaves, and two small fishes: but what are they among so many? And Jesus said, Make the men sit down. Now there was much grass in the place. So the men sat down, in number about five thousand. And Jesus took the loaves; and when he had given thanks, he distributed to the disciples, and the disciples to them that were set down; and likewise of the fishes as much as they would. When they were filled, he said unto his disciples, Gather up the fragments that remain, that nothing be lost. Therefore they gathered *them* together, and filled twelve baskets with the fragments of the five barley loaves, which remained over and

Conforming

above unto them that had eaten. Then those men, when they had seen the miracle that Jesus did, said, This is of a truth that prophet that should come into the world. When Jesus therefore perceived that they would come and take him by force, to make him a king, he departed again into a mountain himself alone.

Genesis 2:10-14 And a river went out of Eden to water the garden; and from thence it was parted, and became into four heads. The name of the first *is* Pison: that *is* it which compasseth the whole land of Havilah, where *there is* gold; And the gold of that land *is* good: there *is* bdellium and the onyx stone. And the name of the second river *is* Gihon: the same *is* it that compasseth the whole land of Ethiopia. And the name of the third river *is* Hiddekel: that *is* it which goeth toward the east of Assyria. And the fourth river *is* Euphrates.

Multiplied 5000 Times Plus

Genesis 2:15-17 And the LORD God took the man, and put him into the garden of Eden to dress it and to keep it. And the LORD God commanded the man, saying, Of every tree of the garden thou mayest freely eat: But of the tree of the knowledge of good and evil, thou shalt not eat of it: for in the day that thou eatest thereof thou shalt surely die.

Action = Reaction – Reaction = Action

Conforming

Genesis 2:18-25 And the LORD God said, *It is* not good that the man should be alone; I will make him an help meet for him. And out of the ground the LORD God formed every beast of the field, and every fowl of the air; and brought *them* unto Adam to see what he would call them: and whatsoever Adam called every living creature, that *was* the name thereof. And Adam gave names to all cattle, and to the fowl of the air, and to every beast of the field; but for Adam there was not found an help meet for him. And the LORD God caused a deep sleep to fall upon Adam, and he slept: and he took one of his ribs, and closed up the flesh instead thereof; And the rib, which the LORD God had taken from man, made he a woman, and brought her unto the man. And Adam said, This *is* now bone of my bones, and flesh of my flesh: she shall be called Woman, because she was taken out of Man. Therefore shall a man leave his father and his mother, and shall cleave unto his wife: and they shall be one flesh. And they were both naked, the man and his wife, and were not ashamed.

Something to think about – after the cross, our lives multiplied.

Matthew 27:11-23 And Jesus stood before the governor: and the governor asked him, saying, Art thou the King of the Jews? And Jesus said unto him, Thou sayest. And when he was accused of the chief priests and elders, he answered nothing. Then said Pilate unto him, Hearest thou not how many things they witness against thee? And he answered him to never a

Conforming

word; insomuch that the governor marvelled greatly. Now at *that* feast the governor was wont to release unto the people a prisoner, whom they would. And they had then a notable prisoner, called Barabbas. Therefore when they were gathered together, Pilate said unto them, Whom will ye that I release unto you? Barabbas, or Jesus which is called Christ? For he knew that for envy they had delivered him. When he was set down on the judgment seat, his wife sent unto him, saying, Have thou nothing to do with that just man: for I have suffered many things this day in a dream because of him. But the chief priests and elders persuaded the multitude that they should ask Barabbas, and destroy Jesus. The governor answered and said unto them, Whether of the twain will ye that I release unto you? They said, Barabbas. Pilate saith unto them, What shall I do then with Jesus which is called Christ? *They* all say unto him, Let him be crucified. And the governor said, Why, what evil hath he done? But they cried out the more, saying, Let him be crucified.

Multiplied Means – To be four times closer, four months closer, four miles closer, four steps closer, four minutes closer, four seconds closer, four inches closer, four times as much.

4 Rivers

Pison – Broad flowing free flowing where the Spirit of the Lord is there is liberty.

Conforming

Gihon – A stream bursting forth – out of your belly shall flow rivers of living water.

Hiddekel – Rapid moving fast behold I come quickly and I have my rewards with me.

Euphrates – That which makes fruit – The Lord said to be fruit full and multiply, He also said you shall know them by their fruit.

Title: Clothed With the Glory of the Lord

Isaiah 40:5 And the glory of the LORD shall be revealed, and all flesh shall see *it* together: for the mouth of the LORD hath spoken *it*.

Isaiah 41:15 Behold, I will make thee a new sharp threshing instrument having teeth: thou shalt thresh the mountains, and beat *them* small, and shalt make the hills as chaff.

Isaiah 43:3-5 For I *am* the LORD thy God, the Holy One of Israel, thy Saviour: I gave Egypt *for* thy ransom, Ethiopia and Seba for thee. Since thou wast precious in my sight, thou hast been honourable, and I have loved thee: therefore will I give men for thee, and people for thy life. Fear not: for I *am* with thee: I will bring thy seed from the east, and gather thee from the west;

Revelations 10:1-11 And I saw another mighty angel come down from heaven, clothed with a cloud: and a rainbow *was* upon his head, and his face *was* as it were the sun, and his feet as pillars of fire: And he had in his hand a little book open: and he set his right foot upon the sea, and *his* left *foot* on the earth, And cried with a loud voice, as *when* a lion roareth: and when he had cried, seven thunders uttered their voices. And when the seven thunders had uttered their voices, I was about to write: and I

Conforming

heard a voice from heaven saying unto me, Seal up those things which the seven thunders uttered, and write them not. And the angel which I saw stand upon the sea and upon the earth lifted up his hand to heaven, And sware by him that liveth for ever and ever, who created heaven, and the things that therein are, and the earth, and the things that therein are, and the sea, and the things which are therein, that there should be time no longer: But in the days of the voice of the seventh angel, when he shall begin to sound, the mystery of God should be finished, as he hath declared to his servants the prophets. And the voice which I heard from heaven spake unto me again, and said, Go *and* take the little book which is open in the hand of the angel which standeth upon the sea and upon the earth. And I went unto the angel, and said unto him, Give me the little book. And he said unto me, Take *it,* and eat it up; and it shall make thy belly bitter, but it shall be in thy mouth sweet as honey. And I took the little book out of the angel's hand, and ate it up; and it was in my mouth sweet as honey: and as soon as I had eaten it, my belly was bitter. And he said unto me, Thou must prophesy again before many peoples, and nations, and tongues, and kings.

Things to Know
Foot – Be ye steadfast unmovable.
Instructions – Little Book
God's voice of thunder spoke through the angel, the seven thunders or spirits. Don'ts write it, just eat it and then say it when I tell you to.

Conforming

Psalms 29:1-9 A Psalm of David. Give unto the LORD, O ye mighty, give unto the LORD glory and strength. Give unto the LORD the glory due unto his name; worship the LORD in the beauty of holiness. The voice of the LORD *is* upon the waters: the God of glory thundereth: the LORD *is* upon many waters. The voice of the LORD *is* powerful; the voice of the LORD *is* full of majesty. The voice of the LORD breaketh the cedars; yea, the LORD breaketh the cedars of Lebanon. He maketh them also to skip like a calf; Lebanon and Sirion like a young unicorn. The voice of the LORD divideth the flames of fire. The voice of the LORD shaketh the wilderness; the LORD shaketh the wilderness of Kadesh. The voice of the LORD maketh the hinds to calve, and discovereth the forests: and in his temple doth every one speak of *his* glory.

It's time for a time out for your games with the Lord. Show up or you will be shut up. The whole world steps when the Lord speaks.

The 7 Thunders or Spirits

1. Behold I come quickly
2. He who hath an ear let him hear what the Spirit of the Lord says unto the Churches
3. I have a two edged sword in my hand get it right or die
4. No ONE can serve two Masters
5. My mercy endures forever; your grace period is up
6. Now is the time to repent and turn to me completely

Conforming

7. Behold I stand at your door, I won't move but you will

Conforming

Title: Freedom Isn't Right to do as We Please it's the Responsibility to do What We Ought to do

Focus Verses:
Romans 6:18-22 Being then made free from sin, ye became the servants of righteousness. I speak after the manner of men because of the infirmity of your flesh: for as ye have yielded your members servants to uncleanness and to iniquity unto iniquity; even so now yield your members servants to righteousness unto holiness. For when ye were the servants of sin, ye were free from righteousness. What fruit had ye then in those things whereof ye are now ashamed? for the end of those things *is* death. But now being made free from sin, and become servants to God, ye have your fruit unto holiness, and the end everlasting life.

Romans 8:2 For the law of the Spirit of life in Christ Jesus hath made me free from the law of sin and death.

Freedom for What:
John 14:6 Jesus saith unto him, I am the way, the truth, and the life: no man cometh unto the Father, but by me.

Conforming

John 8:32 And ye shall know the truth, and the truth shall make you free.

Freedom from What:
Psalms 51:6 Behold, thou desirest truth in the inward parts: and in the hidden *part* thou shalt make me to know wisdom.

Galatians 5:1 Stand fast therefore in the liberty wherewith Christ hath made us free, and be not entangled again with the yoke of bondage.

Freedom to What:
2Corinthians 3:17 Now the Lord is that Spirit: and where the Spirit of the Lord *is,* there *is* liberty.

James 1:25 But whoso looketh into the perfect law of liberty, and continueth *therein,* he being not a forgetful hearer, but a doer of the work, this man shall be blessed in his deed.

Freedom to do What:
James 2:12 So speak ye, and so do, as they that shall be judged by the law of liberty.

1Peter 2:16 As free, and not using *your* liberty for a cloke of maliciousness, but as the servants of God.

Freedom – What's Freedom All About

Freedom – The Right Kind of Freedom:
1Peter 1:12 Unto whom it was revealed, that not unto themselves, but unto us they did minister the things, which are now reported unto you by

Conforming

them that have preached the gospel unto you with the Holy Ghost sent down from heaven; which things the angels desire to look into.

3 Main Points

1. The only true freedom in life comes from Jesus
John 8:36 If the Son therefore shall make you free, ye shall be free indeed.

2. Freedom means making choices
Joshua 24:15 And if it seem evil unto you to serve the LORD, choose you this day whom ye will serve; whether the gods which your fathers served that *were* on the other side of the flood, or the gods of the Amorites, in whose land ye dwell: but as for me and my house, we will serve the LORD.

John 15:5, 6 I am the vine, ye *are* the branches: He that abideth in me, and I in him, the same bringeth forth much fruit: for without me ye can do nothing. If a man abide not in me, he is cast forth as a branch, and is withered; and men gather them, and cast *them* into the fire, and they are burned.

3. Yours or God's
Proverbs 3:1-10 My son, forget not my law; but let thine heart keep my commandments: For length of days, and long life, and peace, shall they add to thee. Let not mercy and truth forsake thee: bind them about thy neck; write them upon the table of thine heart: So shalt thou find favour and good understanding in the

sight of God and man. Trust in the LORD with all thine heart; and lean not unto thine own understanding. In all thy ways acknowledge him, and he shall direct thy paths. Be not wise in thine own eyes: fear the LORD, and depart from evil. It shall be health to thy navel, and marrow to thy bones. Honour the LORD with thy substance, and with the firstfruits of all thine increase: So shall thy barns be filled with plenty, and thy presses shall burst out with new wine.

Conforming

Title: The Demonic Side – Affect of an Unholy Spirit

Focus Verses:
Jude 1:3-8 Beloved, when I gave all diligence to write unto you of the common salvation, it was needful for me to write unto you, and exhort *you* that ye should earnestly contend for the faith which was once delivered unto the saints. For there are certain men crept in unawares, who were before of old ordained to this condemnation, ungodly men, turning the grace of our God into lasciviousness, and denying the only Lord God, and our Lord Jesus Christ. I will therefore put you in remembrance, though ye once knew this, how that the Lord, having saved the people out of the land of Egypt, afterward destroyed them that believed not. And the angels which kept not their first estate, but left their own habitation, he hath reserved in everlasting chains under darkness unto the judgment of the great day. Even as Sodom and Gomorrha, and the cities about them in like manner, giving themselves over to fornication, and going after strange flesh, are set forth for an example, suffering the vengeance of eternal fire. Likewise also these *filthy* dreamers defile the flesh, despise dominion, and speak evil of dignities.

Conforming

6 Golden Nuggets

1. Warning Danger Ahead
2. Are You Ready
3. What's Talking to You
4. Don't Let Circumstances Hold You Down
5. The Darkness in My Mind, That's Still There
6. The Hole in My Eardrum is Gone – I Stop Listening to God

Mind:
Psalms 31:12 I am forgotten as a dead man out of mind: I am like a broken vessel.

Isaiah 26:3 Thou wilt keep *him* in perfect peace, *whose* mind *is* stayed *on thee:* because he trusteth in thee.

Philippians 2:5 Let this mind be in you, which was also in Christ Jesus:

Philipians 1:27 Only let your conversation be as it becometh the gospel of Christ: that whether I come and see you, or else be absent, I may hear of your affairs, that ye stand fast in one spirit, with one mind striving together for the faith of the gospel;

2Corinthians 13:11 Finally, brethren, farewell. Be perfect, be of good comfort, be of one mind, live in peace; and the God of love and peace shall be with you.

2Timothy 1:7 For God hath not given us the spirit of fear; but of power, and of love, and of a sound mind.

Conforming

Unholy Spirit:
1John 2:3-11 And hereby we do know that we know him, if we keep his commandments. He that saith, I know him, and keepeth not his commandments, is a liar, and the truth is not in him. But whoso keepeth his word, in him verily is the love of God perfected: hereby know we that we are in him. He that saith he abideth in him ought himself also so to walk, even as he walked. Brethren, I write no new commandment unto you, but an old commandment which ye had from the beginning. The old commandment is the word which ye have heard from the beginning. Again, a new commandment I write unto you, which thing is true in him and in you: because the darkness is past, and the true light now shineth. He that saith he is in the light, and hateth his brother, is in darkness even until now. He that loveth his brother abideth in the light, and there is none occasion of stumbling in him. But he that hateth his brother is in darkness, and walketh in darkness, and knoweth not whither he goeth, because that darkness hath blinded his eyes.

1John 2:15-21 Love not the world, neither the things *that are* in the world. If any man love the world, the love of the Father is not in him. For all that *is* in the world, the lust of the flesh, and the lust of the eyes, and the pride of life, is not of the Father, but is of the world. And the world passeth away, and the lust thereof: but he that doeth the will of God abideth for ever. Little children, it is the last time: and as ye have heard that antichrist shall come, even now are there many antichrists; whereby we know that it is the last time. They went out from us, but they were not of us; for if they had been of us, they would *no doubt* have continued with us: but *they went out,* that they might be made manifest that they were not all of us. But ye have an unction from the Holy One, and ye know all things. I have not written unto you because ye know not the truth, but because ye know it, and that no lie is of the truth.

1John 4:1-10 Beloved, believe not every spirit, but try the spirits whether they are of God: because many false prophets are gone out into the world. Hereby know ye the Spirit of God: Every spirit that confesseth that Jesus Christ is come in the flesh is of God: And every spirit that confesseth not that Jesus Christ is come in the flesh is not of God: and this is that *spirit* of antichrist, whereof ye have heard that it should come; and even now already is it in the world. Ye are of God, little children, and have overcome them: because greater is he that is in you, than he that is in the world. They are of the world: therefore speak they of the world, and the world heareth them. We are of God: he that knoweth God heareth us; he that is not of God heareth not us. Hereby know we the spirit of truth, and the spirit of error. Beloved, let us love one another: for love is of God; and every one that loveth is born of God, and knoweth God. He that loveth not knoweth not God; for God is love. In this was manifested the love of God toward us, because that God sent his only begotten Son into the world, that we might live through him. Herein is love, not that we loved

Conforming

God, but that he loved us, and sent his Son *to be* the propitiation for our sins.

2John 1:7-12 For many deceivers are entered into the world, who confess not that Jesus Christ is come in the flesh. This is a deceiver and an antichrist. Look to yourselves, that we lose not those things which we have wrought, but that we receive a full reward. Whosoever transgresseth, and abideth not in the doctrine of Christ, hath not God. He that abideth in the doctrine of Christ, he hath both the Father and the Son. If there come any unto you, and bring not this doctrine, receive him not into *your* house, neither bid him God speed: For he that biddeth him God speed is partaker of his evil deeds. Having many things to write unto you, I would not *write* with paper and ink: but I trust to come unto you, and speak face to face, that our joy may be full.

Title: You Can Always Add to a Finished Product

Focus Verses:
Jeremiah 1:4-9 Then the word of the LORD came unto me, saying, Before I formed thee in the belly I knew thee; and before thou camest forth out of the womb I sanctified thee, *and* I ordained thee a prophet unto the nations. Then said I, Ah, Lord GOD! behold, I cannot speak: for I *am* a child. But the LORD said unto me, Say not, I *am* a child: for thou shalt go to all that I shall send thee, and whatsoever I command thee thou shalt speak. Be not afraid of their faces: for I *am* with thee to deliver thee, saith the LORD. Then the LORD put forth his hand, and touched my mouth. And the LORD said unto me, Behold, I have put my words in thy mouth.

1Corinthians 1:27 But God hath chosen the foolish things of the world to confound the wise; and God hath chosen the weak things of the world to confound the things which are mighty;

Conforming

2Thessalonians 2:13 But we are bound to give thanks alway to God for you, brethren beloved of the Lord, because God hath from the beginning chosen you to salvation through sanctification of the Spirit and belief of the truth:

Heavenly Nugget

I can perfect myself more in this finished one that was finished before the foundation of the World was. For we were chosen beyond ourselves.

Finished:
Psalms 40:1-4 To the chief Musician, A Psalm of David. I waited patiently for the LORD; and he inclined unto me, and heard my cry. He brought me up also out of an horrible pit, out of the miry clay, and set my feet upon a rock, *and* established my goings. And he hath put a new song in my mouth, *even* praise unto our God: many shall see *it,* and fear, and shall trust in the LORD. Blessed *is* that man that maketh the LORD his trust, and respecteth not the proud, nor such as turn aside to lies.

Acts 20:24 But none of these things move me, neither count I my life dear unto myself, so that I might finish my course with joy, and the ministry, which I have received of the Lord Jesus, to testify the gospel of the grace of God.

John 5:36 But I have greater witness than *that* of John: for the works which the Father hath given me to finish, the same works that I do, bear witness of me, that the Father hath sent me.

John 17:3-5 And this is life eternal, that they might know thee the only true God, and Jesus Christ, whom thou hast sent. I have glorified thee on the earth: I have finished the work which thou gavest me to do. And now, O Father, glorify thou me with thine own self with the glory which I had with thee before the world was.

The Other Side:
James 1:15 Then when lust hath conceived, it bringeth forth sin: and sin, when it is finished, bringeth forth death.

Chosen:
Isaiah 43:10 Ye *are* my witnesses, saith the LORD, and my servant whom I have chosen: that ye may know and believe me, and understand that I *am* he: before me there was no God formed, neither shall there be after me.

Isaiah 41:8 But thou, Israel, *art* my servant, Jacob whom I have chosen, the seed of Abraham my friend.

Conforming

Psalms 119:30 I have chosen the way of truth: thy judgments have I laid *before me*.

Luke 10:42 But one thing is needful: and Mary hath chosen that good part, which shall not be taken away from her.

John 15:16-19 Ye have not chosen me, but I have chosen you, and ordained you, that ye should go and bring forth fruit, and *that* your fruit should remain: that whatsoever ye shall ask of the Father in my name, he may give it you. These things I command you, that ye love one another. If the world hate you, ye know that it hated me before *it hated* you. If ye were of the world, the world would love his own: but because ye are not of the world, but I have chosen you out of the world, therefore the world hateth you.

John 13:18 I speak not of you all: I know whom I have chosen: but that the scripture may be fulfilled, He that eateth bread with me hath lifted up his heel against me.

Matthew 12:18 Behold my servant, whom I have chosen; my beloved, in whom my soul is well pleased: I will put my spirit upon him, and he shall shew judgment to the Gentiles.

Chose – Their Way:
Isaiah 63:2-4 Wherefore *art thou* red in thine apparel, and thy garments like him that treadeth in the winefat? I have trodden the winepress alone; and of the people *there was* none with me: for I will tread them in mine

anger, and trample them in my fury; and their blood shall be sprinkled upon my garments, and I will stain all my raiment. For the day of vengeance *is* in mine heart, and the year of my redeemed is come.

Focus Verses:
Revelations 21:5 And he that sat upon the throne said, Behold, I make all things new. And he said unto me, Write: for these words are true and faithful.

Revelations 3:12 Him that overcometh will I make a pillar in the temple of my God, and he shall go no more out: and I will write upon him the name of my God, and the name of the city of my God, *which is* new Jerusalem, which cometh down out of heaven from my God: and *I will write upon him* my new name.

Conforming

Title: Working On Something New, Why Don't You Stay out of God's Way

New:
Ecclesiastes 1:9, 10 The thing that hath been, it *is that* which shall be; and that which is done *is* that which shall be done: and *there is* no new *thing* under the sun. Is there *any* thing whereof it may be said, See, this *is* new? it hath been already of old time, which was before us.

2Corinthians 5:16-21 Wherefore henceforth know we no man after the flesh: yea, though we have known Christ after the flesh, yet now henceforth know we *him* no more. Therefore if any man *be* in Christ, *he is* a new creature: old things are passed away; behold, all things are become new. And all things *are* of God, who hath reconciled us to himself by Jesus Christ, and hath given to us the ministry of reconciliation; To wit, that God was in Christ, reconciling the world unto himself, not imputing their trespasses unto them; and hath committed unto us the word of reconciliation. Now then we are ambassadors for Christ, as though God did beseech *you* by us: we pray *you* in Christ's stead, be ye reconciled to God. For he hath made him *to be* sin for us, who knew no sin; that we might be made the righteousness of God in him.

Ephesians 4:21-24 If so be that ye have heard him, and have been taught by him, as the truth is in Jesus: That ye put off concerning the former conversation the old man, which is corrupt according to the deceitful lusts; And be renewed in the spirit of your mind; And that ye put on the new man, which after God is created in righteousness and true holiness.

Colossians 3:5-10 Mortify therefore your members which are upon the earth; fornication, uncleanness, inordinate affection, evil concupiscence, and covetousness, which is idolatry: For which things' sake the wrath of God cometh on the children of disobedience: In the which ye also walked some time, when ye lived in them. But now ye also put off all these; anger, wrath, malice, blasphemy, filthy communication out of your mouth. Lie not one to another, seeing that ye have put off the old man with his deeds; And have put on the new *man,* which is renewed in knowledge after the image of him that created him:

Isaiah 42:8, 9 I *am* the LORD: that *is* my name: and my glory will I not give to another, neither my praise to graven images. Behold, the former things are come to pass, and new things do I declare: before they spring forth I tell you of them.

Conforming

Isaiah 43:18-21 Remember ye not the former things, neither consider the things of old. Behold, I will do a new thing; now it shall spring forth; shall ye not know it? I will even make a way in the wilderness, *and* rivers in the desert. The beast of the field shall honour me, the dragons and the owls: because I give waters in the wilderness, *and* rivers in the desert, to give drink to my people, my chosen. This people have I formed for myself; they shall shew forth my praise.

Isaiah 48:6, 7 Thou hast heard, see all this; and will not ye declare *it?* I have shewed thee new things from this time, even hidden things, and thou didst not know them. They are created now, and not from the beginning; even before the day when thou heardest them not; lest thou shouldest say, Behold, I knew them.

Lamentations 3:21-24 This I recall to my mind, therefore have I hope. *It is of* the LORD'S mercies that we are not consumed, because his compassions fail not. *They are* new every morning: great *is* thy faithfulness. The LORD *is* my portion, saith my soul; therefore will I hope in him.

Title: If the Devil Can Steal Your Joy, He Can Steal Your Victory

Sub Title: If You Keep Your Peace, You Will Keep Your Power

Focus Verses:
3John 1:4, 5 I have no greater joy than to hear that my children walk in truth. Beloved, thou doest faithfully whatsoever thou doest to the brethren, and to strangers;

Things to Know

1. The joy of the Lord is your strength
2. Laughter is like a medicine
3. God's joy is for everyone
4. Let it flow
5. Can laughter be from God? YES and more
6. Where do I start, in all thy ways acknowledge Jesus and He will direct your every step
7. Is it possible for me to really be happy and content, yes but only through Jesus, in relationship

Conforming

Joy:
Jeremiah 15:16 Thy words were found, and I did eat them; and thy word was unto me the joy and rejoicing of mine heart: for I am called by thy name, O LORD God of hosts.

John 15:11 These things have I spoken unto you, that my joy might remain in you, and *that* your joy might be full.

Nehemiah 8:10 Then he said unto them, Go your way, eat the fat, and drink the sweet, and send portions unto them for whom nothing is prepared: for *this* day *is* holy unto our Lord: neither be ye sorry; for the joy of the LORD is your strength.

Psalms 16:11 Thou wilt shew me the path of life: in thy presence *is* fulness of joy; at thy right hand *there are* pleasures for evermore.

Psalms 30:5, 6 For his anger *endureth but* a moment; in his favour *is* life: weeping may endure for a night, but joy *cometh* in the morning. And in my prosperity I said, I shall never be moved.

Psalms 43:4 Then will I go unto the altar of God, unto God my exceeding joy: yea, upon the harp will I praise thee, O God my God.

Isaiah 61:7 For your shame *ye shall have* double; and *for* confusion they shall rejoice in their portion: therefore in their land they shall possess the double: everlasting joy shall be unto them.

Conforming

Matthew 25:21-23 His lord said unto him, Well done, *thou* good and faithful servant: thou hast been faithful over a few things, I will make thee ruler over many things: enter thou into the joy of thy lord. He also that had received two talents came and said, Lord, thou deliveredst unto me two talents: behold, I have gained two other talents beside them. His lord said unto him, Well done, good and faithful servant; thou hast been faithful over a few things, I will make thee ruler over many things: enter thou into the joy of thy lord.

James 1:2-4 My brethren, count it all joy when ye fall into divers temptations; Knowing *this,* that the trying of your faith worketh patience. But let patience have *her* perfect work, that ye may be perfect and entire, wanting nothing.

1John 1:6-9 If we say that we have fellowship with him, and walk in darkness, we lie, and do not the truth: But if we walk in the light, as he is in the light, we have fellowship one with another, and the blood of Jesus Christ his Son cleanseth us from all sin. If we say that we have no sin, we deceive ourselves, and the truth is not in us. If we confess our sins, he is faithful and just to forgive us *our* sins, and to cleanse us from all unrighteousness.

Laughter:
Ecclesiastes 2:1, 2 I said in mine heart, Go to now, I will prove thee with mirth, therefore enjoy pleasure: and, behold, this also *is* vanity. I said of laughter, *It is* mad: and of mirth, What doeth it?

Conforming

Psalms 126:1-6 A Song of degrees. When the LORD turned again the captivity of Zion, we were like them that dream. Then was our mouth filled with laughter, and our tongue with singing: then said they among the heathen, The LORD hath done great things for them. The LORD hath done great things for us; *whereof* we are glad. Turn again our captivity, O LORD, as the streams in the south. They that sow in tears shall reap in joy. He that goeth forth and weepeth, bearing precious seed, shall doubtless come again with rejoicing, bringing his sheaves *with him.*

Proverbs 1:24-28 Because I have called, and ye refused; I have stretched out my hand, and no man regarded; But ye have set at nought all my counsel, and would none of my reproof: I also will laugh at your calamity; I will mock when your fear cometh; When your fear cometh as desolation, and your destruction cometh as a whirlwind; when distress and anguish cometh upon you. Then shall they call upon me, but I will not answer; they shall seek me early, but they shall not find me:

Title: God in Thee Unexpected

Sub Title: Not Seen Yet Known = From the Spiritual to the Natural and Then from the Natural to the Spiritual

Focus Verses:
1Corinthians 14:36-40 What? came the word of God out from you? or came it unto you only? If any man think himself to be a prophet, or spiritual, let him acknowledge that the things that I write unto you are the commandments of the Lord. But if any man be ignorant, let him be ignorant. Wherefore, brethren, covet to prophesy, and forbid not to speak with tongues. Let all things be done decently and in order.

To give it back to God, so he can have control of it, so it won't have control of you.

Heavenly Nugget

When we call those things to the expected from the unexpected we speak them into their see form – From the unforeseen, eye realm.

Conforming

But you have to have on the right uniform. = Being in Jesus' order.

Uniform Means – Heavenly always the same form, manner or degree, not varying or being variable of the same form with others. Conforming to one rule or made, consistent in conduct or though pattern.

Psalms 110:4-6 The LORD hath sworn, and will not repent, Thou *art* a priest for ever after the order of Melchizedek. The Lord at thy right hand shall strike through kings in the day of his wrath. He shall judge among the heathen, he shall fill *the places* with the dead bodies; he shall wound the heads over many countries.

Colossians 2:1-8 For I would that ye knew what great conflict I have for you, and *for* them at Laodicea, and *for* as many as have not seen my face in the flesh; That their hearts might be comforted, being knit together in love, and unto all riches of the full assurance of understanding, to the acknowledgement of the mystery of God, and of the Father, and of Christ; In whom are hid all the treasures of wisdom and knowledge. And this I say, lest any man should beguile you with enticing words. For though I be absent in the flesh, yet am I with you in the spirit, joying and beholding your order, and the stedfastness of your faith in Christ. As ye have therefore received Christ Jesus the Lord, *so* walk ye in him: Rooted and built up in him, and stablished in the faith, as ye have been taught, abounding therein with thanksgiving. Beware lest any man spoil you through philosophy and vain deceit, after the tradition of men, after the rudiments of the world, and not after Christ.

Job 33:4-6 The Spirit of God hath made me, and the breath of the Almighty hath given me life. If thou canst answer me, set *thy words* in order before me, stand up. Behold, I *am* according to thy wish in God's stead: I also am formed out of the clay.

Psalms 50:21-23 These *things* hast thou done, and I kept silence; thou thoughtest that I was altogether *such an one* as thyself: *but* I will reprove thee, and set *them* in order before thine eyes. Now consider this, ye that forget God, lest I tear *you* in pieces, and *there be* none to deliver. Whoso offereth praise glorifieth me: and to him that ordereth *his* conversation *aright* will I shew the salvation of God.

2Kings 20:1-6 In those days was Hezekiah sick unto death. And the prophet Isaiah the son of Amoz came to him, and said unto him, Thus saith the LORD, Set thine house in order; for thou shalt die, and not live. Then he turned his face to the wall, and prayed unto the LORD, saying, I beseech thee, O LORD, remember now how I have walked before thee in truth and with a perfect heart, and have done *that which is* good in thy sight. And Hezekiah wept sore. And it came to pass, afore Isaiah was gone out into the middle court, that the word of the LORD came to him, saying, Turn again, and tell Hezekiah the captain of my people, Thus saith the LORD, the God of David thy father, I have

Conforming

heard thy prayer, I have seen thy tears: behold, I will heal thee: on the third day thou shalt go up unto the house of the LORD. And I will add unto thy days fifteen years; and I will deliver thee and this city out of the hand of the king of Assyria; and I will defend this city for mine own sake, and for my servant David's sake.

Title: The Sweep, Don't Get Swept Under

Sub Title: You Better Leave God's People Alone

Focus Verses:
Isaiah 43:1-4 But now thus saith the LORD that created thee, O Jacob, and he that formed thee, O Israel, Fear not: for I have redeemed thee, I have called *thee* by thy name; thou *art* mine. When thou passest through the waters, I *will be* with thee; and through the rivers, they shall not overflow thee: when thou walkest through the fire, thou shalt not be burned; neither shall the flame kindle upon thee. For I *am* the LORD thy God, the Holy One of Israel, thy Saviour: I gave Egypt *for* thy ransom, Ethiopia and Seba for thee. Since thou wast precious in my sight, thou hast been honourable, and I have loved thee: therefore will I give men for thee, and people for thy life.

Main Meat:
Zephaniah 1:1-18 The word of the LORD which came unto Zephaniah the son of Cushi, the son of Gedaliah, the son of Amariah, the son of Hizkiah, in the days of Josiah the son of Amon, king of Judah. I will utterly consume all *things* from off the land, saith the LORD. I will consume man and beast; I will consume the

Conforming

fowls of the heaven, and the fishes of the sea, and the stumblingblocks with the wicked; and I will cut off man from off the land, saith the LORD. I will also stretch out mine hand upon Judah, and upon all the inhabitants of Jerusalem; and I will cut off the remnant of Baal from this place, *and* the name of the Chemarims with the priests; And them that worship the host of heaven upon the housetops; and them that worship *and* that swear by the LORD, and that swear by Malcham; And them that are turned back from the LORD; and *those* that have not sought the LORD, nor enquired for him. Hold thy peace at the presence of the Lord GOD: for the day of the LORD *is* at hand: for the LORD hath prepared a sacrifice, he hath bid his guests. And it shall come to pass in the day of the LORD'S sacrifice, that I will punish the princes, and the king's children, and all such as are clothed with strange apparel. In the same day also will I punish all those that leap on the threshold, which fill their masters' houses with violence and deceit. And it shall come to pass in that day, saith the LORD, *that there shall be* the noise of a cry from the fish gate, and an howling from the second, and a great crashing from the hills. Howl, ye inhabitants of Maktesh, for all the merchant people are cut down; all they that bear silver are cut off. And it shall come to pass at that time, *that* I will search Jerusalem with candles, and punish the men that are settled on their lees: that say in their heart, The LORD will not do good, neither will he do evil. Therefore their goods shall become a booty, and their houses a desolation:

they shall also build houses, but not inhabit *them;* and they shall plant vineyards, but not drink the wine thereof. The great day of the LORD *is* near, *it is* near, and hasteth greatly, *even* the voice of the day of the LORD: the mighty man shall cry there bitterly. That day *is* a day of wrath, a day of trouble and distress, a day of wasteness and desolation, a day of darkness and gloominess, a day of clouds and thick darkness, A day of the trumpet and alarm against the fenced cities, and against the high towers. And I will bring distress upon men, that they shall walk like blind men, because they have sinned against the LORD: and their blood shall be poured out as dust, and their flesh as the dung. Neither their silver nor their gold shall be able to deliver them in the day of the LORD'S wrath; but the whole land shall be devoured by the fire of his jealousy: for he shall make even a speedy riddance of all them that dwell in the land.

8 Points to Be Seen

1. The devil's hidden people
2. Those who bow down to false gods; sun, moon, different shapes in the clouds, etc
3. Those who say it with their mouths but their hearts are far from it
4. So they swear by their god
5. God has chosen His own beyond themselves
6. They even dress to serve their own god
7. They only come to bring confession in the Lords house

Conforming

8. Judah Means Praise – Jerusalem Means – Home or a place of peace. You have to have Jesus to have them, but remember He has to have you first

Title: Watch Out for the One Who Turns 2 Great Wonders – Both Good but ONE Turned Evil

Sub Title: God's Few Chosen, ONE Way Chose God's Way

Focus Verses:
Isaiah 14:12-15 How art thou fallen from heaven, O Lucifer, son of the morning! *how* art thou cut down to the ground, which didst weaken the nations! For thou hast said in thine heart, I will ascend into heaven, I will exalt my throne above the stars of God: I will sit also upon the mount of the congregation, in the sides of the north: I will ascend above the heights of the clouds; I will be like the most High. Yet thou shalt be brought down to hell, to the sides of the pit.

Revelations 12:1-11 And there appeared a great wonder in heaven; a woman clothed with the sun, and the moon under her feet, and upon her head a crown of twelve stars: And she being with child cried, travailing in birth, and pained to be delivered. And there appeared another wonder in heaven; and behold a great red

Conforming

dragon, having seven heads and ten horns, and seven crowns upon his heads. And his tail drew the third part of the stars of heaven, and did cast them to the earth: and the dragon stood before the woman which was ready to be delivered, for to devour her child as soon as it was born. And she brought forth a man child, who was to rule all nations with a rod of iron: and her child was caught up unto God, and *to* his throne. And the woman fled into the wilderness, where she hath a place prepared of God, that they should feed her there a thousand two hundred *and* threescore days. And there was war in heaven: Michael and his angels fought against the dragon; and the dragon fought and his angels, And prevailed not; neither was their place found any more in heaven. And the great dragon was cast out, that old serpent, called the Devil, and Satan, which deceiveth the whole world: he was cast out into the earth, and his angels were cast out with him. And I heard a loud voice saying in heaven, Now is come salvation, and strength, and the kingdom of our God, and the power of his Christ: for the accuser of our brethren is cast down, which accused them before our God day and night. And they overcame him by the blood of the Lamb, and by the word of their testimony; and they loved not their lives unto the death.

Matthew 1:16-25 And Jacob begat Joseph the husband of Mary, of whom was born Jesus, who is called Christ. So all the generations from Abraham to David *are* fourteen generations; and from David until the carrying away into

Babylon *are* fourteen generations; and from the carrying away into Babylon unto Christ *are* fourteen generations. Now the birth of Jesus Christ was on this wise: When as his mother Mary was espoused to Joseph, before they came together, she was found with child of the Holy Ghost. Then Joseph her husband, being a just *man,* and not willing to make her a publick example, was minded to put her away privily. But while he thought on these things, behold, the angel of the Lord appeared unto him in a dream, saying, Joseph, thou son of David, fear not to take unto thee Mary thy wife: for that which is conceived in her is of the Holy Ghost. And she shall bring forth a son, and thou shalt call his name JESUS: for he shall save his people from their sins. Now all this was done, that it might be fulfilled which was spoken of the Lord by the prophet, saying, Behold, a virgin shall be with child, and shall bring forth a son, and they shall call his name Emmanuel, which being interpreted is, God with us. Then Joseph being raised from sleep did as the angel of the Lord had bidden him, and took unto him his wife: And knew her not till she had brought forth her firstborn son: and he called his name JESUS.

Revelations 7:11-17 And all the angels stood round about the throne, and *about* the elders and the four beasts, and fell before the throne on their faces, and worshipped God, Saying, Amen: Blessing, and glory, and wisdom, and thanksgiving, and honour, and power, and might, *be* unto our God for ever and ever. Amen. And one of the elders answered, saying

Conforming

unto me, What are these which are arrayed in white robes? and whence came they? And I said unto him, Sir, thou knowest. And he said to me, These are they which came out of great tribulation, and have washed their robes, and made them white in the blood of the Lamb. Therefore are they before the throne of God, and serve him day and night in his temple: and he that sitteth on the throne shall dwell among them. They shall hunger no more, neither thirst any more; neither shall the sun light on them, nor any heat. For the Lamb which is in the midst of the throne shall feed them, and shall lead them unto living fountains of waters: and God shall wipe away all tears from their eyes.

Title: I Spoke it and it Was Done, I Commanded it and it Stood Fast

Sub Title: And it Came to Pass

Focus Verses:
Psalms 32:7-11 Thou *art* my hiding place; thou shalt preserve me from trouble; thou shalt compass me about with songs of deliverance. Selah. I will instruct thee and teach thee in the way which thou shalt go: I will guide thee with mine eye. Be ye not as the horse, *or* as the mule, *which* have no understanding: whose mouth must be held in with bit and bridle, lest they come near unto thee. Many sorrows *shall be* to the wicked: but he that trusteth in the LORD, mercy shall compass him about. Be glad in the LORD, and rejoice, ye righteous: and shout for joy, all *ye that are* upright in heart.

Psalms 33:9 For he spake, and it was *done;* he commanded, and it stood fast.

Conforming

1. And it came to pass after God said

Genesis 1:1-3 In the beginning God created the heaven and the earth. And the earth was without form, and void; and darkness *was* upon the face of the deep. And the Spirit of God moved upon the face of the waters. And God said, Let there be light: and there was light.

Genesis 1:6 And God said, Let there be a firmament in the midst of the waters, and let it divide the waters from the waters.

Genesis 1:9 And God said, Let the waters under the heaven be gathered together unto one place, and let the dry *land* appear: and it was so.

Genesis 1:11 And God said, Let the earth bring forth grass, the herb yielding seed, *and* the fruit tree yielding fruit after his kind, whose seed *is* in itself, upon the earth: and it was so.

2. As I received my instructions from the Lord

As They	As They Thought
Soon As	As They Turned
That While	As They Walked
That When	As They Listen
They Heard	As They Talked
They Saw	As They Went Up
As They Seen	When They Praised
As They Did	When They Sang
When They Obeyed	As They Spoke
	While They Slept

Conforming

Main Meat:
2Timothy 3:1-17 This know also, that in the last days perilous times shall come. For men shall be lovers of their own selves, covetous, boasters, proud, blasphemers, disobedient to parents, unthankful, unholy, Without natural affection, trucebreakers, false accusers, incontinent, fierce, despisers of those that are good, Traitors, heady, highminded, lovers of pleasures more than lovers of God; Having a form of godliness, but denying the power thereof: from such turn away. For of this sort are they which creep into houses, and lead captive silly women laden with sins, led away with divers lusts, Ever learning, and never able to come to the knowledge of the truth. Now as Jannes and Jambres withstood Moses, so do these also resist the truth: men of corrupt minds, reprobate concerning the faith. But they shall proceed no further: for their folly shall be manifest unto all *men*, as theirs also was. But thou hast fully known my doctrine, manner of life, purpose, faith, longsuffering, charity, patience, Persecutions, afflictions, which came unto me at Antioch, at Iconium, at Lystra; what persecutions I endured: but out of *them* all the Lord delivered me. Yea, and all that will live godly in Christ Jesus shall suffer persecution. But evil men and seducers shall wax worse and worse, deceiving, and being deceived. But continue thou in the things which thou hast learned and hast been assured of, knowing of whom thou hast learned *them;* And that from a child thou hast known the holy scriptures, which are able to make thee wise unto salvation through faith which is in Christ Jesus. All

Conforming

scripture *is* given by inspiration of God, and *is* profitable for doctrine, for reproof, for correction, for instruction in righteousness: That the man of God may be perfect, throughly furnished unto all good works.

Thought: Betrayal

There is a high form of betrayal and a low form. The Word of God says against thee Lord and thee only have I sinned and done this evil, in thy sight O' Lord – Lying, cheating, stealing, backbiting, deceiving or being deceptive is a plant that grows into the tree of betrayal. Then the tree has become the giver of betrayal.

Thinking it, talking about it to long will mostly lead to doing it, the further the seed is planted the deeper it takes root.

Then once it has rooted, it says let me out of here, it's time for me to do what I the Lord was planted inside of you to do good or evil.

The Lord said he created us for His Glory to show forth His good works, to help others to lead others to Jesus, to how His real love that they never had before. Real love conquers all and that's Jesus on the inside of you, the real Jesus – There is only ONE!

To Betray Means – To lead astray, seduce, to deliver to an enemy by treachery to fail or desert in time of need to prove false.

Conforming

Jesus said Betray Means – Putting other things and people before him all the time , letting your trying to serve two masters have it's way, or letting bitter and sweet water of the Word and World come out of you.

Do Giver Means – Whatever you are doing right or wrong are giving you a part of it. It's planting and sewing into your life for better or bitterness. To help you go to Heaven or help you dive straight into hell. You will make that choice one way or the other.

Focus Verses:
Ephesians 4:29-32 Let no corrupt communication proceed out of your mouth, but that which is good to the use of edifying, that it may minister grace unto the hearers. And grieve not the holy Spirit of God, whereby ye are sealed unto the day of redemption. Let all bitterness, and wrath, and anger, and clamour, and evil speaking, be put away from you, with all malice: And be ye kind one to another, tenderhearted, forgiving one another, even as God for Christ's sake hath forgiven you.

Thought: The Part That You Left Out, God Works in Cans Not Can't

Nehemiah 9:25-38 And they took strong cities, and a fat land, and possessed houses full of all goods, wells digged, vineyards, and oliveyards, and fruit trees in abundance: so they did eat, and were filled, and became fat, and delighted themselves in thy great goodness. Nevertheless they were disobedient, and rebelled against

Conforming

thee, and cast thy law behind their backs, and slew thy prophets which testified against them to turn them to thee, and they wrought great provocations. Therefore thou deliveredst them into the hand of their enemies, who vexed them: and in the time of their trouble, when they cried unto thee, thou heardest *them* from heaven; and according to thy manifold mercies thou gavest them saviours, who saved them out of the hand of their enemies. But after they had rest, they did evil again before thee: therefore leftest thou them in the hand of their enemies, so that they had the dominion over them: yet when they returned, and cried unto thee, thou heardest *them* from heaven; and many times didst thou deliver them according to thy mercies; And testifiedst against them, that thou mightest bring them again unto thy law: yet they dealt proudly, and hearkened not unto thy commandments, but sinned against thy judgments, (which if a man do, he shall live in them;) and withdrew the shoulder, and hardened their neck, and would not hear. Yet many years didst thou forbear them, and testifiedst against them by thy spirit in thy prophets: yet would they not give ear: therefore gavest thou them into the hand of the people of the lands. Nevertheless for thy great mercies' sake thou didst not utterly consume them, nor forsake them; for thou *art* a gracious and merciful God. Now therefore, our God, the great, the mighty, and the terrible God, who keepest covenant and mercy, let not all the trouble seem little before thee, that hath come upon us, on our kings, on our princes, and on our priests, and on our prophets, and on our

Conforming

fathers, and on all thy people, since the time of the kings of Assyria unto this day. Howbeit thou *art* just in all that is brought upon us; for thou hast done right, but we have done wickedly: Neither have our kings, our princes, our priests, nor our fathers, kept thy law, nor hearkened unto thy commandments and thy testimonies, wherewith thou didst testify against them. For they have not served thee in their kingdom, and in thy great goodness that thou gavest them, and in the large and fat land which thou gavest before them, neither turned they from their wicked works. Behold, we *are* servants this day, and *for* the land that thou gavest unto our fathers to eat the fruit thereof and the good thereof, behold, we *are* servants in it: And it yieldeth much increase unto the kings whom thou hast set over us because of our sins: also they have dominion over our bodies, and over our cattle, at their pleasure, and we *are* in great distress. And because of all this we make a sure *covenant,* and write *it;* and our princes, Levites, *and* priests, seal *unto it.*

Nehemiah 10:1 Now those that sealed *were,* Nehemiah, the Tirshatha, the son of Hachaliah, and Zidkijah,

Nehemiah 10:28, 29 And the rest of the people, the priests, the Levites, the porters, the singers, the Nethinims, and all they that had separated themselves from the people of the lands unto the law of God, their wives, their sons, and their daughters, every one having knowledge, and having understanding; They clave to their brethren, their nobles, and entered into a

Conforming

curse, and into an oath, to walk in God's law, which was given by Moses the servant of God, and to observe and do all the commandments of the LORD our Lord, and his judgments and his statutes;

Your Part You Left Out

1. God's covenant you agreed to
2. Dedication, commitment, truthfulness
3. Who you really beloved in
4. Your promise and promises to God
5. Giving up your own will to do His never the less not my will be done O' Lord but thine.

More of you and less of me always

The Lord said stop having track feet, when it comes to His Word. Be still and know that I am God, stop timing Me.

When you are doing what you want to do. You are glued to the nude. You have no time limit; TV, sports, gossip, talking about others, computer time, phone talk or gossip, sex texting bringing phones in My Holy Place, then playing games on them you and your children, leave all that ungodliness in the outside of my Holy Place.

If I the Lord can't take care of it then you truly can't.

Conforming

Focus Verses:
John 15:9 As the Father hath loved me, so have I loved you: continue ye in my love.

John 15:16 Ye have not chosen me, but I have chosen you, and ordained you, that ye should go and bring forth fruit, and *that* your fruit should remain: that whatsoever ye shall ask of the Father in my name, he may give it you.

Thought: If You Are Going to War You Better Have an Inside Man Who Can't Be Seen Or Heard.

1. He makes the difference
2. He tells you what you can't see
3. He helps you move in the right positions for full victory
4. He warns you of your enemies plan
5. He never fails
6. He never sleeps
7. He won't tell your plans to anyone

You Must Listen to the Inside Man:
For Life or death, no one knows what the inside man will do or has plans to do until.

1Kings 17:2-9 And the word of the LORD came unto him, saying, Get thee hence, and turn thee eastward, and hide thyself by the brook Cherith, that *is* before Jordan. And it shall be, *that* thou shalt drink of the brook; and I have commanded the ravens to feed thee there. So he went and did according unto the word of the LORD: for he went and dwelt by the brook Cherith, that *is* before Jordan. And the ravens

Conforming

brought him bread and flesh in the morning, and bread and flesh in the evening; and he drank of the brook. And it came to pass after a while, that the brook dried up, because there had been no rain in the land. And the word of the LORD came unto him, saying, Arise, get thee to Zarephath, which *belongeth* to Zidon, and dwell there: behold, I have commanded a widow woman there to sustain thee.

The inside man will tell you all you don't have to be there, just listen to the inside man.

2Kings 6:8-23 Then the king of Syria warred against Israel, and took counsel with his servants, saying, In such and such a place *shall be* my camp. And the man of God sent unto the king of Israel, saying, Beware that thou pass not such a place; for thither the Syrians are come down. And the king of Israel sent to the place which the man of God told him and warned him of, and saved himself there, not once nor twice. Therefore the heart of the king of Syria was sore troubled for this thing; and he called his servants, and said unto them, Will ye not shew me which of us *is* for the king of Israel? And one of his servants said, None, my lord, O king: but Elisha, the prophet that *is* in Israel, telleth the king of Israel the words that thou speakest in thy bedchamber. And he said, Go and spy where he *is,* that I may send and fetch him. And it was told him, saying, Behold, *he is* in Dothan. Therefore sent he thither horses, and chariots, and a great host: and they came by night, and compassed the city about. And when the servant of the man of God was risen early, and gone forth, behold, an host compassed the city both with horses and chariots. And his servant said unto him, Alas, my master! how shall we do? And he answered, Fear not: for they that *be* with us *are* more than they that *be* with them. And Elisha prayed, and said, LORD, I pray thee, open his eyes, that he may see. And the LORD opened the eyes of the young man; and he saw: and, behold, the mountain *was* full of horses and chariots of fire round about Elisha. And when they came down to him, Elisha prayed unto the LORD, and said, Smite this people, I pray thee, with blindness. And he smote them with blindness according to the word of Elisha. And Elisha said unto them, This *is* not the way, neither *is* this the city: follow me, and I will bring you to the man whom ye seek. But he led them to Samaria. And it came to pass, when they were come into Samaria, that Elisha said, LORD, open the eyes of these *men,* that they may see. And the LORD opened their eyes, and they saw; and, behold, *they were* in the midst of Samaria. And the king of Israel said unto Elisha, when he saw them, My father, shall I smite *them?* shall I smite *them?* And he answered, Thou shalt not smite *them:* wouldest thou smite those whom thou hast taken captive with thy sword and with thy bow? set bread and water before them, that they may eat and drink, and go to their master. And he prepared great provision for them: and when they had eaten and drunk, he sent them away, and they went to their master. So the bands of Syria came no more into the land of Israel.

Conforming

You must have the inside man; to be like Me, to worship Me in Spirit and My Truth.

John 4:24 God *is* a Spirit: and they that worship him must worship *him* in spirit and in truth.

John 14:1-4 Let not your heart be troubled: ye believe in God, believe also in me. In my Father's house are many mansions: if *it were* not *so,* I would have told you. I go to prepare a place for you. And if I go and prepare a place for you, I will come again, and receive you unto myself; that where I am, *there* ye may be also. And whither I go ye know, and the way ye know.

John 14:7-9 If ye had known me, ye should have known my Father also: and from henceforth ye know him, and have seen him. Philip saith unto him, Lord, shew us the Father, and it sufficeth us. Jesus saith unto him, Have I been so long time with you, and yet hast thou not known me, Philip? he that hath seen me hath seen the Father; and how sayest thou *then,* Shew us the Father?

John 14:15-18 If ye love me, keep my commandments. And I will pray the Father, and he shall give you another Comforter, that he may abide with you for ever; *Even* the Spirit of truth; whom the world cannot receive, because it seeth him not, neither knoweth him: but ye know him; for he dwelleth with you, and shall be in you. I will not leave you comfortless: I will come to you.

Conforming

John 14:25-29 These things have I spoken unto you, being *yet* present with you. But the Comforter, *which is* the Holy Ghost, whom the Father will send in my name, he shall teach you all things, and bring all things to your remembrance, whatsoever I have said unto you. Peace I leave with you, my peace I give unto you: not as the world giveth, give I unto you. Let not your heart be troubled, neither let it be afraid. Ye have heard how I said unto you, I go away, and come *again* unto you. If ye loved me, ye would rejoice, because I said, I go unto the Father: for my Father is greater than I. And now I have told you before it come to pass, that, when it is come to pass, ye might believe.

Thought: There is a Difference, Use God's Eyes:
There is a way that seemeth right to man, but is end is death. I will send them a strong delusion to believe a lie because they would not believe My truth. When it's God's, right there is a flow into flowing even in times of all chaos going on. When it's not God, it's always a push until pushing the wrong ways. It never sets right in your Spirit or heart; we just keep pushing the truth away, until our own lie becomes out truth, then the thing that we believe in almost destroyed us except for Jesus' love for us. God's anointing puts and keeps you in His flow; your fleshly doings keeps you pushing all the wrong buttons. Remember this – Your flesh is the want your spirit is the need to get and stay right with Jesus.
Amen

Conforming

Focus Verses:
John 4:24 God *is* a Spirit: and they that worship him must worship *him* in spirit and in truth.

Mark 8:34, 35 And when he had called the people *unto him* with his disciples also, he said unto them, Whosoever will come after me, let him deny himself, and take up his cross, and follow me. For whosoever will save his life shall lose it; but whosoever shall lose his life for my sake and the gospel's, the same shall save it.

Thought: If You Don't Kill Yourself, Your Address Will Not be in Heaven With Jesus:

You must dial M for murder, Me for your murder. P.S. You must die, die, and die my beloved. I showed you how on the cross, then you can raise up in Me with Me.

Introduction

You ask; how do I do it? It's Easy. You must do what it says, in order for it to work, right or wrong, God's or evil. To live or die you must learn how to follow instructions for it to work right. Follow it all the way through, not part of it. For all that's in your World is your lust of your flesh. You last that's in your eye and your pride in your life.

Ezekiel 3:20 Again, When a righteous *man* doth turn from his righteousness, and commit iniquity, and I lay a stumblingblock before him, he shall die: because thou hast not given him warning, he shall die in his sin, and his righteousness which he hath done shall not be remembered; but his blood will I require at thine hand.

In Genesis 2:17 it says if you disobey God you will surely die.

To those who minister God's Word forever,
Exodus 28:43 And they shall be upon Aaron, and upon his sons, when they come in unto the tabernacle of the congregation, or when they come near unto the altar to minister in the holy *place;* that they bear not iniquity, and die: *it shall be* a statute for ever unto him and his seed after him.

Jesus said in John 8:24 if you don't believe in Him, you will die in your sins and go to hell. In 1st Corinthians 15:31 Jesus said you must put your ugly flesh to death daily, or it will show off the way you like it to.

Main Meat:
Romans 8:1-14 *There is* therefore now no condemnation to them which are in Christ Jesus, who walk not after the flesh, but after the Spirit. For the law of the Spirit of life in Christ Jesus hath made me free from the law of sin and death. For what the law could not do, in that it was weak through the flesh, God sending his own Son in the likeness of sinful flesh, and for sin, condemned sin in the flesh: That the righteousness of the law might be fulfilled in us, who walk not after the flesh, but after the Spirit. For they that are after the flesh do mind

Conforming

the things of the flesh; but they that are after the Spirit the things of the Spirit. For to be carnally minded *is* death; but to be spiritually minded *is* life and peace. Because the carnal mind *is* enmity against God: for it is not subject to the law of God, neither indeed can be. So then they that are in the flesh cannot please God. But ye are not in the flesh, but in the Spirit, if so be that the Spirit of God dwell in you. Now if any man have not the Spirit of Christ, he is none of his. And if Christ *be* in you, the body *is* dead because of sin; but the Spirit *is* life because of righteousness. But if the Spirit of him that raised up Jesus from the dead dwell in you, he that raised up Christ from the dead shall also quicken your mortal bodies by his Spirit that dwelleth in you. Therefore, brethren, we are debtors, not to the flesh, to live after the flesh. For if ye live after the flesh, ye shall die: but if ye through the Spirit do mortify the deeds of the body, ye shall live. For as many as are led by the Spirit of God, they are the sons of God.

Word Helper:
1Corinthians 1:13 Is Christ divided? was Paul crucified for you? or were ye baptized in the name of Paul?

Galatians 5:24 And they that are Christ's have crucified the flesh with the affections and lusts.

Conforming

Galatians 2:20 I am crucified with Christ: nevertheless I live; yet not I, but Christ liveth in me: and the life which I now live in the flesh I live by the faith of the Son of God, who loved me, and gave himself for me.

Romans 6:6 Knowing this, that our old man is crucified with *him,* that the body of sin might be destroyed, that henceforth we should not serve sin.

You will be betrayed to help crucify you.

Matthew 26:2 Ye know that after two days is *the feast of* the passover, and the Son of man is betrayed to be crucified.

You will show Christ if you die to your flesh.

Mark 15:32 Let Christ the King of Israel descend now from the cross, that we may see and believe. And they that were crucified with him reviled him.

Crucify Means – To put to death, to destroy the power of or mortify, to torture, to treat cruelly, extreme painful punishment.

Mortify Means – To destroy the strength or functioning of, to subdue or deaden the body, to subject, to severe and vexing embarrassment or shame, Denial of bodily passions and appetites.

Conforming

Focus Verse:
John 1:34 And I saw, and bare record that this is the Son of God.

Thought: The Only Everlasting Light

Main Meat:
John 1:1-34 In the beginning was the Word, and the Word was with God, and the Word was God. The same was in the beginning with God. All things were made by him; and without him was not any thing made that was made. In him was life; and the life was the light of men. And the light shineth in darkness; and the darkness comprehended it not. There was a man sent from God, whose name *was* John. The same came for a witness, to bear witness of the Light, that all *men* through him might believe. He was not that Light, but *was sent* to bear witness of that Light. *That* was the true Light, which lighteth every man that cometh into the world. He was in the world, and the world was made by him, and the world knew him not. He came unto his own, and his own received him not. But as many as received him, to them gave he power to become the sons of God, *even* to them that believe on his name: Which were born, not of blood, nor of the will of the flesh, nor of the will of man, but of God. And the Word was made flesh, and dwelt among us, (and we beheld his glory, the glory as of the only begotten of the Father,) full of grace and truth. John bare witness of him, and cried, saying, This was he of whom I spake, He that cometh after me is preferred before me: for he was before me. And of his fulness have all we

received, and grace for grace. For the law was given by Moses, *but* grace and truth came by Jesus Christ. No man hath seen God at any time; the only begotten Son, which is in the bosom of the Father, he hath declared *him*. And this is the record of John, when the Jews sent priests and Levites from Jerusalem to ask him, Who art thou? And he confessed, and denied not; but confessed, I am not the Christ. And they asked him, What then? Art thou Elias? And he saith, I am not. Art thou that prophet? And he answered, No. Then said they unto him, Who art thou? that we may give an answer to them that sent us. What sayest thou of thyself? He said, I *am* the voice of one crying in the wilderness, Make straight the way of the Lord, as said the prophet Esaias. And they which were sent were of the Pharisees. And they asked him, and said unto him, Why baptizest thou then, if thou be not that Christ, nor Elias, neither that prophet? John answered them, saying, I baptize with water: but there standeth one among you, whom ye know not; He it is, who coming after me is preferred before me, whose shoe's latchet I am not worthy to unloose. These things were done in Bethabara beyond Jordan, where John was baptizing. The next day John seeth Jesus coming unto him, and saith, Behold the Lamb of God, which taketh away the sin of the world. This is he of whom I said, After me cometh a man which is preferred before me: for he was before me. And I knew him not: but that he should be made manifest to Israel, therefore am I come baptizing with water. And John bare record, saying, I saw the Spirit descending

Conforming

from heaven like a dove, and it abode upon him. And I knew him not: but he that sent me to baptize with water, the same said unto me, Upon whom thou shalt see the Spirit descending, and remaining on him, the same is he which baptizeth with the Holy Ghost. And I saw, and bare record that this is the Son of God.

Help me Lord to jump out of my place into your place. Jesus cannot embrace your sin but He will embrace His love for you. That's why He said He had to set us apart not from being around as to not being a part of them.

The Bible said they came among us, but they left from us, because they were not of us. The light will always out shine the darkness. Darkness will never get along with light, t hates light. It always wants to kill the light or shut it up. It acts like it's listening but really it despises it. It can't have fellowship with it (darkness). If we are locked into Jesus the right way we are told to be by Him. Then we wouldn't keep on going out side His holiness to do what feels good to our flesh. If your key won't work any more, throw it away and use Jesus' key. It will never fail, but you have to enter in.

We have three different nature parts of Spirit in us. The only everlasting light
            and One Holy Part
                God
      Ours-------|------Mommy
              Daddy

Conforming

Once we come to that understanding of serving right or wrong, we must and will choose the ONE we will feed the most to reap alive the most.

Remember this – Your flesh is the want and your spirit is the need.

If you are ugly on the inside you are ugly on the out side – take a Godly look.

You can't dress it up

The eyes of the Lord are every where beholding the good and the evil.

Thought: God Said it but God's Gifts Comes Without Repentance

It could be this or it could be that. It could be a little or it could be a lot. It could be his or hers. It could be yes or no. It could be right or wrong.

It could be your good or God's good. It could be your right or God's right.

It's one thing everybody needs to know and come to understand, that whatever God says it is. It will be just the way He said it will be.

Just like at the beginning, God said let there be and it was so. When He said it and how He said it at that time He spoke it to be not before, something we all need you got to have some, the necessity of an enemy to help you grow.

Conforming

Read First – Word Helpers:
Matthew 13:24 Another parable put he forth unto them, saying, The kingdom of heaven is likened unto a man which sowed good seed in his field:

Matthew 13:31 Another parable put he forth unto them, saying, The kingdom of heaven is like to a grain of mustard seed, which a man took, and sowed in his field:

Matthew 13:33 Another parable spake he unto them; The kingdom of heaven is like unto leaven, which a woman took, and hid in three measures of meal, till the whole was leavened.

Focus Verses:
Matthew 13:34, 35 All these things spake Jesus unto the multitude in parables; and without a parable spake he not unto them: That it might be fulfilled which was spoken by the prophet, saying, I will open my mouth in parables; I will utter things which have been kept secret from the foundation of the world.

Matthew 13:11 He answered and said unto them, Because it is given unto you to know the mysteries of the kingdom of heaven, but to them it is not given.

Thought: How's Your Wisdom

Conforming

Main Meat:
Matthew 13:18-23 Hear ye therefore the parable of the sower. When any one heareth the word of the kingdom, and understandeth *it* not, then cometh the wicked *one,* and catcheth away that which was sown in his heart. This is he which received seed by the way side. But he that received the seed into stony places, the same is he that heareth the word, and anon with joy receiveth it; Yet hath he not root in himself, but dureth for a while: for when tribulation or persecution ariseth because of the word, by and by he is offended. He also that received seed among the thorns is he that heareth the word; and the care of this world, and the deceitfulness of riches, choke the word, and he becometh unfruitful. But he that received seed into the good ground is he that heareth the word, and understandeth *it;* which also beareth fruit, and bringeth forth, some an hundredfold, some sixty, some thirty.

Are you walking on water or are you still sinking in your bath tub, from the cares of this world or what some say.

In all thy getting, get my understanding says the Lord. If it's standing over you, you don't have my understanding.

My ways are not like yours; My thoughts are not like yours, from as far as you can see or imagine. You should be learning how to stand over it instead of it standing over you. Obedience comes first, and then learns how to follow the instructions. Everything in this life

Conforming

and the one you are preparing for. They both have instructions Heaven and Hell.

If the Lord gave instructions from Genesis to Revelations and most of all He set people in place, every where to give you instructions good or evil. Then He gave you the best and only choice that would help keep you alive, ME!

So whose report will you choose to be love life or death?

Close:
Matthew 13:36-43 Then Jesus sent the multitude away, and went into the house: and his disciples came unto him, saying, Declare unto us the parable of the tares of the field. He answered and said unto them, He that soweth the good seed is the Son of man; The field is the world; the good seed are the children of the kingdom; but the tares are the children of the wicked *one;* The enemy that sowed them is the devil; the harvest is the end of the world; and the reapers are the angels. As therefore the tares are gathered and burned in the fire; so shall it be in the end of this world. The Son of man shall send forth his angels, and they shall gather out of his kingdom all things that offend, and them which do iniquity; And shall cast them into a furnace of fire: there shall be wailing and gnashing of teeth. Then shall the righteous shine forth as the sun in the kingdom of their Father. Who hath ears to hear, let him hear.

Conforming

To everything there is a beginning and an end except me says the Lord. I am the beginning and the end. There was nothing before Me and there can and will be nothing after Me.

Conforming

Title: Learn How to See it Like Jesus

Sub Title: See Life, God's Plan Always Works

Focus Verses:
John 11:25, 26 Jesus said unto her, I am the resurrection, and the life: he that believeth in me, though he were dead, yet shall he live: And whosoever liveth and believeth in me shall never die. Believest thou this?

What I knew got me where I was. What I know in the Lord got me where I am today.

Theme – You must die to have real life in and with Christ Jesus forever.

John 11:26 And whosoever liveth and believeth in me shall never die. Believest thou this?

Unbelief and doubt stinks in Jesus' sight.

John 11:39 Jesus said, Take ye away the stone. Martha, the sister of him that was dead, saith unto him, Lord, by this time he stinketh: for he hath been *dead* four days.

John 11:23 Jesus saith unto her, Thy brother shall rise again.

Conforming

Martha tried to tell Him what she knew in John 11: 24 like a lot of us do.

John 11:24 Martha saith unto him, I know that he shall rise again in the resurrection at the last day.

Learn ho to know nothing, and then Jesus can teach you what's right His way.

You blindness will only lead you to more blindness, which leads you straight to hell's fire forever – NON –STOP!

Certain Man – Positive, know for sure to establish beyond doubt, the chosen one or one's.

Focus Verse:
John 15:16 Ye have not chosen me, but I have chosen you, and ordained you, that ye should go and bring forth fruit, and *that* your fruit should remain: that whatsoever ye shall ask of the Father in my name, he may give it you.

Die daily to your flesh.

Thought: The Inside Man, but He Has to Have You First

John 15:1-27 I am the true vine, and my Father is the husbandman. Every branch in me that beareth not fruit he taketh away: and every *branch* that beareth fruit, he purgeth it, that it may bring forth more fruit. Now ye are clean through the word which I have spoken unto

Conforming

you. Abide in me, and I in you. As the branch cannot bear fruit of itself, except it abide in the vine; no more can ye, except ye abide in me. I am the vine, ye *are* the branches: He that abideth in me, and I in him, the same bringeth forth much fruit: for without me ye can do nothing. If a man abide not in me, he is cast forth as a branch, and is withered; and men gather them, and cast *them* into the fire, and they are burned. If ye abide in me, and my words abide in you, ye shall ask what ye will, and it shall be done unto you. Herein is my Father glorified, that ye bear much fruit; so shall ye be my disciples. As the Father hath loved me, so have I loved you: continue ye in my love. If ye keep my commandments, ye shall abide in my love; even as I have kept my Father's commandments, and abide in his love. These things have I spoken unto you, that my joy might remain in you, and *that* your joy might be full. This is my commandment, That ye love one another, as I have loved you. Greater love hath no man than this, that a man lay down his life for his friends. Ye are my friends, if ye do whatsoever I command you. Henceforth I call you not servants; for the servant knoweth not what his lord doeth: but I have called you friends; for all things that I have heard of my Father I have made known unto you. Ye have not chosen me, but I have chosen you, and ordained you, that ye should go and bring forth fruit, and *that* your fruit should remain: that whatsoever ye shall ask of the Father in my name, he may give it you. These things I command you, that ye love one another. If the world hate you, ye know that it hated me before *it hated* you. If ye were of the world, the world would love his own: but because ye are not of the world, but I have chosen you out of the world, therefore the world hateth you. Remember the word that I said unto you, The servant is not greater than his lord. If they have persecuted me, they will also persecute you; if they have kept my saying, they will keep yours also. But all these things will they do unto you for my name's sake, because they know not him that sent me. If I had not come and spoken unto them, they had not had sin: but now they have no cloke for their sin. He that hateth me hateth my Father also. If I had not done among them the works which none other man did, they had not had sin: but now have they both seen and hated both me and my Father. But *this cometh to pass,* that the word might be fulfilled that is written in their law, They hated me without a cause. But when the Comforter is come, whom I will send unto you from the Father, *even* the Spirit of truth, which proceedeth from the Father, he shall testify of me: And ye also shall bear witness, because ye have been with me from the beginning.

Introduction

God is love He that knoweth not God knoweth not love.

I give an inside peace which passeth all other understanding.

Conforming

1John 2:15-17 Love not the world, neither the things *that are* in the world. If any man love the world, the love of the Father is not in him. For all that *is* in the world, the lust of the flesh, and the lust of the eyes, and the pride of life, is not of the Father, but is of the world. And the world passeth away, and the lust thereof: but he that doeth the will of God abideth for ever.

It's strange how many Christians say that they have Jesus, but their lifestyle and behavior don't line up with His Word, His will and His way. Which way we like to pick and choose our yes's we love trying to. If God like, moves by you. The only thing that moves God is faith and compassion. The compassion in you that tells Him you want it all for real and need His help to breakout of your ungodly spirit of bondage. The Bible says that it's Christ in you; your only hope of deliverance, empowerment, guidance, freedom, endurance, real love and going home to Glory with Him. Your breath is vital inside of you, if it's not there, you will die. If you lose too much blood at once you will die. A heart attack could kill you instantly if Jesus didn't step in. So if Jesus is not on the inside of you with His fullness, then you are already dead. He has to all day everyday. The inside man, there can only be one.

Nuggets from Heaven

Thought: No One Else Could, from the Beginning of This World. Jesus Has Been in His Business of Bringing a Great Measure of Certainty and Peace of Mind to Every Family.

Conforming

Thought: Christ Like Mind; Having a Clear and Effective Decision Making Frame of Mind Has Always Been Important Even More so, in Times Like These.

Thought: The Right Help, Jesus Does Not Need Any Outside Help to Take Care of His Business. He Takes Care of it His Way. The Old Fashioned Jesus – Sufficient Way, Not Our self-sufficient Way.

Thought: Get Some,
A Strong Sense of Holy Purpose
A Clear Set of Godly Values
A Long Term Perspective or Outlook on Life
Independent and Accountable Thinking
Be Built for All Times and All People to Help

In my life I felt for years that I didn't know what to do. So I kept on doing wrong. Even my right was wrong. Then came Jesus, Born-Again.

Thought: What Makes Jesus Different

It would take a million life times to tell you and more. But to start off, Jesus can't lie or He can't die.

He has the best protection plan and life insurance plan for you life. There is none stronger, bigger or more loving.

Jesus created everything and everybody for His purpose.

Conforming

He said I go away, but I'll come back to you. Really He never left, it's called supernatural. He said I'll leave the real Me with you and in you. Then I can be everywhere at once, can you? I see everything and everybody at once, can you? What can man do that I can do? Nothing! What can man try to do, that I can't undo? Nothing! Can man give you eternal life? NO. See Me and live.

Thought: Helps

Planning a secure financial future for yourself and your family is an important decision – guess what you can't make it by yourself, need real help? Call Jesus and dial 1.

Finding the right life insurance company to help you do that is equally important in all thy ways, check with Jesus first. Not all insurance companies are the same not all gods are real try Jesus.

Here are a few of the ways Jesus serves you better and keeps you safer.

1. He keeps you from seen and unseen danger, natural and spiritual.
2. Jesus was attacked for you to be protected.
3. He was bruised for your healing.
4. He became dumb so, you wouldn't have to.
5. He became poor so you don't have to stay that way.
6. He is the giver of all things so you don't have to steal, cheat or kill.

Conforming

7. He took on our chaos, so we could have His peace that passes all understanding.

Be Prepared!

In hard times, troubled times and in times of crises, I would like to humbly remind you again. Just like I learned before time, that Jesus is the only one built for times like these. He is the only one who is strong enough to lead you through. So you won't stay there, the rest of your life and become, homeless or Godless, which will leave you being Heaven-less.

Thought: Reach

Reach beyond the break. Reach beyond whatever and whoever.

Then reach beyond it forever and see Jesus. He said I will never leave you or forsake you. But you have to want to come back to Jesus, He's drawing you. Just reach up beyond whatever it is in your life and Jesus will do the rest.

The Lord Said Put This Nugget in Place,
Thought: It All Comes Back to You

In the beginning God made man in His image and likeness. That's all man could do was good. Then man made choice to disobey God. Then that have him the ability he thought to do or not to do. It all comes back to you. We all make mistakes, but we have the right or wrong

Conforming

choice to keep making the same one's over and over.

With or without Jesus you will make mistakes, but without Him on the inside of you, you don't have the real power to stop making the same ones over and over. Then comes more to help keep you where you are and push you in deeper and deeper until it all comes back to you and on you.

Then who are you going to do, His will or your kill.

Thought: Do You Have the Acts or Are You Just Acting

Acts 1:1-20 The former treatise have I made, O Theophilus, of all that Jesus began both to do and teach, Until the day in which he was taken up, after that he through the Holy Ghost had given commandments unto the apostles whom he had chosen: To whom also he shewed himself alive after his passion by many infallible proofs, being seen of them forty days, and speaking of the things pertaining to the kingdom of God: And, being assembled together with *them*, commanded them that they should not depart from Jerusalem, but wait for the promise of the Father, which, *saith he*, ye have heard of me. For John truly baptized with water; but ye shall be baptized with the Holy Ghost not many days hence. When they therefore were come together, they asked of him, saying, Lord, wilt thou at this time restore again the kingdom to Israel? And he said unto them, It is not for you to know the times or the seasons, which the Father hath put in his own power. But ye shall receive power, after that the Holy Ghost is come upon you: and ye shall be witnesses unto me both in Jerusalem, and in all Judaea, and in Samaria, and unto the uttermost part of the earth. And when he had spoken these things, while they beheld, he was taken up; and a cloud received him out of their sight. And while they looked stedfastly toward heaven as he went up, behold, two men stood by them in white apparel; Which also said, Ye men of Galilee, why stand ye gazing up into heaven? this same Jesus, which is taken up from you into heaven, shall so come in like manner as ye have seen him go into heaven. Then returned they unto Jerusalem from the mount called Olivet, which is from Jerusalem a sabbath day's journey. And when they were come in, they went up into an upper room, where abode both Peter, and James, and John, and Andrew, Philip, and Thomas, Bartholomew, and Matthew, James *the son* of Alphaeus, and Simon Zelotes, and Judas *the brother* of James. These all continued with one accord in prayer and supplication, with the women, and Mary the mother of Jesus, and with his brethren. And in those days Peter stood up in the midst of the disciples, and said, (the number of names together were about an hundred and twenty,) Men *and* brethren, this scripture must needs have been fulfilled, which the Holy Ghost by the mouth of David spake before concerning Judas, which was guide to them that took Jesus. For he was numbered with us, and had

Conforming

obtained part of this ministry. Now this man purchased a field with the reward of iniquity; and falling headlong, he burst asunder in the midst, and all his bowels gushed out. And it was known unto all the dwellers at Jerusalem; insomuch as that field is called in their proper tongue, Aceldama, that is to say, The field of blood. For it is written in the book of Psalms, Let his habitation be desolate, and let no man dwell therein: and his bishoprick let another take.

Acts 2:1-7 And when the day of Pentecost was fully come, they were all with one accord in one place. And suddenly there came a sound from heaven as of a rushing mighty wind, and it filled all the house where they were sitting. And there appeared unto them cloven tongues like as of fire, and it sat upon each of them. And they were all filled with the Holy Ghost, and began to speak with other tongues, as the Spirit gave them utterance. And there were dwelling at Jerusalem Jews, devout men, out of every nation under heaven. Now when this was noised abroad, the multitude came together, and were confounded, because that every man heard them speak in his own language. And they were all amazed and marvelled, saying one to another, Behold, are not all these which speak Galilaeans?

Introduction

Jesus said a part from me being on the inside of you, you could do nothing. You must be Born-Again of the water and of My Spirit, or

Conforming

you can't enter into My Spiritual Kingdom or understanding to know the right way of reading or ministering My Word.

The Words I speak are Spirit and life. For I am a Spirit and if you are going to worship Me and obey Me you must be born of Me.

Your real act will give you away. Just wait it's crying to get out. Bitter and sweet can't come out of the truly Born-Again vessel, not mine.

The whole world is a stage and everybody plays a part. The stage is set then the curtain goes up, but who are they seeing. There are two ways to move, with the Acts or with an Act.

Act Means – To produce an effect to perform a function anything done, being done or to be done or trying to serve two masters.

Thought: The Shake Down

The shake down, the Lord said let Me get it all out.

You ask all of what Lord? You out of you so I can lead you right with my eyes and way. You have been shaken up. You're shaken to the left and right. You were shaken backward and forward. Now let Me your Lord and God shake you down. That you might take root in me and come up to My level, your right full place in Me.

Conforming

Shake Down Means to

Settle down; make a full search of, to bring about a reproduction of a testing under operating conditions of something new for possible faults or defects.

Word Helpers

Usury is a Form of Exhortation

Nehemiah 5:6-13 And I was very angry when I heard their cry and these words. Then I consulted with myself, and I rebuked the nobles, and the rulers, and said unto them, Ye exact usury, every one of his brother. And I set a great assembly against them. And I said unto them, We after our ability have redeemed our brethren the Jews, which were sold unto the heathen; and will ye even sell your brethren? or shall they be sold unto us? Then held they their peace, and found nothing *to answer*. Also I said, It *is* not good that ye do: ought ye not to walk in the fear of our God because of the reproach of the heathen our enemies? I likewise, *and* my brethren, and my servants, might exact of them money and corn: I pray you, let us leave off this usury. Restore, I pray you, to them, even this day, their lands, their vineyards, their oliveyards, and their houses, also the hundredth *part* of the money, and of the corn, the wine, and the oil, that ye exact of them. Then said they, We will restore *them*, and will require nothing of them; so will we do as thou sayest. Then I called the priests, and took an oath of them, that they should do according to this promise. Also I shook my lap, and said, So God shake out every man from his house, and from his labour, that performeth not this promise, even thus be he shaken out, and emptied. And all the congregation said, Amen, and praised the LORD. And the people did according to this promise.

2Thessalonions 2:1-3 Now we beseech you, brethren, by the coming of our Lord Jesus Christ, and *by* our gathering together unto him, That ye be not soon shaken in mind, or be troubled, neither by spirit, nor by word, nor by letter as from us, as that the day of Christ is at hand. Let no man deceive you by any means: for *that day shall not come,* except there come a falling away first, and that man of sin be revealed, the son of perdition;

Luke 21:26, 27 Men's hearts failing them for fear, and for looking after those things which are coming on the earth: for the powers of heaven shall be shaken. And then shall they see the Son of man coming in a cloud with power and great glory.

Job 38:13 That it might take hold of the ends of the earth, that the wicked might be shaken out of it?

Matthew 23:12 And whosoever shall exalt himself shall be abased; and he that shall humble himself shall be exalted.

Conforming

2Corinthians 12:20, 21 For I fear, lest, when I come, I shall not find you such as I would, and *that* I shall be found unto you such as ye would not: lest *there be* debates, envyings, wraths, strifes, backbitings, whisperings, swellings, tumults: *And* lest, when I come again, my God will humble me among you, and *that* I shall bewail many which have sinned already, and have not repented of the uncleanness and fornication and lasciviousness which they have committed.

James 4:6-8 But he giveth more grace. Wherefore he saith, God resisteth the proud, but giveth grace unto the humble. Submit yourselves therefore to God. Resist the devil, and he will flee from you. Draw nigh to God, and he will draw nigh to you. Cleanse *your* hands, *ye* sinners; and purify *your* hearts, *ye* double minded.

1Peter 5:5-7 Likewise, ye younger, submit yourselves unto the elder. Yea, all *of you* be subject one to another, and be clothed with humility: for God resisteth the proud, and giveth grace to the humble. Humble yourselves therefore under the mighty hand of God, that he may exalt you in due time: Casting all your care upon him; for he careth for you.

James 4:10 Humble yourselves in the sight of the Lord, and he shall lift you up.

Conforming

The Ten Commandments as God See's Them

17 Points

Exodus 34:1-17 And the LORD said unto Moses, Hew thee two tables of stone like unto the first: and I will write upon *these* tables the words that were in the first tables, which thou brakest. And be ready in the morning, and come up in the morning unto mount Sinai, and present thyself there to me in the top of the mount. And no man shall come up with thee, neither let any man be seen throughout all the mount; neither let the flocks nor herds feed before that mount. And he hewed two tables of stone like unto the first; and Moses rose up early in the morning, and went up unto mount Sinai, as the LORD had commanded him, and took in his hand the two tables of stone. And the LORD descended in the cloud, and stood with him there, and proclaimed the name of the LORD. And the LORD passed by before him, and proclaimed, The LORD, The LORD God, merciful and gracious, longsuffering, and abundant in goodness and truth, Keeping mercy for thousands, forgiving iniquity and transgression and sin, and that will by no means clear *the guilty;* visiting the iniquity of the fathers upon the children, and upon the children's children, unto the third and to the fourth *generation.* And Moses made haste, and bowed his head toward the earth, and

Conforming

worshipped. And he said, If now I have found grace in thy sight, O Lord, let my Lord, I pray thee, go among us; for it *is* a stiffnecked people; and pardon our iniquity and our sin, and take us for thine inheritance. And he said, Behold, I make a covenant: before all thy people I will do marvels, such as have not been done in all the earth, nor in any nation: and all the people among which thou *art* shall see the work of the LORD: for it *is* a terrible thing that I will do with thee. Observe thou that which I command thee this day: behold, I drive out before thee the Amorite, and the Canaanite, and the Hittite, and the Perizzite, and the Hivite, and the Jebusite. Take heed to thyself, lest thou make a covenant with the inhabitants of the land whither thou goest, lest it be for a snare in the midst of thee: But ye shall destroy their altars, break their images, and cut down their groves: For thou shalt worship no other god: for the LORD, whose name *is* Jealous, *is* a jealous God: Lest thou make a covenant with the inhabitants of the land, and they go a whoring after their gods, and do sacrifice unto their gods, and *one* call thee, and thou eat of his sacrifice; And thou take of their daughters unto thy sons, and their daughters go a whoring after their gods, and make thy sons go a whoring after their gods. Thou shalt make thee no molten gods.

1. Ask yourself, who brought you out of your house of bondage, was it them, things, money or Me. If it was Me, who gave you knowledge to gain, then who did it. If it was Me who told you a part from Me you should do nothing –

Conforming

who did it? It was Me who said, by Me you move, you love and have your being – then who did it. I gave you breath.

Genesis 2:7 And the LORD God formed man *of* the dust of the ground, and breathed into his nostrils the breath of life; and man became a living soul.

Job 12:10 In whose hand *is* the soul of every living thing, and the breath of all mankind.

So Who Did It

2. The Lord said stop going after everything that has a hot link or that has a banana split, they don't have enough of anything to make you happy or keep you safe from seen or unseen danger. Only I can do that.

3. The Lord said – don't put your trust in people or things that you can't see, everything like Me or who cannot be every where at once like Me.... Movie stars, fast cars, the world's fast life, and your money image or tree image or false man Christ image. Things and people can only present themselves as being god. But you need to learn that there is no other I. I will show you.

4. I am the same yesterday, today and forever. If I destroyed a whole generation then I will do the same today of them that hate Me and disobey Me. But to those who love Me and keep my Commandments I will show you mercy.

Conforming

5. Stop saying I swear to god and lying.

6.-7. In your heart you can't swear by anything because it's all God's. Don't say God is your witness if you aren't living anything. Don't lie to the Holy Ghost.

8. The Lord said, be ye holy for I am holy, not just on your Church day but everyday should be a Jesus day to you. You can't act or look holy on your Church day only. It takes the real Holy Ghost to help make you and keep you holy in God's sight, not man's – man see's temporal and God see's eternal.

9. Don't do everything else under the sun with you day off and then expect for Me to bless it. My time is My time and theirs is theirs. Give Me mine you need it. I don't. The rocks will cry out if you don't. The animals will prophesy if you don't, they already do it every day listen and learn.

10. You need to learn to rest in me and do nothing. Some of you are like a water facet in a baseball park, every time someone turns it on you are running.

11. You can't work seven days and leave God out. If you do you will find a hole in everything you do. Give God His time due to Him.

12. There is a curse on you for not obeying and honoring your father and mother, natural and Spiritual ones.

If some of you don't have either of them, then that's why the Lord gave you Spiritual ones to help lead and guide you to His truth.

13. Yourself or others by keeping out of you life. That's murder shalt not shed someone else's blood except in war.

14. Thou shalt not commit adultery, naturally, spiritually.

15. Thou shalt not steal you life, your soul belongs to Jesus, not you. He and Him alone went to Calvary bled, died and arose up for you. Your life is not your own, it was brought forth with a price, before you were formed in your mother's womb.

16. False Witness – Do not support a lie, not even for any price.

17. Thou shalt not covet – don't be wanting for what's not yours. Wanting turns into despise and it turns into jealousy and it turns into doing something about it that leads to taking it by force or undermining the other person to get it.

Conforming

Thought: There is Only ONE Expert

Let the Holy Ghost make you an expert. You can never be one without Him, known or unknown to your flesh. The flesh wars against the Spirit for control or ruler-ship. Your gifts and talents didn't come from you, they came from Jesus.

When you read the Bible - the Word of God it talks back to you. Because the truth always stays with you, even if you push it away, it always tries to get in to stay in. The Lord said my ways are not like your ways. Your understanding is not like mine. If I don't give you my understanding of anything or everything, then your understanding of it is wrong. Good or Bad. In all that you do see me first. I was before all things and people. Then I only knew you before you were formed in your mother's belly. How can you know more than me, fool?

Psalms 14:1-7 To the chief Musician, *A Psalm of David. The fool hath said in his heart, There is no God. They are corrupt, they have done abominable works, there is none that doeth good. The LORD looked down from heaven upon the children of men, to see if there were any that did understand, and seek God. They are all gone aside, they are all together become filthy: *there is* none that doeth good, no, not one. Have all the workers of iniquity no knowledge? who eat up my people *as* they eat bread, and call not upon the LORD. There were they in great fear: for God *is* in the generation of the righteous. Ye have shamed the counsel of the poor, because the LORD *is* his refuge. Oh that the salvation of Israel *were come* out of Zion! when the LORD bringeth back the captivity of his people, Jacob shall rejoice, *and* Israel shall be glad.

Thought: The Breakdown of Acts 2:1-13

Acts 2:1-13 And when the day of Pentecost was fully come, they were all with one accord in one place. And suddenly there came a sound from heaven as of a rushing mighty wind, and it filled all the house where they were sitting. And there appeared unto them cloven tongues like as of fire, and it sat upon each of them. And they were all filled with the Holy Ghost, and began to speak with other tongues, as the Spirit gave them utterance. And there were dwelling at Jerusalem Jews, devout men, out of every nation under heaven. Now when this was noised abroad, the multitude came together, and were confounded, because that every man heard them speak in his own language. And they were all amazed and marvelled, saying one to another, Behold, are not all these which speak Galilaeans? And how hear we every man in our own tongue, wherein we were born? Parthians, and Medes, and Elamites, and the dwellers in Mesopotamia, and in Judaea, and Cappadocia, in Pontus, and Asia, Phrygia, and

Conforming

Pamphylia, in Egypt, and in the parts of Libya about Cyrene, and strangers of Rome, Jews and proselytes, Cretes and Arabians, we do hear them speak in our tongues the wonderful works of God. And they were all amazed, and were in doubt, saying one to another, What meaneth this? Others mocking said, These men are full of new wine.

1. The day of God's greatest power was given to man. Jesus living on the inside of you, if you let Him do it, His right.

2. Then came the supernatural experience.

3. The Holy Spirit came in a different form.

4. Then they were all filled with Jesus you must stay filled.

5. Then Jesus had His own witness there.

6. Then the Lord gave them understanding of the tongues, He had them speaking in.

7.-11. They were confounded or mixed up in their own understanding of the supernatural or Spiritual workings of God.

12.-13. They were so confused that they called it what they thought it was. Like some of us do, when we don't have the real deal Holy Ghost or when we are satisfied where we are in the Lord and don't want to grow to glow in Him any more.

Conforming

Thought: The Lord Said Stop Being Crossways, There are Two Ways to be Crossways

1. Hot tempered overly angry, mean tempered or bad tempered or just ugly tempered.

2. Your life style can be two different ways or more, because of different spirits in you. To help you to project different personalities; you could be one way in the morning, then your other part comes out later or your real you come out when you can't have it your way which is crossways.

To cross someone is to wrong them deeply to deceive them deeply or manipulate them often. Some of you know about your crossways of dressing, your hidden secret that God knows about. Your crossways can cover a lot or you can let Jesus destroy it once and for all, confess, repent, then turn away from it in your heart. Then let the only power that can stop it deliver you and help you can stay delivered.

Some crossways are self-righteousness ways; I, I, I, Me, Me, Me, I know it all and have all the right answers. God showed me this, well He's going to show you, you first, if you really listen to Him.

Jesus said your ways need to be like His. If not they are your own crossways. That's why you must be Born – Again and filled with Jesus on the inside of you. Make sure you get more and

Conforming

more of Jesus everyday to learn how to stay in His way.

You will feed what you really want the most and you will starve what you really want to get rid of the most.

You will do one or the other.

Remember this, your flesh is the want your spirit is the need. How will you cross this pathway and who with? His one way or with your crossways, you will choose.

Title: Religion

Sub Title: Jesus Said Give Me What's Mine and Give Caesar What's His

Focus Verses:
Acts 25:1-19 Now when Festus was come into the province, after three days he ascended from Caesarea to Jerusalem. Then the high priest and the chief of the Jews informed him against Paul, and besought him, And desired favour against him, that he would send for him to Jerusalem, laying wait in the way to kill him. But Festus answered, that Paul should be kept at Caesarea, and that he himself would depart shortly *thither*. Let them therefore, said he, which among you are able, go down with *me,* and accuse this man, if there be any wickedness in him. And when he had tarried among them more than ten days, he went down unto Caesarea; and the next day sitting on the judgment seat commanded Paul to be brought. And when he was come, the Jews which came down from Jerusalem stood round about, and laid many and grievous complaints against Paul, which they could not prove. While he answered for himself, Neither against the law of the Jews, neither against the temple, nor yet against Caesar, have I offended any thing at all. But Festus, willing to do the Jews a pleasure,

Conforming

answered Paul, and said, Wilt thou go up to Jerusalem, and there be judged of these things before me? Then said Paul, I stand at Caesar's judgment seat, where I ought to be judged: to the Jews have I done no wrong, as thou very well knowest. For if I be an offender, or have committed any thing worthy of death, I refuse not to die: but if there be none of these things whereof these accuse me, no man may deliver me unto them. I appeal unto Caesar. Then Festus, when he had conferred with the council, answered, Hast thou appealed unto Caesar? unto Caesar shalt thou go. And after certain days king Agrippa and Bernice came unto Caesarea to salute Festus. And when they had been there many days, Festus declared Paul's cause unto the king, saying, There is a certain man left in bonds by Felix: About whom, when I was at Jerusalem, the chief priests and the elders of the Jews informed *me, desiring to have* judgment against him. To whom I answered, It is not the manner of the Romans to deliver any man to die, before that he which is accused have the accusers face to face, and have licence to answer for himself concerning the crime laid against him. Therefore, when they were come hither, without any delay on the morrow I sat on the judgment seat, and commanded the man to be brought forth. Against whom when the accusers stood up, they brought none accusation of such things as I supposed: But had certain questions against him of their own superstition, and of one Jesus, which was dead, whom Paul affirmed to be alive.

Conforming

In other words, you let religious people serve Me in their own man made way and you Christ like saints, serve Me in Spirit and in truth.

Word Helpers

Colossians 2:16-23 Let no man therefore judge you in meat, or in drink, or in respect of an holyday, or of the new moon, or of the sabbath *days:* Which are a shadow of things to come; but the body *is* of Christ. Let no man beguile you of your reward in a voluntary humility and worshipping of angels, intruding into those things which he hath not seen, vainly puffed up by his fleshly mind, And not holding the Head, from which all the body by joints and bands having nourishment ministered, and knit together, increaseth with the increase of God. Wherefore if ye be dead with Christ from the rudiments of the world, why, as though living in the world, are ye subject to ordinances, (Touch not; taste not; handle not; Which all are to perish with the using;) after the commandments and doctrines of men? Which things have indeed a shew of wisdom in will worship, and humility, and neglecting of the body; not in any honour to the satisfying of the flesh.

James 1:19-27 Wherefore, my beloved brethren, let every man be swift to hear, slow to speak, slow to wrath: For the wrath of man worketh not the righteousness of God. Wherefore lay apart all filthiness and superfluity of naughtiness, and receive with meekness the engrafted word, which is able to save your souls. But be ye doers of the word, and not hearers only, deceiving your own selves. For if any be a hearer of the word, and not a doer, he is like unto a man beholding his natural face in a glass: For he beholdeth himself, and goeth his way, and straightway forgetteth what manner of man he

Conforming

was. But whoso looketh into the perfect law of liberty, and continueth *therein,* he being not a forgetful hearer, but a doer of the work, this man shall be blessed in his deed. If any man among you seem to be religious, and bridleth not his tongue, but deceiveth his own heart, this man's religion *is* vain. Pure religion and undefiled before God and the Father is this, To visit the fatherless and widows in their affliction, *and* to keep himself unspotted from the world.

James 2:1 My brethren, have not the faith of our Lord Jesus Christ, *the Lord* of glory, with respect of persons.

Religion is a man made organizations that promotes man's way of serving God. But having pure religion is having the standard (Jesus) and having a relationship with Him, moving into a love walk with Him. Man made religion comes without the Holy Ghost. Relationship comes with it.

Jesus said man made religion will send you straight to hell. Pure religion is having a pure God living on the inside of you. Jesus said if you have not My Spirit, then you are not Mine. Yes I created you as I did everything, but you must be Born-Again of My Spirit and dipped in My blood and washed through the watering of My Word. Then fire baptized in the Holy Ghost to burn out all of you, your fleshly way of thinking and doing your worldly standard.

Then having an on growing relationship and Lordship with Me to be in Me.

Conforming

I have to have you first before you can have Me really. I choose you , give all and receive Me fully in faith forever forsake all and follow Me.

There is a way that seemeth right to man but it's end is hell.

Conforming

Final Thought: Who's in Control

John 10:27 My sheep hear my voice, and I know them, and they follow me:

Ephesians 4:13, 14 Till we all come in the unity of the faith, and of the knowledge of the Son of God, unto a perfect man, unto the measure of the stature of the fulness of Christ: That we *henceforth* be no more children, tossed to and fro, and carried about with every wind of doctrine, by the sleight of men, *and* cunning craftiness, whereby they lie in wait to deceive;
Eph 4:15 But speaking the truth in love, may grow up into him in all things, which is the head, *even* Christ:

The devil cannot use anything against you that He doesn't have control over you with, if your steps are ordered by God. Then it will be formed but it won't prosper it's there but it has no power over you, if Jesus is in control over your life. But if you like playing in the devil's playground, then you have to play with His toys. They are death, hell and the grave. The Lord saith it would be better if you were hot or cold. Whoever you feed or entertain the most has the most control over you. Jesus said you can't serve two masters. He said you will love me or hate me. Jesus said you can't have Me

Conforming

and all of your daily pleasures and hidden pleasures too.

You will leave one for the other and the Lord said it just might be Him. God forbid.

I told you not to go around whoring, stop giving My vessel away. I the Lord Jesus Christ died and arose for you no one else could. Amen.

May You Be Blessed As You Find Your Way, **CONFORMING TO THE MIND OF CHRIST**.

Conforming

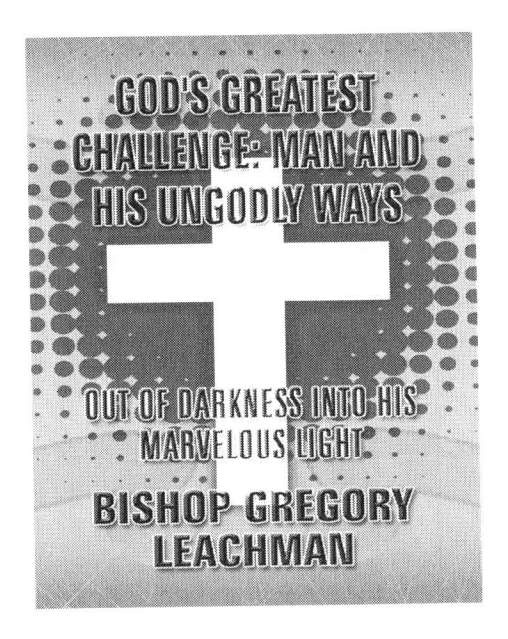

66 Page Book "Gregory Leachman is a Bishop of God that has experienced hardship like very few have. He tells the story in *God's Greatest Challenge: Man and His Ungodly Ways* as he helps use his experiences to teach others about God's goodness. *God's Greatest Challenge: Man and His Ungodly Ways* is a true life story: It all started when he was a child. Thrown in the Nile River, rejected, thrown away by a mother who did not understand who or what she had. From Egypt to Egypt to live with the King of Kings. As a teenager; he was in Church but for the wrong reasons. Then came years of bondage, life in the streets until he was under the streets. Then Jesus came as He did before. How many times? Then the church hurt to hurting churches. Then the road to bring the chosen one's chosen. The Pastor always and every day a people's Pastor. Then to the next level in Christ his Bishop. The Lord placed his bishopric on him May 4, 2007 to the glory of His Name. We hope you enjoy this impactful book."

ISBN: 9781630005801 Order Your Copy Today
www.revivalwavesofglory.com

Made in the USA
Charleston, SC
04 March 2013